AUDREY COHEN COLLEGE LIBRARY
75 Varick St. 12th Floor
New York, NY 10013

The Effective Advancement Professional

Management Principles and Practices

Duane L. Day
Principal
Day & Associates
Orange, California

AN ASPEN PUBLICATION®
Aspen Publishers, Inc.
Gaithersburg, Maryland
1998

The authors have made every effort to ensure the accuracy of the information herein. However, appropriate information sources should be consulted, especially for new or unfamiliar procedures. It is the responsibility of every practitioner to evaluate the appropriateness of a particular opinion in the context of actual clinical situations and with due considerations to new developments. Authors, editors, and the publisher cannot be held responsible for any typographical or other errors found in this book.

Library of Congress Cataloging-in-Publication Data

Day, Duane L.
The effective advancement professional:management principles and practices/Duane L. Day.
p. cm.
Includes bibliographical references and index.
ISBN 0-8342-1040-1 (hardcover)
1. Management. I. Title.
HD31.D333 1998
658—dc21
97-39246
CIP

Copyright © 1998 by Aspen Publishers, Inc.
All rights reserved.

Aspen Publishers, Inc., grants permission for photocopying for limited personal or internal use. This consent does not extend to other kinds of copying, such as copying for general distribution, for advertising or promotional purposes, for creating new collective works, or for resale. For information, address Aspen Publishers, Inc., Permissions Department, 200 Orchard Ridge Drive, Suite 200, Gaithersburg, Maryland 20878.

Cover courtesy of Massachusetts College of Pharmacy and Allied Health Sciences, Boston, Massachusetts. Historical photos courtesy of National Library of Medicine.

Orders: (800) 638-8437
Customer Service: (800) 234-1660

About Aspen Publishers • For more than 35 years, Aspen has been a leading professional publisher in a variety of disciplines. Aspen's vast information resources are available in both print and electronic formats. We are committed to providing the highest quality information available in the most appropriate format for our customers. Visit Aspen's Internet site for more information resources, directories, articles, and a searchable version of Aspen's full catalog, including the most recent publications: **http://www.aspenpub.com**
  Aspen Publishers, Inc. • The hallmark of quality in publishing
  Member of the worldwide Wolters Kluwer group.

Editorial Services: Ruth Bloom
Library of Congress Catalog Card Number: 97-39246
ISBN: 0-8342-1040-1

Printed in the United States of America

1 2 3 4 5

*For Charmaine
Friend, Partner, Wife*

Contents

Preface vii

Foreword x

Chapter 1— **Nature and Function of Management for Advancement** 1
    Management Defined and Illustrated 2
    Managers Are Made, Not Born 3
    There May Be Many Levels of Managers 5
    What Are the Functions of the Advancement Manager? 6

Chapter 2— **The Scope of Advancement Activities** 39
    Historical Background 39
    Government's Role 40
    Private Philanthropy 41
    Public Affairs 60
    Government or Church Relations 63
    Publications 65
    Alumni Relations 67

Chapter 3— **Structuring Advancement Activities** 71
    Advancement Manager and CEO or Board 71
    Advancement Manager and Organizational Units 76
    Advancement Staff Relationships 88

Chapter 4— **The Language of Management** 93
    Mission 94

	Vision	96
	Policy	98
	Procedure	101
	Goals and Objectives	102
	Priority	106
Chapter 5—	**The Manager and Communications**	**109**
	Models of Communication	109
	Quality of Communication	112
	Staying in Touch	118
	Conflict	121
	Conflict Resolution	121
	Organizational Communication	125
Chapter 6—	**The Manager and Technology**	**131**
	Evolutionary Process	132
	Acquiring Communications Technology	134
	Acquiring Information Technology	136
	Choosing the Best System	137
	Conversion	139
	On-Line Uses of Information Technology	140
	Problems	141
Chapter 7—	**The Manager and Planning**	**145**
	Strategic Planning	146
	Who Is Involved in Creating a Strategic Plan?	147
	The Elements of the Strategic Plan	149
	Plan Implementation	166
Chapter 8—	**The Manager and Motivation**	**169**
	Staff Composition	169
	Job Security	170
	Financial Incentives	172
	Career Growth and Advancement	177
	Achievement	179
	Recognition	181
	Management Theories about Motivation	184
Chapter 9—	**The Manager and Change**	**189**
	Reactionary Tactics	191
	Positive Tactics	196

    External Change 204
    Readiness for Change 206

Chapter 10—The Manager and Ethics 209
    Ethics Defined 211
    The Development of Ethics: Views from Religion
      and Philosophy 211
    Codes of Ethics 214
    Donors' Expectations of Advancement Staff 220
    Advancement Manager's Fiduciary Responsibility 222
    Law and Ethics 225
    Ethics and Character 227
    Appendix A 233

Chapter 11—Manager or Leader? 245
    Leadership Defined 246
    Managers and Leaders 248
    The Fallacy of Charisma, the Paradox of Followership 250
    Leadership Traits and Skills: the Right Stuff 252
    Situational Theories of Leadership 254
    Influence, Power, and Authority 260
    Nature or Nurture: Can Leadership Be Taught? 262
    Leadership Models, Theories, and the Advancement
      Manager 262

Chapter 12—Evaluating the Advancement Manager 265
    From Traits to Systems: The Evolution of Performance
      Evaluation 266
    What Constitutes Success for the Advancement
      Manager? 267
    Advancement Managers' Fundamental Competencies 269
    The Elusive Nonprofit Bottom Line 271
    Informal Evaluations 273
    Formal Evaluations 274
    Tying Evaluation Results to Rewards 279
    Career Advancement 280

Index 283

PREFACE

As conceived, *The Effective Advancement Professional* was intended for the men and women who manage one or all of the elements of advancement operations within the organizations of America's independent sector. I hoped that the book might serve as a reference from which counsel might be sought as the conundrums attendant to the advancement manager's roles presented themselves.

The dominant practice in the advancement world of promoting successful practitioners to management positions argued persuasively for the need for such a work. The management literature addressed to those in the discipline related to advancement has been relatively sparse and has tended to be fragmented—a chapter here, a couple of paragraphs there, and an article someplace else.

I approached the writing of this book keenly aware, also, of the high level of aspiration among many of my colleagues in advancement. Large numbers of successful development officers and public affairs professionals wanted to move into management ranks but found little to help them prepare for their hoped-for roles. And so I imagined that this work might serve to support the career aspirations of advancement officers.

As the work unfolded and I spoke about the book to vice presidents, directors of development, executive directors, and volunteer leaders, I was surprised to be told again and again that the audience for the material I was writing was larger than I had imagined:

- "Directors of development have to know how to manage if they're going to be able to do their jobs. They must communicate, motivate, deal with change . . . the responsibilities you're addressing don't belong to the boss alone."
- "I stumbled through one managemen position making more mistakes than I care to admit. I finally got fired. I'm a development director now, but I'm

about to get another chance at managing, and I can use all the help I can get. I've got to get it right this time."
- "As chairman of the board of a youth-serving agency, I need to work comfortably with the E.D. He's not much of a manager, but he knows kids and kids' programs, and he raises money. Your book may provide us some common ground and help our relationship develop."

Apparently, the subject of management for advancement speaks to interests that go beyond the vision that originally shaped this work. I hope, therefore, that whoever picks up this book and turns its pages will find material which serves some of their interests and meets a few of their professional needs.

The thoughtful—for that matter, the casual—reader will readily understand that serious and detailed volumes have been written on many of the subjects addressed in these chapters: communications, technology, motivation, change, and so forth. What has been attempted in these chapters is to represent some of the cogent thinking on the topics at hand and to make that thinking available in a form accessible to and pertinent for advancement professionals.

Other material discussed in the text—the nature and scope of advancement activities, structuring advancement, evaluating the advancement manager—has received scant attention in print. I have tried to bring disciplined thought to bear on these topics based on general management literature and my own experiences and those of my colleagues.

This is not a typical fund-raising book. There is no "how to" attention paid to cultivation and solicitation, direct mail, telefunds, grants, or planned gifts. Those of us who work in advancement are advantaged by a flood of recent works that deal with the techniques of our calling. I'm grateful for the growing literature in our field.

Nor does this book speak, except in passing, of those friends and donors who make possible our organizations and the work we do. I am convinced that there is a profound sense in which those who support the institutions of the third sector shape the character of this nation. The absence of donors and volunteers from the pages of this book in no way diminishes my/our indebtedness to those who give and those who serve. They commit to the missions of nonprofit organizations out of the conviction that their efforts make for a better world. They are right.

As I reflect on my indebtedness to them, I am struck by the many to whom I owe much in the crafting of this book. So many have contributed to the ideas and experiences which have gone into this book. A few must be recognized for their contributions. Dr. Jerry Mandel at the University of California, Irvine, and Loretta Stock Haught of Aspen Publishers believed in the need for a book on managing the advancement enterprise and agreed that I was the one to write it. Henry and Lilly Colossi made their desert retreat available to me so that I could write uninterruptedly for days at a time. Lainie Lareau, my long-suffering secretary, translated my scribbling on yellow pages (yes, I write by hand) to produce a transcript. Brian Lawver of California State University, Long Beach, guided me through the thickets of technology and software conversions. Patti Ten Eyck, my youngest daughter and mother of two of my grandchildren, did some of the research that found its way into this book. The gifted Dr. Mary Schmitz, a valued associate of the firm of Day & Associates, made monumental contributions in researching sources and shaping the ideas that have found their way into these pages.

I also want to recognize my wife and partner, Charmaine. During the long months of writing, months that were also occupied with the needs of clients on a busy consulting practice, she encouraged and supported my efforts beyond all reasonable expectation. Charmaine willingly accepted responsibilities and shouldered burdens that would have been mine, but for the demands of the book. *The Effective Advancement Professional* would never have seen the light of day were it not for her help.

I am deeply grateful to all of you.

Finally, this word to my colleague advancement professionals: may you always surpass all your goals.

Duane L. Day

FOREWORD

I came to my work in advancement by a long and winding route. On the way, I was a university instructor, then a professor, a dean, a businessperson (briefly), a development officer, and, finally, an advancement manager. When at last I had come to the field, I set about identifying the factors that contribute to success in advancement—not just personal or career success, but success for the institutions of the voluntary sector, in both short- and long-range terms.

It was apparent to me that efforts to raise funds produced widely varied results. Some organizations appeared to garner all the support they needed. Others worked hard and struggled mightily but were never able to fund their programs at levels that reached parity with comparable institutions. Something was missing in the structure and function of the under-performing advancement shops.

Over time, I began to shape some answers as to why some succeeded and others did not:

- the quality and reputation of the organization seeking voluntary support
- the compelling nature of "the case" for support
- the strength of volunteer leadership
- the size and ability of the advancement staff
- the vision and sophistication of senior advancement management
- the commitment to a well-thought-out philosophy of advancement

Those aren't bad answers; I made speeches in which I prescribed for advancement success based on those factors.

More years in the field, more exposure to more advancement programs, and more reflection led me to the disquieting conclusion that there were other factors that went into the "success equation" for advancement. Scores of organizations I knew well were of high quality, committed to important things, with good leadership, employing numbers of able people, but barely scraping by. Those organizations told their stories, cultivated and solicited their friends, but were relegated to the "get-by" level of philanthropic support. They stood in sharp contrast to other organizations that seemed, in my purview and in the harsh terms of a colleague, to be "money machines." Contributions abounded for the latter organizations; dollars flowed; prospects responded, openhandedly, to volunteer and staff challenges.

Trying to avoid the fate of the one and emulate the success of the other, I finally came to understand an important difference between the two. The advancement efforts of the successful institutions were focused: they knew what they were about; their efforts grew from an understanding of institutional aims; they were marked by organized staff and volunteer efforts; they acknowledged the importance and worth of the people—volunteers and staff—charged with securing philanthropic dollars. In short, successful advancement programs were *managed* programs: their actions were intentional; their people were thoughtfully arrayed across the range of organizational needs; their dollar expenditures were rationally directed; their internal and external relationships were carefully—even artfully— designed. By way of comparison, the operations of the less successful organizations conveyed a slap-dash quality; "hit and miss" appeared to be the dominant strategy. They moved in a crisis state.

As I came to that realization, slowly, I admit, the content of my speeches began to change; more important, the nature of my personal management style underwent a metamorphosis. Organization, case, leadership, and staff remained important realities in my vision of requisites for organizational success; now, however, that vision was augmented by my understanding of management and my belief in the concept of system. System became a dominant theme in my speeches and a preoccupation of my daily work-related efforts.

As I speak of an advancement system, I have in mind a gestalt—an approach to managing the philanthropic enterprise in which operations are seamless, in which each part feeds into each other part. System means that the individual efforts of staff members are supported by others and are, in turn, the support of others. In an advancement system, people and funds are deployed in ways determined by the organization's mission and the commitments growing from that mission. Donors and prospective donors are colleagues in efforts to support and energize the institution.

To employ an analogy, my understanding of the work of advancement grew from one in which it was as though staff and volunteers comprised a group of soloists, to one in which their several voices were blended into a choir, producing a result greater than that which could have been created by individual parts. That change or growth in my understanding of advancement leadership had important concomitants. Support services for volunteers and staff took on greater importance, ways of supporting staff required re-thinking, and projection of future activities came to shape current initiatives. What I discovered, along the way, was that integrated advancement services keyed growing philanthropic results.

Some months ago, Loretta Stock Haught of Aspen Publishers asked me to identify for her a gap in the literature available to advancement professionals. Thinking of my own journey, I said immediately, "managing advancement" and then went on, at rather greater length than Loretta might have liked, to speak of the systems approach to management in the search for philanthropic success. When asked about a person who might be qualified to write a book representing that point of view, one who could produce a book that was rigorous yet grounded in the realities of our discipline, I said, "Duane Day is the only person I know who is capable of authoring the book that is needed." Aspen Publishers ultimately charged Day with authoring the advancement management book I had suggested. I am, I'm proud to say, co-conspirator in this project.

Over many years I have known the author as a skilled resource development consultant. Indeed, Duane has served me on several occasions and serves the institution for which I still work. His pen is facile, his reading wide, his interests catholic. When working with him, I have discovered that he is rarely content with a one-time event; he seeks reasons, he systematizes, he finds ways to replicate unanticipated results. He learns by his efforts, and he raises philanthropic gifts. He is passionate in his commitment to philanthropy. Duane is, as a friend described him, "the thinking man's fund raiser." He is the only person I know in this field who could have written this book.

The Effective Advancement Professional: Management Principles and Practices has exceeded my expectations. It is a ground-breaking effort to define and shape the work of the advancement manager, and it establishes, beyond question, that sound, informed management practice is the ground on which stands success in the advancement enterprise.

As the reader works through the chapters of this study, managers are encountered doing and deciding to the benefit of their institutions. Techniques for recruiting, hiring, and evaluating are set within the context of the manager's daily effort. The discussion of the specialties characteristic of contemporary advancement offices illumines the wide-ranging responsibilities that fall to the manager. The exposition of the alternatives facing the advancement manager when considering an organizational structure that may best serve the institution is worth the price of the entire book—and it stands nearly alone in the literature of advancement.

And so it goes, through communication, planning, motivation, change, ethics. A friend asked, "Is this the kind of book one will read at a sitting?" "I don't know," was my answer, "I did." My speculation, however, is that most who approach the discussions that comprise this work will read it through, then place it on their shelves, only to remove it and re-consult it repeatedly as the business of managing brings to the fore its daily conundrums. The advancement manager reading this book will come to realize how important it is to understand the philosophy behind the system in use; moreover, the manager will see that it is very important, in fact virtually a necessity, for the manager to communicate this philosophy to advancement staff, to the organization's leadership, and to key volunteer support. It is the only way to build and sustain a truly successful advancement program in today's world.

I can envision the reader perusing the section on planning as he or she seeks to project the institutional future. I'm certain that the thoughtful words on compensation will be consulted repeatedly by the manager with limited resources for salary enhancements. The contrasts and comparisons between the advancement manager and the leader may well mold career commitments.

Managing advancement can be a daunting experience. The demand to increase fund-raising results for most of our philanthropic organizations is now a way of life. Often those of us who have been thrust into management roles in advancement have not had appropriate training in management, have not thought through the approach we will take to our complex jobs, have discovered very little literature on the subject, and have found too few seminars or workshops on this role. *The Effective Advancement Professional* is a book that answers our questions about the role. Our profession has long needed a book such as this. Now that it is here it should be read again and again by advancement managers and those who aspire to achieve to the role.

Duane Day has made an invaluable contribution to the future of advancement. I urge you to make this book your most trusted advisor.

Jerry E. Mandel, PhD
Vice Chancellor
University of California, Irvine

CHAPTER 1

Nature and Function of Management for Advancement

The men and women who have been charged with the responsibility of managing the advancement function in nonprofit, public service organizations and institutions have good reason to take pride in what they do. Theirs is the critical task of ensuring that their organizations develop, with their publics, the psychic and financial support necessary to ensure that those organizations are able to accomplish their several missions. To a remarkable degree they are accomplishing that task. And this they are doing in a social, historical, and political environment in which change seems the only constant. The laws relating to the treatment of contributions and of institutions receiving contributions; the roles of the federal and state governments in education, health, and care for the needy; and the posture of religion vis-à-vis the nation's social agenda all are subject to public discussion as the new century commences. The decisions flowing from those discussions have profound impact on the efforts of the advancement manager.

If the external environments in which managers of the advancement function operate are in flux, so too are the internal environments. The technologic/electronic revolution has changed the way we do philanthropy and its associated activities. The organization and structure of nonprofit organizations are undergoing many of the same changes as organizations in the for-profit sector and produce, it might be added, the same insecurities. The very definition of philanthropy is "up for grabs" with the emergence of public-private partnerships, program-related investments, and cause-related marketing.

In the face of the obvious pressures resulting from the contexts in which today's advancement managers are required to operate, they are achieving remarkable—and, some might say, wholly unexpected—results across the length and breadth of the nation. Public affairs offices are succeeding in getting more media attention and more in-depth coverage in the media of issues of importance to their organization. Alumni* groups are securing financial and other support from ever-growing percentages of graduates. Social change groups are widening their circles of influence and meeting many of the challenges they were created to address. And the level of voluntary support for the organizations of America's third sector grows, relentlessly it seems, year after year.

Pride of accomplishment, among managers of advancement, is well earned but hard won.

This book is about managing the advancement function, and this chapter seeks to provide the conceptual framework for the manager who works in advancement. After proposing a definition of management, the chapter explores activities in which managers engage, looks at management levels and roles, identifies a variety of specific management functions, and discusses institutional culture with specific reference to staff, donors, and the wider community.

MANAGEMENT DEFINED AND ILLUSTRATED

Management is the utilization of resources—people, funds, and time—to accomplish agreed-upon organizational purposes. It may be argued that this definition is foreshortened, that it starts and ends in the middle. Where does the definition of management encompass such important realities as planning? acquiring the financial resources required of the job? evaluating efforts? projecting results? relating to other functions in the institution or organization?

Each of these issues is discussed in some detail in the pages that follow, and each is important. All of the functions implied in the questions above, however, relate to the processes that surround management rather than to the act(s) of management itself. Management has to do with the utilization of a complex of resources, as the following examples illustrate.

The vice-president for advancement arranges to see one of his development directors. The director has missed meetings with prospective donors. She has tried to lead campaign meetings without an agenda. She has not provided volunteers with promised written materials. She has failed to return phone calls. The vice-president has counseled her, at length, about job performance and has told the development director that the effort put forth is unsatisfactory. Finally, on this occasion, the vice-president tells the director that she is being separated. That act on the part of the vice-president is an act of management; it has to do with resource utilization. Because time, money, and people all are in limited supply, the vice-president has decided that organizational ends will be compromised if the decision to terminate employment is not taken and that someone else can be found who will provide a better use of limited resources.

---

*To promote a greater ease of reading, the plural alumni is used when referring to both the male and female graduates of institutions of higher education.

The assistant administrator of the medical center, who has just commenced his work as the manager of the advancement function, has been told that one of his staff members is "impossible," will never become a successful development officer, and will have to be terminated. When he meets with the staff member in question, he says, "Let's forget about the job for now. I want to get acquainted with you and to have you get to know me." Over the next few weeks he meets repeatedly with this development officer. Trust grows, and with it, enthusiasm for the job grows. Soon, the development officer's performance takes on a brighter aspect. A small campaign is launched and rapidly reaches and then surpasses its modest goal. The officer plans new initiatives. That, too, is management, and it is resource utilization. The assistant administrator determined that he would test the information about his staff member before acting on it, and in the process of testing, determined that the development officer could help the organization reach its goals.

The assistant vice-president responsible for publications is overwhelmed with internal requests for the services of her two excellent graphic artists. The result is that departments are having to wait unconscionable periods of time to have their design work completed. The department heads have grown angry that their work is so long delayed, and they have started to take their work to outside artists. A brief review reveals that outsourcing graphic design is costing the institution far more than it would cost if it could be done internally. The assistant vice-president prepares a request for budget augmentation for her graphics operation, which would allow her to place another artist on the payroll on a half-time basis. This, too, has to do with effective resource utilization, and it is illustrative of a manager at work managing.

There are, to be sure, many factors that impact on management and a wide variety of process steps that feed into sound management. But the advancement manager who understands that daily work is about the use of the resources at his or her disposal has faced the realities of the job.

MANAGERS ARE MADE, NOT BORN

Managers are persons who are appointed to their positions by the institutional authority, are responsible for the utilization of the resources provided them, ensure that tasks are carried out through the efforts of those in their charge, and are held responsible for achieving results.

Most advancement managers are named to their positions as a result of perceived excellence in one or more of the activities associated with advancement. They tend to come from previous responsibilities within advancement: fund raising or public affairs. In those occasional instances in which a president, other senior level administrator, or board has appointed an advancement manager who lacks a background in a discipline associated with advancement, the record is replete with instances of failure.

Relatively few persons working in advancement have had extensive formal education specific to their work assignments. Public affairs professionals would appear to be the exception: a high percentage of public affairs officers working in the nonprofit arena have earned college or university degrees in communications or journalism prior to their employment in advancement. Fund-raisers, alumni officers, government affairs professionals, and researchers, for the most part, have been graduated from university programs in the social sciences or humanities and have developed and honed their advancement skills on the job. Most often, they have supplemented their job experiences with training sessions provided by professional organizations. Many advancement professionals have come to their work from careers in education, business, the church, and so forth. Although formal academic programs in philanthropy are growing in America's colleges and universities, they remain few in number and limited in enrollment.

The result is that persons are hired by institutions to undertake assignments in advancement, provided with brief orientation or training, and set to work. Studies suggest that many if not most flounder and leave the field in short order; the average length of stay in fund raising for a new hire is less than two years. Some, however, find their assignments challenging and their rewards motivational. They remain in the field, acquire the skills and knowledge required of their work, commit long hours to their assignments, and make career commitments to institutional philanthropy. A significant number of such advancement employees move from one institution to another (and make, for themselves and their families, useful, rewarding careers). A few stand out; they raise a little more in contributions for their employing organizations most years. They go to the professional meetings, they read the literature of advancement, they cultivate and ask, they write and speak, and they publish.

It is from among the latter that advancement managers are most often identified and named to their management roles. The fact that advancement operations in the United States have been as successful as they are argues for the effectiveness (if not the sophistication) of current practice. But the fact that many advancement managers have entered into their jobs with an existential understanding of at least one of the advancement disciplines but little background in or preparation for management, argues for the acquisition of the same level of thoughtful understanding and disciplined practice of management skills as went into the acquisition of advancement techniques.

As in other fields of endeavor, it is common for informal leaders to arise in advancement staffs; these are men and women to whom their colleagues turn for advice and counsel. They are important components of virtually every successful staff operation, and those informal leaders often serve as vital adjuncts to advancement managers. But this book addresses management, and it is important to remember that managers are appointed to their positions by the leadership of their organizations and, thus, act on behalf of and with the authority of the organization. Managers of advancement may have skills and knowledge identical to those possessed by informal leaders, or they may develop those skills and thus earn similar regard as that afforded informal leaders, but managers are, and remain, different because they have been draped with the mantle of institutional authority.

All advancement staff members have some responsibility for using resources to accomplish their work: support staff, computers, time, and so forth. The manager differs in that he or she is responsible for allocating advancement resources among all members of the staff. The manager determines who on the staff gets what, how much, and when. Those determinations may be, and often are, as straightforward as the assignment of office space or the identification of appropriate support staff. They may be, and often are, as complex (albeit sometimes intuitive) as deciding which staff member is best qualified to see which prospect or whose dollar goal was inappropriately determined.

The advancement manager, it should be clear, accomplishes much work through others. To be sure, many managers are, themselves, active members of the advancement team. They solicit contributions, write case statements, prepare articles, meet with press, lobby legislators, and so forth. However, by virtue of the fact that they are managers, their defining functions have to do with enabling and directing the work of others. The size of advancement operations varies greatly across the nonprofit world; some managers have three or four staff members reporting to them, others more than a hundred. However many there are, it belongs to the manager to accomplish at least a portion of the work of the organization through others. The manager, no matter what the level of energy and commitment, no matter how skillful and experienced, cannot be a lone ranger. The manager operates with and through the efforts of others—the advancement staff.

In the end, the manager is responsible to his or her superiors for the results obtained. If the organizational goal for contributions is two million dollars and the staff has raised one million, the advancement manager is the one who is brought to account. There may be good reasons for the failure to reach the goal. The goal may have been based on wishes rather than reason. But it is the manager who bears the responsibility. The manager may explain or apologize. The manager cannot blame someone else.

THERE MAY BE MANY LEVELS OF MANAGERS

As noted above, advancement staffs vary widely in size. In large research universities it is not uncommon for the advancement staff to number 200 and more. In social service agencies, it is typical that only a small handful is charged with all of the organization's advancement operations. In those circumstances in which many staff members are involved, several managers frequently work under the authority of one senior level manager (see Figure 1–1). It is apparent from this organization chart that this advancement operation has at least three levels of management within the structure: vice-president, four assistant vice-presidents, and several directors with staff reporting to each. That is a function of the reality that no single manager can effectively direct the efforts of dozens of persons.

The differences among the levels of management have to do with the scope of authority and responsibility. In our example, the vice-president for advancement has overall responsibility for the totality of advancement operations. The assistant vice-presidents have specific responsibilities, that is, for development, public affairs, alumni relations, and governmental affairs. Their degree of authority differs also in that none of the assistant vice-presidents has authority over the others at the same level. The responsibilities of the directors with staff is yet more limited, and so too is the scope of their authority.

A significant difference in managerial expectations in the nonprofit, as compared to the for-profit organization, world is that advancement managers are expected, even required, to develop and maintain good relationships with nonemployees: in the case of universities, these may be graduates, donors, press, legislators, and so forth; in medical centers, these may be physicians, third-party payers, employer groups; in agencies, these may be clients, parents, referral sources, and so forth.

The levels of management in small organizations are significantly more limited than in the above example. The scope and authority principles remain the same, however (see Figure 1–2). In this illustration, the executive director has overall responsibility and full authority, presumably granted by the agency's board of trustees. The development director and the program director each has specific responsibility and real but limited authority. (In the agency depicted, the editor of the newsletter is a volunteer, indicated by a dotted line.)

WHAT ARE THE FUNCTIONS OF THE ADVANCEMENT MANAGER?

The advancement manager has five main functions: planning, personnel administration, evaluating, budgeting, and representing.

Planning

Advancement has frequently been criticized as an activity so heavily dependent on chance as to be resistant to appropriate management. A well-known advance-

Nature and Function of Management for Advancement 7

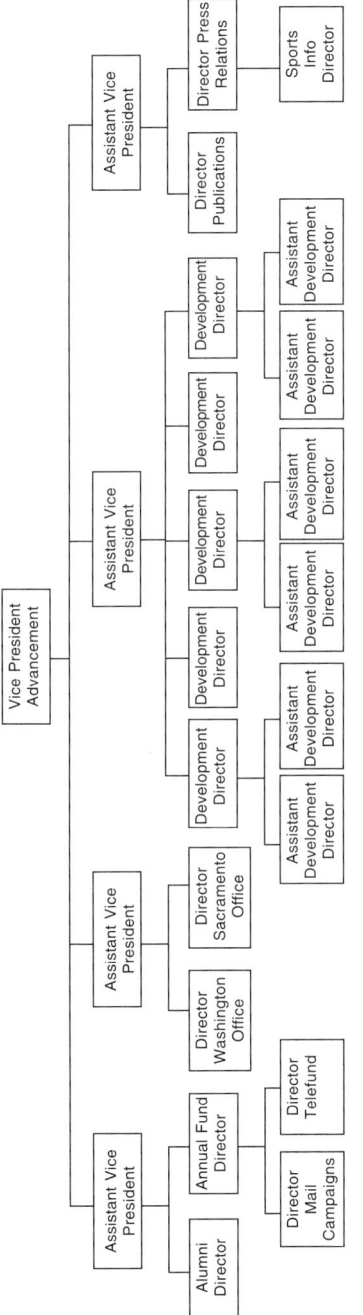

Figure 1–1 Advancement staff organization chart for a large, complex organization

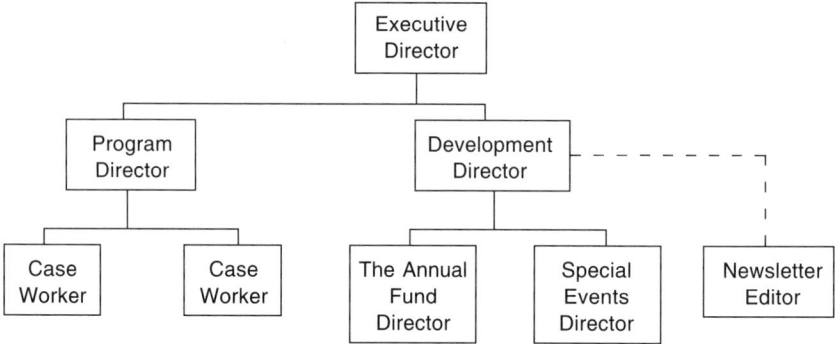

Figure 1–2 Advancement staff organization chart for a small organization

ment consultant, in decrying that supposed dependence, is fond of announcing, "Serendipity is not an advancement strategy." It is certainly true that many universities and colleges have derived significant financial benefit from the unexpected deaths of long-forgotten alumni. Similarly, favorable media coverage for educational institutions often is occasioned by successful football or basketball teams—circumstances well beyond the control of the advancement office. Medical centers have, not infrequently, been the recipients of wide public notice when celebrities have had health problems addressed within their walls. As our consultant implies with his aphorism, however, such events are no substitute for thoughtful planning. Chance is a slender reed on which to build philanthropic support.

Planning will be addressed in a later chapter. The advancement manager should be clear about the differences between strategic and tactical planning. Strategic planning deals with large (one is tempted to say global) issues. The strategic plan usually projects operations for a significant period of time—three years, five, ten; it addresses the advancement operation within the larger institutional context and within the environment in which the organization operates. Strategic planning looks at the competition. It typically has about it the quality of aspiration. The creation of a strategic plan acceptable to the institution and the advancement constituencies will usually have involved representative groups giving sizeable amounts of time to crafting the plan.

Tactical planning is more modest in scope. It may focus on a single prospect and deal with ways to involve that lone prospect so as to secure support for a specific project. It may be directed toward one event in the life of the organization and focus on the elements that are essential to making that event successful: media coverage, attendance, quality control, and so forth.

Tactical planning is marked by a short time frame and specific purposes; strategic planning is characterized by extended concerns and overall purposes.

Tactical plans may define what it is that the advancement manager does on a daily or weekly basis; strategic plans may be months or even years in preparation, involve many people representing many interests, and intended to direct the total operation over the course of a number of years.

It is instructive to note the ways in which the military use these terms. When they speak of strategic plans, they refer to planning for an entire theater of operations or an entire conflict (the strategic bombers stationed in England through much of World War II were tasked with destroying the capacity of the Nazi regime to wage war in Europe). The tactical issues, however, from a military point of view, are those that address a single operation, often a specific battlefield, and involve a minimal use of personnel and other resources (the tactical fighters in World War II were comprised of smaller aircraft flying missions that were directed against limited targets). Tactical or strategic, the overall purpose of planning is always the same: to determine how best to deploy resources to achieve a desired purpose.

Exhibit 1–1 identifies issues that must be addressed in the tactical planning process as that process involves an individual, corporate, or foundation prospect. Although the questions posed in Exhibit 1–1 refer to a potential request for funds from a single prospective donor, similar questions may be posed for the tactical plans leading to activities relating to other advancement needs such as media relations, alumni activities, or governmental relations.

In similar cases, the careful and results-oriented advancement manager will want—and require—thoughtful preparation for the individual activities of staff that, taken together, feed into overall success. The manager understands and expects similar understanding from staff, that is, that advancement efforts are thoughtfully designed to produce desired results.

The benefits of such planning are readily apparent:

- focused purpose
- appropriate and agreed-upon staff assignments
- identified support
- prospect readiness
- relevant time constraints

Personnel Administration

The emphasis of this chapter on the nature of management holds, that management has to do with resource utilization and that managers appointed to their positions work through others. Such a view places major focus on the manager's efforts with staffs and on the staff members with whom managers work.

Exhibit 1–1 Issues to be addressed in tactical planning process

```
 1. Identified project                                    _____
      Case statement prepared                             _____
      Case statement distributed                          _____
 2. Donor name, address                                   _____
 3. Largest previous gift                                 _____
 4. Date of previous gift                                 _____
      Staff member                                        _____
 5. Contribution desired                                  _____
 6. Time frame                                            _____
 7. Response to last ask                                  _____
      Date                                                _____
 8. Donor identified reasons for results of last ask      _____
 9. Staff to be assigned, current ask                     _____
10. Desired support, name                                 _____
11. Fall-back position                                    _____
                                                          _____
                                                          _____
                                                          _____
12. Cultivation activities planned                        _____
                                                          _____
                                                          _____
                                                          _____
13. Cultivation undertaken, dates                         _____
                                                          _____
                                                          _____
                                                          _____
14. Briefing material prepared                            _____
```

Virtually without exception, managers of advancement will insist that their efforts, successful or failing, are dependent on the quality of their staffs—those they hire, assign, supervise, compensate, train, motivate, and evaluate. It is a matter of considerable consternation, therefore, when the advancement staff experiences rapid and continuing turnover. Although many managers of the advancement function surrender the responsibility for recruiting and selecting new staff members to committees or human resource offices, it is clear that they do so at considerable risk to successful operations. To make that point in another way, if the advancement manager wants and needs quality staff, the manager must be personally involved in the recruitment/selection process.

The key that opens the door to effective efforts in the personnel arena is the job description. The manager will accept responsibility for putting pen to paper or mouse to screen in order to put in words with unmistakable meanings the tasks to be undertaken by the incumbent in a particular advancement staff position. The job description will include job title, reporting relations, specific job responsibilities, skills necessary, educational or other requirements, and position classification or compensation level (see Exhibit 1–2).

It is not sufficient to utilize a "one size fits all" or general job description. The more specific the job description, the more useful it will be at every point along the way of personnel administration: selection, assignment, evaluation, promotion, and compensation. The manager who is unable to be specific in preparing a job description is not ready to hire a new staff member. The following example illustrates the unnecessary loss of good staff because of poor job descriptions.

The author, some years ago, had taken a new job. On his first morning of work, he arrived on the campus about 30 minutes early. Walking down the hall toward his office, he heard voices raised in anger—shouts and curses. Opening the door to the suite, he found his executive secretary and his assistant involved in a terrible argument. With a few embarrassed words of apology to their new boss, the antagonists left and went to their respective work stations. During the morning, each came to offer explanations for the argument; though the explanations were at variance from one another, it seemed that the disagreement and its near violence stemmed from a lack of clarity about job responsibilities. Before lunch that day, the author went to the Human Resources Department to review the job descriptions for the executive secretary and the assistant. To his amazement, both job descriptions were identical and both were dated 10 years earlier.

Although this situation was unusual, it is clear that any attempt that might have been made to solve the problems that led to the argument was effectively thwarted by the lack of current, specific, and differentiated job descriptions. Unfortunately both antagonists left the institution, of their own volition, in a matter of weeks, and their considerable talents were lost.

Recruitment

It is probably accurate to say that, for most organizations, recruitment to positions in advancement is undertaken largely through advertisements placed in the classified section of newspapers of general circulation. A brief review of classified ads in weekend editions of the newspapers in most metropolitan areas will reveal many job opportunities listed for fund raisers, development officers, public affairs professionals, and so forth. That those advertisements produce candidates for vacant positions is certain; it is not uncommon for a single ad placed in the classified section of a metropolitan area newspaper to produce dozens of résumés. One of the problems encountered by reliance on the classified section is that many of the respondents to such ads are more interested in finding a job than they are in making a career in advancement: the job experiences the respondents cite frequently are not germane to the position the manager seeks to fill, and the understanding of what is entailed in a professional position in

Exhibit 1–2 Sample job description for the director of development at a university

JOB DESCRIPTION, DIRECTOR OF DEVELOPMENT, SCHOOL OF ENGINEERING, XYZ UNIVERSITY

The Director of Development of the School of Engineering is responsible for raising contributed funds in support of the academic and research missions of the school. The incumbent reports directly to the associate vice-president for development of the university and is expected to develop and maintain cooperative relations with the other development officers, the dean and faculty of the school, and actual and potential benefactors.

Job responsibilities

1. The director of development will be familiar, in detail, with the major initiatives of the school that require contributions support.
2. He/she will develop a thorough understanding of previous gifts to the school: amounts, purposes, donors, etc.
3. The incumbent will build relationships with past donors (individuals, corporations, and foundations) and will cultivate relationships with potential future donors.
4. The director of development will establish and maintain communication with:
    past donors
    potential donors
    the dean of the school
    the faculty of the school
    the associate vice-president
    colleague development officers
5. He/she will actively solicit contributions to the programs of the school.
6. The incumbent will make active and appropriate use of the support staff and services provided by the Office of University Advancement including prospect research, corporate and foundation relations, media relations, and alumni affairs.
7. The director of development will submit annually a development plan to the associate vice-president for development and the dean of the school. The plan will identify, in detail, the activities to be pursued, the strategies to be utilized, primary donors to be solicited, resources required, etc.
8. He/she will file monthly reports of activities with the associate vice-president for development. The monthly reports will be filed in timely fashion and in the form prescribed by the associate vice-president. Additionally, he/she will meet with the associate vice-president and the dean on a mutually agreed schedule.
9. The director of development will understand that he/she will have a dollar goal for funds to be raised and will work to meet that goal.
10. He/she may be assigned other specific responsibilities from time to time and will address those responsibilities with diligence.

continues

> **Exhibit 1–2** continued
>
> **Skills/abilities required**
>
> - the ability to write and speak, in the English language, in a fashion that clearly communicates meaning
> - the skills required to drive an automobile
> - the ability to make appropriate use of a personal computer
> - interest in and concern for building cooperative working relationships
> - understanding of the missions of a modern university
> - demonstrated belief in the philanthropic enterprise
> - an energy level consistent with the demands of the position
>
> **Educational and/or other requirements**
>
> - obtained a degree from a four-year college (graduate work and degrees will be understood as a "plus")
> - demonstrated history of professional accomplishment
> - knowledge of the literature and trends associated with contemporary philanthropy
> - an active interest in and positive response to the ideas and culture of the time
>
> **Position classification**
>
> The Director of Development of the School of Engineering holds the classification Administrator III. The compensation range for the classification is $ _____ to $ _____ .

advancement is frequently limited. But, and it is an important but, such advertisements do provide a candidate pool.

Job announcements in publications related to advancement tend to result in fewer respondents, but among those who do respond, there is usually a higher percentage of persons who report qualifications specifically related to advancement. Among such publications are *Chronicle of Philanthropy*, *Fund Raising Management*, *Non Profit News*, and the various newsletters published by the regional chapters of the National Society of Fund Raising Executives (NSFRE). Because of publication schedules, job announcements in professional advancement publications tend to take longer to produce a viable candidate pool.

Another potential recruitment avenue that shouldn't be overlooked is the professional press related to specific disciplines. Advancement officers working in the museum world will, as a matter of course, read the publications related to that world. An advancement manager serving a museum will find that a job announcement in a museum-related publication may result in identified applicants who know advancement and who understand the specifics of the museum environment. The same may be said, of course, for many of the arenas in which advancement managers operate: hospitals, performing arts, the sciences, and so forth.

Not to be forgotten as a useful recruitment device is word of mouth. A direct telephone call to one or more colleagues during which the available job is briefly described and related information is shared (experience desired, compensation offered) frequently results in suggestions of names of persons who are seeking to move or may be persuaded to do so. A follow-up phone call to the persons suggested will enable the manager to measure the interest—perhaps the suitability—of the potential candidates.

Oral announcements of job openings at professional meetings—NSFRE, CASE (Council for the Advancement and Support of Education), AHP (Association for Healthcare Philanthropy)—may find the manager with a small handful of business cards by meeting's end. Once again, follow-up conversations on the phone with those potential candidates whose cards have been received will allow the advancement manager to measure the depth of interest and gauge the "fit."

One successful advancement manager says, "I interview all the time, whether I have position openings or not." He goes on to point out that it is his belief that his most important job is to find skillful and committed people to do advancement work in his institution. He has instructed his administrative assistant that everyone who calls for an interview should be accommodated. That manager maintains a small private file of high potential candidates with which he "seeds" his candidate pools when he is looking to add to or replace staff.

Another highly regarded manager of advancement argues that it helps to have names in mind to add to a candidate pool. She says, "I often will encourage a candidate who has finished second in one job search to become a candidate for my very next opening. You would be surprised at how often that works and produces, for us, a very competent employee."

Advancement managers agree that few, if any, factors in their work have a more direct and immediate impact on effective operations than the quality of staff. Recruitment is where the identification of quality staff members commences; in those places in which productive advancement staff members are found, recruitment has been thoughtfully conceived and executed.

Selection

The identification and employment of persons to work in one of the advancement function areas follows on the creation of a candidate pool, the reduction of that pool to qualified persons, and interviews in which skills, attitudes, and commitments are tested and weighed. Straightforward as that process seems, in the last two decades, advancement offices—and other offices—throughout the nonprofit world in the United States have been faced with an additional requirement: to make employment opportunities available to persons representative of ethnic minorities, the disabled population, or the gender disadvantaged. It is not the purpose of this text to engage in discussion of or to take positions regarding what has been described as affirmative action. For a time, affirmative action enjoyed broad—perhaps majority—public support; more recently, the practice has been under question. Whether affirmative action and the employment policies flowing therefrom remain a federal mandate as this book is read, some facts are clear:

- The United States has metamorphosed in recent decades from a largely white, male-dominated society to one that is diverse in both cultural and gender terms.
- Relationship issues, important to advancement success, imply the value of building staffs that are representative of society.
- Advancement staffs, and their leadership, have not adequately reflected society as a whole nor the population on which institutions will depend, in future years, for support.

One related factor of importance is the growing feminization of advancement. In the past 15 years or so, employment among advancement professionals has moved from well over 50 percent male to near 70 percent female; employment of ethnic minorities in advancement lags far behind.

Should the manager's employing institution have, or be responsive to, strong policies relating to the employment of persons representative of "protected classes," selection of new employees will be "tilted" toward such persons in their activities. With or without such considerations, selection of quality, motivated staff members remains a critical element in successful management. The process involves five steps:

1. Screening persons in the candidate pool for position requirements
2. Identifying those to be interviewed
3. Interviewing
4. Deciding
5. Negotiating and hiring

The discussion that follows addresses the process elements, identified above, in sequence.

Screening and identifying. If the advancement manager services a small agency with only one or two levels of management, he or she will review the records of the applicants for the available position and will make determination of those whose materials (résumé or application) report qualifications sufficient to proceed to interview. (The basic internal document used to make such determination is the job description, an example of which is found in Exhibit 1–2 and described at the beginning of the section titled "Personnel Administration.")

In the event the manager serves a large organization or institution, it may be appropriate to entrust the initial screening of those in the candidate pool to the Human Resources Office. What that office will be asked to determine—and the only thing they will determine—is if the records provided by a given candidate demonstrate that the candidate meets the minimum requirements as spelled out in the job description and the recruitment notice. The records of those who possess the desired qualifications will be passed along to the advancement manager, who will screen yet again to determine which applicants, among those who meet the minimum requirements, are to be interviewed.

The effect of the screening described in the above paragraphs is the creation of an interview pool. Those who are designated for interview will be called and invited to meet the interviewer or interview team at a designated time and place.

Who should interview the persons who comprise the interview pool? The most important interviewer is, almost always, the manager to whom the potential employee will report; this manager has not only the right but the responsibility to meet and evaluate all of the candidates for the vacant position. The manager may wish (or it may be characteristic of the organizational culture) to include other persons on an interview panel: other development officers, department heads from areas outside advancement, board members, or volunteers who have specific knowledge of the area in which the new advancement staff member will work. The interview panel will be most effective if it is kept relatively small: five may be the maximum number of members comprising an effective interview pool.

It is common, if the pool of persons to be interviewed is large (eight or ten), for the interview to be conducted in two or even three steps. After the initial round of interviews, the pool may be narrowed to three to five candidates from which the successful job candidate will emerge. Although an interview panel may provide important assistance to the advancement manager (several perspectives, varying insights), the final selection decision belongs to the advancement manager alone. The manager must take ownership of the final decision even and especially in those circumstances in which the manager has been persuaded by panel members to select, for employment, a candidate who was not the manager's first choice. Exhibit 1–3 contains a search protocol for advancement staff in a large university.

Interviewing and deciding. The moment in which an applicant comes face to face with an interviewer (or an interview team) is difficult for both parties. The prospective employee presumably wants the job for which records and an interview request have been submitted. The advancement manager, similarly, will bring to the interview hopes of identifying and employing a gifted and committed staff member. It is remarkable, given the aspirations involved, that so many interviews are less than satisfying: candidates who have not adequately prepared themselves for evaluation by the employing organization; managers who sit before candidates with limited understanding of what it is they seek in new

Exhibit 1–3 Search protocol for advancement staff

PROTOCOL FOR SELECTION OF DEVELOPMENT OFFICERS

I. Determination of job description and expectations

The associate vice-president for development and the dean of the college meet to determine the responsibilities, expectations, and priorities associated with the position. The minimum qualifications for candidates applying for the position are agreed upon. They jointly develop a job description.

II. Personnel credential screening

Initial responses to the job announcement are directed to staff personnel services. Staff personnel services representatives undertake the minimum requirement screening process. This screening eliminates candidates who do not meet the minimum requirements specified in the job description.

III. Screening interview

Applications and credentials of qualified candidates are sent to the associate vice-president for review. From these candidates, the associate vice-president selects, for screening interview, those who appear to be most qualified and who most closely match the needs of the position. The screening interview panel includes the associate vice-president, the dean or director, and one (or more) peer development officer(s).

IV. Screening interview

Selected candidates are invited to participate in a screening interview. The associate vice-president offers the candidate background information and an overview of the history, structure, and function of the position. The associate vice-president also provides the candidate with an understanding of the process and time line for the completion of recruitment. The dean provides background on the college.

Each university representative asks questions from a prepared list. The associate vice-president offers the candidate the opportunity to tell members of the panel anything not covered in the interview that the candidate wants the panel to know.

Each candidate is rated by each of the interviewers on the standard form prepared for this purpose. The most highly rated candidates (the top five) are invited to return for a final interview.

V. Final interview

The most highly rated candidates are asked to spend one day on campus. The day includes private meetings with the dean, with an appropriate group from within the college or unit as determined by the dean, and with the associate vice-president. Each candidate will also meet with at least one additional development colleague.

---

continues

18   THE EFFECTIVE ADVANCEMENT PROFESSIONAL

Exhibit 1–3 continued

> The associate vice-president checks the selectees' references and the references of other candidates as required and shares the results with the dean.
>
> After these meetings, each candidate is rated again. When all final interviews are concluded, the candidates are ranked. The vice-president of university advancement will meet and negotiate terms and conditions with the top-rated candidate and, after consultation with the dean and associate vice-president, will make the appointment for the university.
>
> **VI. Regrets**
>
> Candidates not selected for the available position will be notified and appropriate regrets extended by staff personnel services.

employees or the skills and abilities they wish to find in the persons interviewed. It is as though both—candidate and employing manager alike—are waiting for lightning to strike.

This book is not directed to advancement candidates or staff members, but it would seem obvious that potential employees will want to have learned, before interview, something of the organization to which they are applying and of the position they seek. What is equally apparent is that the interviewing manager will have prepared the interview to maximize the acquisition of information from job candidates. Too frequently, interviews take place "off the top of the head."

The interview that begins, and sometimes concludes, with the interviewer rehearsing information contained in the résumé—"I see you spent two years with United Way. Is that right?"—does not provide the advancement manager with the information needed to make wise hire/no hire decisions. Employment interviews can be among the most direct and consequential interactions a manager and a staff member ever have. Each brings expectations to the interview. As those realities relate to the manager, they require, for realization of the potential of the interview, an expenditure of time and an investment of intellect to devise questions that will provide the raw material for quality decision making.

Successful interviews begin with introductions and a few words of easy conversation ("Did you have trouble finding us?" "Was this time and day convenient for you or did you have to re-arrange your schedule?" etc.) designed to ease the candidate (and the interviewers) into the substantive parts of the interview. The candidate also should be given, at the outset, information that will provide answers to several unspoken, but important preliminary, questions: How much time has been allotted for this interview? What is the nature of the selection process? When is it anticipated that the new hire will commence work? And, if the interview is being conducted by a panel, what are the names of and the positions held by the members of the panel? Such questions, answered by the interviewer(s) at the outset will enable the candidate to contextualize responses and, thus, focus responses to questions asked.

It is appropriate, and in some circumstances a legal requirement, that all of the candidates for a given position be asked similar, if not identical, questions. (In a litigious society, an unsuccessful candidate may seek legal redress if he or she believes that the questioning process was carried out in an unfair or biased fashion.)

There are, at root, three kinds of questions that may be asked in an employment interview: (a) the question of fact, (b) the probing question, and (c) the follow-up question. Each serves to provide the interviewer with information useful to the decision process. The *question of fact*, as indicated above, will not simply rehearse the data available in the résumé. Rather, it will build on that information.

Wrong: "I see you worked at United Way. Is that right?"

Better: "When you were at United Way, did you have occasion to be involved in the planning and implementation of special events?"

Wrong: "Your vitae indicates that you were the public relations director at Collinwood Hospital. How long were you there?"

Better: "When you were at Collinwood Hospital, did you have opportunity to plan press conferences? Tell me about them."

Wrong: "As a student at the university, was history your major field of study?"

Better: "As a history major at the university, you must have considered careers related to that discipline. How do you see history relating to your current career track? Why did you choose to work in the field of advancement?"

The applicant is likely to expound on all of the questions of fact illustrated in the "better" answers above, and the questioner will, by employing such a factual questioning pattern, learn a great deal more about the interviewee than is contained in the résumé. What is learned will become important to the employment equation that the manager is addressing.

The *probing question* tends to be open ended. It deals less in fact and more in style, attitude, and commitment. Candidates' answers to probing questions tend to be extended and, frequently, complex. They may, when posed, produce a measure of discomfort for the person being interviewed, but the answers provided will enable the advancement manager to understand the applicant and to weigh job suitability.

Example: "After ten years at Winthrop College, you are now, by your application for this position, contemplating leaving that institution. Such a decision can't have been reached lightly. Will you tell me about your willingness to move?"

Example: "The capital campaign that your current employer recently concluded was successful. I'd be interested in knowing the part you played in that campaign and your feelings on its successful completion."

Example: "The press coverage of the clinic scandal was extensive and very negative. As the director of press relations, you must have had a difficult time. In retrospect, is there anything you would have done differently?"

The *follow-up question* bears similarities to the probing question: it often requires an extended response and it may produce a measure of discomfort for the interviewee. The follow-up question is defined as a query building on something the applicant has said in response to a previous question. Such a line of questioning is designed to elicit further information or explication of an idea or an attitude expressed in response to an earlier question.

Example: "You said that you want to work with people. Does that mean that there have been periods in your career when you didn't work with people? Tell me, please, what your statement means."

Example: "Your previous response indicated some dissatisfaction with your recent job assignments. I don't know the details; will you discuss your unhappiness at greater length?"

Example: "I sense some discomfort about your relationship with your current supervisor. I understand that can happen . . . would you feel comfortable in telling me about your discomfort?"

The interview is a function of discovery. It addresses the question, "What can I learn, of value, about those persons who might work for me?" The issue for the advancement manager, too rarely put into words, is: "What have I discovered about the several candidates that will assist me in making an employment decision that will benefit my organization and my department?" In short, the advancement manager does not acquire information from candidates to satisfy curiosity. Every piece of information acquired in the screening and interview process is utilized to the end of making a responsible employment decision. Some questions are, therefore, "out of bounds" and inappropriate. Questions pertaining to marital status, number and age of children, religious affiliation, and sexual orientation have all been held to be outside the scope of information managers may legitimately seek during the selection process. They must, therefore, be avoided. Some applicants will choose to volunteer information of the type described; the interviewer is under no obligation to stop a candidate from providing personal data unbidden. Information thus learned, however, is to play no part in the selection decision.

Decisions to hire are made in a variety of ways. If the applicant interviews have been undertaken by a team, the decision process will differ from that where there is a single interviewer.

The interviewer(s) will have kept careful notes of each of the interviews. When five, six, or ten persons have been interviewed, it is extremely difficult, without notes, to recall what each applicant said in response to each question. Vague impressions are an insufficient basis on which to make the hire/no hire determination. If an interview panel has been utilized, the chairperson (preferably the advancement manager) will encourage a general discussion of the several candidates during which the notes of panel members will be reviewed and responses evaluated. Some interview panels function almost as though they were members of a jury: they ballot on the suitability of the applicants. That formal process is, more frequently, avoided by the interview panel in favor of informal discussion: "I like the way Susan answered the question about . . ." "Clifford's preparation for the interview suggests that . . ." It is a common experience on interview panels for decisions to become obvious as panel members' discussion unfolds. On the other hand, it is not unheard of for interview panels to become deadlocked—split between two or even three candidates. In a deadlocked situation, the advancement manager will be called on to determine whether he or she should move forward to a decision, wait for a few days, or re-open the search. The parties to the deadlock, the positions they hold, and the manager's own preference will feed into the resolution of the deadlock. In those circumstances in which the manager is the only one who has done the interviewing, the factors that go into the decision will be weighed in his or her mind alone.

Job requirements are the baseline against which employment decisions are made. Does the applicant show promise, based on past performance and current attitudes as discerned in the interview, of being able to meet the demands imposed by the position in question? If more than one candidate meets the baseline requirements—as revealed in the records submitted and the interview—are the position requirements prioritized? How? To what end? Which candidate meets which priority requirements? The employment interview is undertaken to evaluate potential employees against the requirements determined as critical to acceptable performance on a specific and identified job. Hard facts must play the prominent role in that part of the selection process: education, training, past performance, reputation as discerned from recommendations, responses to direct questions. Becuase advancement operations are always relationship-intensive and, therefore, require the ability to deal with other persons to accomplish purposes, the question of "chemistry" almost always comes into play when employment decisions are to be made.

As popularly posed, the chemistry issue deals with fit. Age, appearance, dress, style, language, and attitude are components of the issue. The advancement manager and the interview team will not ignore chemistry, but it becomes an issue only as it is posed about those candidates who meet and surpass the "hard fact" requirements. When choosing among those whose skills are responsive to identified job requirements, the advancement manager may invoke chemistry issues in the final decision; when faced with two candidates, one of whom meets the position requirements and the other of whom seems to offer the "right chemistry" without having met job requirements, the disciplined advancement manager will decide for the applicant whose preparation, experience, and interviews are consistent with job demands.

Negotiating and hiring. Institutions and organizations of the voluntary sector vary widely in their policies relating to employment. Some require the actual hiring of a staff member to take place through the Human Resources Office. Others place the negotiation and hire responsibilities at the next level above the supervising manager. Still others insist that hiring be placed on the shoulders of the person who will actually supervise the new employee.

Wherever the employment responsibility rests, there are several issues that must be discussed and agreed upon by the organization and the proposed new employee. These include:

- salary
- hours of work
- vacation
- fringe benefits—health insurance, retirement, etc.
- physical examination—is it required?
- start date
- place of work
- support staff
- status—probationary to permanent
- evaluations, salary review
- memberships in professional organizations
- training/education opportunities
- expenses
- contractual relationship or "at will"

For the most part, each of the above items is self-explanatory, and the employing organization will long since have established its own practices, policies, and procedures with respect to the listed items. It remains for the person doing the hiring to identify thoroughly, for the potential employee, the position of the organization on each. Nothing damages an employee's relationship with the employer more seriously than the belief that the employee was promised one thing when hired only to discover that what is received is something different. The event identified as the negotiation and hire is the time to achieve clear and agreed-upon understanding. In those cases in which understanding and agreement cannot be reached, the hiring should be aborted.

A few words must be spoken about compensation. Advancement personnel who have worked in other institutions will come to a new position with a general understanding of the level of compensation that position will support. Specific numbers (i.e., what is desired and what will be offered) may be at variance; they may separate employee and employer by several hundred or a few thousand dollars. The manager (or the hiring authority) will measure the costs associated with or implied by a vacant advancement position, the price involved in the search procedure, and the salary request made by the prospective employee. Compensation decisions will flow from thoughtful analysis and comparisons. Simultaneous with that evaluation, the manager will review salaries paid to current staff members. There are—or may be—circumstances in which the person charged with hiring will identify and offer to a new employee a beginning compensation that is inconsistent with the compensation of current staff members (either higher or lower); in the main, that will not be the case. New employees will commence their employment with salaries that are like those paid to staff already in place, albeit a bit lower. In large, bureaucratic, sophisticated organizations, salary levels tend to fall within compensation classes and the manager's decision about salary will be made within identified upper and lower limits. The negotiation, at the time of hire, will thus be within preset limits.

For new hires who come from jobs outside of advancement, the potential for conflict between expectations and possibility is great indeed. At this writing, with a nationwide readership, the author is unprepared, and indeed unable, to suggest appropriate rates of pay. Table 1–1 may suggest some parameters within which the advancement manager may feel confident of conformity to national patterns.

The percentages identified in Table 1–1 are intended to suggest ranges and not to be normative. They must be measured against and incorporated into the total budget for advancement in any given year. The growth of compensation for advancement professionals will not occur without regard to the contributions, commitments, and needs of support staff or of other advancement staff.

Training

Advancement staff members do not come to their positions as fully realized professionals with the employing organization, no matter their previous prepara-

Table 1-1 Suggested salary parameters

New hire	Starting compensation (% in excess)	After one year (% increase)
Little experience	10–20 of senior support staff	3–8
Mid-level professional	25–35 of senior support staff	0–8
Experienced professional	$33^1/_3$–45 of senior support staff	0–10
Highly regarded professional	20–40 of lowest paid advancement professional	0–12

tion or accomplishments. Nor does the advancement manager. It is important to introduce the subject of training and education of the advancement staff member in this chapter because it is one of the manager's important and continuing functions.

The environment changes, as do the laws regulating philanthropy; institutional needs are seen in new terms, and prospects have varying characteristics. The drive and dynamic with which gifted advancement professionals are marked, no matter how brightly burning today, may be reduced to an ember tomorrow by circumstances and time. The opportunity to meet colleagues in other places, to hear new ideas (or old ideas freshly stated), and to think at length in an organized fashion is necessary to keep alive the flame of passion and replenish the fuel of energy and effort. All of the foregoing argue for a commitment, on the part of the advancement manager, to training.

Advancement budget that is expended on professional memberships and training is money invested in future success. The NSFRE, through regional and national meetings, training programs, and certification preparation is near at hand for all advancement staff members. Annual membership fees, though more than pocket change, amount to a sum approaching insignificance (less than a dollar a day per member) and serve to open the door for members to myriad learning opportunities. CASE memberships require nothing by way of fees for individual staff members, based, as they are, on institutional affiliation. CASE provides scores of short-course training programs, annually, across the nation and in the several regions with special (reduced) fees for staff from member institutions. These training programs offered by NSFRE and CASE are of sufficient breadth and depth to address the training and education of the most junior, beginning advancement staff member, and of those preparing themselves for vice-presidencies in fund-raising organizations of historic significance.

In recent years, a significant number of quality training opportunities for advancement staff have appeared on the scene offered by organizations that are not membership organizations. Colleges and universities across the United States, either in their degree sequences or through their extended education programs, regularly announce courses in philanthropy-related disciplines: direct mail, planned giving, major gifts, publications, media relations, and so forth. Many institutions of higher education, even if they do not make available degrees in philanthropy, provide certificate programs.

Independent organizations (some for-profit, others nonprofit) offer short-course learning opportunities directed at advancement staff members or those seeking to be employed in advancement positions. Of special note in this regard is the Indiana University Center for Philanthropy, which provides instruction in Indiana and in selected sites throughout the nation. Similarly, the Los Angeles–based Grantsmanship Center (now a quarter century old) provides advancement training programs in California and throughout the country.

The value of participation in classes and workshops designed to hone the skills of the advancement staff member goes well beyond the formal content. The participants get to know and exchange ideas with peers charged with similar responsibilities and, thus, to create networks of similarly tasked individuals who are available to render advice, counsel, and emotional support as needs arise. The staffer sent to a training session comes to understand that he or she is worth an investment by his or her employer of time and money for future effectiveness. The sending organization (the employing institution) is valued for willingness to invest in staff potential. Voluntary sector organizations, of whatever size, find that the commitment for training of a sum of 3 percent to 5 percent of budgeted professional salaries will have a pay-off in advancement effectiveness equal to several times the actual dollars expended. In most instances improved results are readily apparent after the training as the following example illustrates.

It was nearly a whim that Constance chose to attend a workshop on in-kind gifts at an NSFRE-sponsored Fund Raising Day. The instructor—not particularly dynamic or glib, but obviously knowledgeable—had garnered experience and achieved success in securing gifts of goods. At the time, Constance was pursuing support for a child care center for her employing university and incorporated the ideas with which she was presented into her fund-raising plan. Less than two months after Fund Raising Day, she had secured commitments for heating and air conditioning, landscaping, and musical instruments for the center, nearly $60,000 in contributions for an employee training expenditure of less than $300. Similar stories of the pay-off flowing out of training experience can be cited in such diverse areas as public relations, grantsmanship, planned giving, publications, major gifts, and so forth.

An immediate benefit does not always follow advancement staff training; it does, however, happen with sufficient frequency to be noteworthy; the energy flowing from participation in training programs drives many participants to new levels of effort that offer the potential for extraordinary achievement.

Among organizations and institutions with multiple advancement staff members, in-house training—supplementing training offered by outside organizations—is of increasing importance. Often undifferentiated (i.e., with all advancement staff members being exposed to identical material), other institutions offer staff training programs on a responsibility or discipline-specific basis. The former approach has the advantage of emphasizing wholeness ("We're part of the team"), which may promote appreciation for the efforts of colleagues. The latter enables the training to be results driven (i.e., specific and focused; "Here's how you do that . . .").

Recognition of the value of staff training varies widely among advancement managers and the organizations that employ them. It cannot be denied that external training programs vary widely in their effectiveness; those organizations that make a significant commitment to and investment in the education and training of advancement staff argue that the overall impact of their investment is dollar effective even as occasional training failures are admitted. One university advancement manager of 20 said, "Given the choice of funds sufficient to hire another development officer or an equal sum to spend on training, I'd opt for the training. In the long run, the training will be of greater help to my institution by creating more productive staff members."

Motivation

Utilizing the human resources at the disposal of the advancement manager requires thoughtful and continuing attention to the issues associated with motivation. Because this book later addresses motivation and the relationship of management to leadership, several of the important management theories touching on employee motivation are discussed here.

Employees, whatever their arena of responsibility, bring to their work many kinds of needs: physiological (food, shelter, clothing), social (companionship and interaction), psychological (esteem by self and others). Maslow's well-known "hierarchy of needs,"[1] as a conceptual framework, should be required reading, and his concepts and words should be periodically reviewed by every advancement manager. The fact is that needs drive behavior; not all employees act on the same need at identical intensity levels at all times. The staff member who has inherited money is less likely to be motivated by the fact that the job provides funds with which to buy food and pay the mortgage than by the need to make a contribution to society or the need to build and maintain strong relationships. On the other hand, the employee who faces an overwhelming financial burden (e.g., a desperately ill husband) will be heavily invested in the economic factors related to employment. The skillful advancement manager will note the differences and adjust behavior and words to the needs of both.

Motivation may be seen in two dimensions: self-motivation and external motivation. Some managers discount what goes on within the employee and focus their energies on what they impose *on* the employee (detailed reports, stringent oversight of hours, harsh directives). It is not to be denied that external factors are at work in shaping employee behavior and performance; neither, however, is it to be denied that the factors that drive most staff members stem, in large measure, from personal needs as perceived by the individual employee. The manager who seeks to tap into the power of those driving forces (i.e., the manager who cares about the potential for employee self-motivation) will spend time with and come to know those for whom he or she is responsible. The content of the time spent with employees and the feelings and attitudes received and understood become factors of major importance. One skilled advancement manager scheduled time every two weeks for a one-on-one meeting with each individual member of her staff, but she required the staff member to submit an agenda for their meeting several days in advance, and refused to entertain any discussion, during this scheduled meeting, of matters outside the published agenda. Further, the manager determined that she would see staff only in scheduled meetings. Aside from those meetings, her door was closed. Far from building supportive relationships with her staff during her meetings with them, she succeeded in alienating them. The result, over time, was that staff insisted that she be replaced.

How different was the experience of another advancement manager who, similarly, met face to face with staff members on a biweekly basis. He let staff control the meetings; if they wanted to talk about family or recreation, he was comfortable and entered into the spirit of the subject matter they brought to the meetings. He didn't lose sight of job assignments or goals because he maintained careful and thorough records. The manager was skillful at taking information provided in apparent casual conversation and tilting it toward advancement efforts. He created task forces among the members of his staff and gave the task forces substantive issues to address. He allotted budget for professional memberships, distributed training money to benefit all, and promoted from within. When this manager left the institution for which he worked, the staff—though sad at his departure—was prepared to assume leadership.

The differences between the two managers are small—they both met, one on one, with staff every two weeks. The one, however, related to staff in a rigid, institutional manner as though they were mere automatons; the other related to the several and distinct staff personalities as valued colleagues. The latter manager, during his tenure, saw advancement results grow by a factor of four. Motivation is often a function of valuing staff and the differences in need and circumstance among staff members.

At another level, it is to be noted that employee motivation may be related to very concrete realities: compensation, time off, recognition of worth, promotional opportunities. As important as warm and close relationships are between and among staff members and manager, they are "sealed" by objective factors. Although organizational policy may prohibit the disclosure of specific salaries for the several employees on a staff, there are few secrets among advancement staff members. Most employees know what most other employees are paid, if not precisely, then within a narrow range. Many advancement staff members suspect, often with good and valid reason, that their compensation is inappropriate when levels of responsibility and performance are measured against others. Even the most committed advancement professional, sensing—or knowing—that his or her salary is not commensurate with value delivered, will become dissatisfied. The policy based on that reality is *not* one that insists that all advancement staff members are to be compensated identically; rather it is (1) that there is a compensation policy understood by all (not "top of the head" reactions to salary issues); (2) that the administration of the policy is consistent and predictable; (3) that staff members, understanding the compensation policy, are enabled to anticipate a salary growth, within broad parameters; and (4) that provision is made for extraordinary salary increases for staff members who have demonstrated extraordinary efforts and results.

In the same manner, the staff member who has been caught up in—and has met—unusual time demands (the special events director who has worked 70 or 80 hours a week in preparation for the opening performances in a new performing arts venue; the director of public affairs who has committed 16 to 18 hours a day to the organization's needs in addressing a crisis) associated with a work assignment will be affirmed (and grateful) when the manager says, "Why don't you take a couple of days off? You deserve it, and I won't charge it to your vacation account." Although a strict interpretation of personnel policy might conclude that such a "boon" is outside the prerogatives of the manager, the effective manager will understand that so long as special consideration is equitably provided to all deserving staff, such actions are well within an appropriate range of action.

In a manner hard to understand, too many advancement managers withhold oral expressions of approval. It is a fact, scarcely to be contested, that advancement personnel work in arenas in which appreciation is rare, disappointments frequent. Despite the fact that most managers of the advancement function have been promoted from staff positions in advancement (in which they have coped with failures, "noes," and discouragement), the mantle of authority, once draped, often brings with it amnesia about the value of commendation and the emotional support it provides for those who have met discouragement, rejection, or disappointment. Words of encouragement from the boss mean a great deal and often motivate a staff member to double and redouble efforts.

Promotional opportunities, made available to able and hard-working staff-in-place, are among the most important motivators of employees. The temptation to hire from outside is always great when a new job—a step up—becomes available. It is understandable that a manager might determine that he or she needs to discover who is "out there," who might bring new insights, sophisticated skills, and fresh commitment to the institution. It is yet more understandable when the quirks and foibles of current staff are compared to the challenges of the promotional position. However, belief in present staff and their potential, when promotions come available, coupled with willingness to put a member of the staff in a position of increased responsibility, serves to demonstrate, for all staff, that their efforts are appreciated; that they are not, as Sisyphus was, doomed to push a huge boulder up a mountain forever without hope of rescue.

Many major, for-profit corporations have made promotion from within a corporate policy and have reaped the benefit of that policy from the resulting employee. One such business has made it a point to tell their first-level supervisors, "When you hire someone, don't just look at that person's potential to replace you, ultimately; hire people who have the capacity to succeed to your boss's job." For 75 years that corporation has been a leader in its industry; motivated employees have been the corporation's "secret."

It is a matter of fact that a high rate of employee turnover is one of the endemic problems for advancement offices. The reasons are complex and frequently resistant of solution. However, it is apparent that many men and women in advancement do not see a career path for themselves in their current situations. The practices of the institutions for which they work do not provide assurances that quality efforts will be rewarded by promotional opportunities. The perceptive employee, understanding that he or she is doomed to his position forever, will, understandably, be open to other job possibilities. It is true that not all staff members are prepared for or deserving of promotion. Still, the advancement manager who selects staff wisely, provides ample training opportunities, compensates appropriately, and offers appropriate emotional support will create an employee complement, at least some of whom will have developed the traits necessary for upward mobility and a commitment to stay with the employing institution.

Evaluating

Known by several names—performance reviews, performance appraisals, employee evaluations—the process of evaluating staff is one that few advancement managers and fewer employees embrace with joy. However, employees who know where they stand in the eyes of the boss—and thus the institution—perform at higher levels of effectiveness than those who do their jobs without feedback.

Most large organizations have specific policies in place regarding the evaluation of employees, and procedures are spelled out about the manner in which evaluations are to be carried out. Although those policies and procedures tend to vary widely, they all seem to include the following: employee evaluations will be done, they will be done at identified intervals (semi-annually or annually), they will form the basis for compensation decisions, and they will be made part of the employee's permanent personnel record. Most organizations have adopted forms for use in the evaluation process, require that the written evaluation be accompanied by a face-to-face discussion, and allow the employee to file a written response to the evaluation.

Some managers have, in recent years, taken to requiring their employees to evaluate themselves before the manager does so, even to the point of completing the relevant form, writing the comments required in the form, and then submitting the self-completed form to the manager for review, comment, and amendment. Such a requirement has the advantage of bringing the employee into the evaluation process. Some, however, feel that the practice implies an abdication of managerial responsibility by suggesting that the manager doesn't know enough about the employee to make sound evaluative judgments.

It is important that the advancement manager let employees know that evaluation time is approaching and ask for any specific suggestions the staff member might have for inclusion on the form or in the process. At the same time, the manager may be able to identify a period of time ("the third week of next month") when the appraisal interview will be scheduled.

Although evaluation forms display wide differences in categories addressed, most forms include questions requiring that the manager weigh (1) the job performance of the individual staff member against the job requirements (see previous section on job description) and (2) that personal traits and behavior (teamwork, attitude, judgment) be measured against some unspecified but presumably desirable standard (see Exhibit 1–4). It is characteristic for the forms to include questions to which responses are sought on numeric (1 to 5) or adjectival (excellent, good, etc.) scales. Most appraisal forms provide spaces for comments following the responses to so-called "objective" questions. (The form reproduced in the figure was chosen because it is representative, not because of perceived excellence.) It is an unusual evaluative process that does not require or afford the opportunity to the manager to identify future activities that will minimize employee negatives and maximize growth and performance. As important as the focus on past activities may be in the evaluation process, of even greater importance are the prescriptive elements identified in the appraisal. Written comments appear to have greater impact on employee performance than checkmarks on a scale. Performance appraisals require the best efforts of the advancement manager as he or she evaluates past performance and projects desirable future activities and behaviors.

Although efforts are made to assure objectivity in the institutional policies and procedures relating to evaluation, it is recognized that, to a large degree, employee evaluation is a subjective process. Feelings, attitudes, relationships, and expectations, all subjective factors, play prominent roles in evaluating employee performance. Some managers are simply tougher or more critical than others in weighing employee efforts. Others define the standards of "excellent," "good," or "meets standards," and so forth in different ways. Those differentials inevitably

Nature and Function of Management for Advancement

Exhibit 1-4 Performance appraisal

Employee Name _____ Title_____			
Department_____			
Reason for Review:	Annual_____	Promotion_____	
	Merit_____	End of Probation_____	
Date of last appraisal_____		Next appraisal_____	
Rating Definitions	O=Outstanding	Employee is recognized as performing in a manner that is superior in all respects.	
	V=Very Good	Performance clearly exceeds most position requirements	
	G=Good	Performance meets standards of job	
	I=Improvement Required	In identified areas, performance is deemed deficient	
	U=Unsatisfactory	Performance is generally below levels required	
Reliability	The employee can be relied on to perform assigned tasks	O _____ V _____ G _____ I _____ U _____	Comments
Job Knowledge	The technical understanding and skills brought to the position	O _____ V _____ G _____ I _____ U _____	
Adaptability	Demonstrated willingness to be flexible in response to position demands	O _____ V _____ G _____ I _____ U _____	
Quality	The overall acceptability of the work undertaken	O _____ V _____ G _____ I _____ U _____	

continues

Exhibit 1–4 continued

Quantity	The productiveness of employee	O _____ V _____ G _____ I _____ U _____
Creativity	Demonstrated ability to approach assignments utilizing new/fresh approaches	O _____ V _____ G _____ I _____ U _____
Accessibility	The degree to which the employee is available—punctuality, attendance, etc.	O _____ V _____ G _____ I _____ U _____
Initiative	The extent to which the employee seeks out job assignments, undertakes to expand professional skills	O _____ V _____ G _____ I _____ U _____
Relationships	Demonstrated ability to work cooperatively with co-workers, supervisors, community supporters	O _____ V _____ G _____ I _____ U _____

Provide answers to each of the following questions:

1. What are specific accomplishments of the employee since the last written review?

2. Areas identified in which improvement is needed.

3. Recommendations for changed responsibilities.

4. Recommendations for activities providing for career advancement or personal growth.

continues

Exhibit 1–4 continued

My evaluation of _____(name)_____ overall job performance is:

Outstanding _____   Good _____
Very Good _____   Improvement Required _____
Unsatisfactory _____

Date of written review _____ Date of review discussion _____

Follow-up requested/desired? _____
Date of follow-up _____

Reviewer's Signature _____ Date _____

Employee's Signature _____ Date _____
(Employee may arrange to add additional comments to this review)

Signature of Reviewer's Supervisor _____ Date _____

---

mean that the essay parts of the appraisal (comments) will carry a heavy cargo of meaning. All employees, if not all managers, understand that reality.

The appraisal interview is an important opportunity for the manager and the staff member to reach understanding about the past and in preparation for the future. Management style and tone, along with content, are important in the accomplishment of a fruitful evaluation interview. Ample time should be set aside for the interview; 10 or 15 minutes are simply insufficient for an encounter that addresses a staff member's career, compensation, and future direction. Circumstances vary, and so do people, but the allocation of 45 minutes to an hour for the appraisal interview should be a minimum commitment. The staff member will have been prepared for the interview by having been informed ahead of time that the performance appraisal will take place.

The style adopted by the manager, in most cases, should be one of concern and counsel. After the exchange of pleasantries, the manager reviews the form, first to identify the subjects covered and second to report on the scores allotted and the comments made. The advancement manager talks through the areas of both commendation and concern, trying not to read the material word for word. The manager should encourage comments from the staff member, listen to disagreements, and offer to amend the document as necessary or appropriate. Recommendations for salary enhancements and new performance requirements, as identified on the evaluation form, will be shared in specific terms. The employee will be informed of his or her right to prepare written comments of disagreement or explanation to be incorporated in the appraisal form and that the employer's comments will be made part of the permanent personnel record.

One of the problems associated with employee evaluations is that managers, all too frequently, give a high rating to an employee only to discover later that the employee is performing at a level that is unsatisfactory. Under such circumstances, the manager may find it difficult or even impossible to terminate that employee until there has been one or more appraisals noting and documenting the unsatisfactory performance. It is well understood that the manager will be required, by organizational personnel policies, to document problem areas in employee performance. What is not so widely understood is that the manager must, similarly, be prepared to document reasons for high ratings on appraisals. Feelings or "hunches" are not a sufficient basis for marks given in the employee evaluation process.

Human resource literature is clear that managers place themselves at a singular disadvantage if the only feedback given occurs at appraisal time. When an employee does something well, or makes an error of significance, the effective manager will comment on that fact to the employee at a time near to the event. Brief notes maintained by the manager about each staff member and the manager's interactions with the employee will provide the information necessary to prepare a detailed and helpful performance appraisal.

Thought also should be given to the place in which evaluation interviews take place. Many effective managers schedule those interviews in places other than their personal offices. The office may, subliminally, suggest power and authority in a way that inhibits useful interaction. The organization's cafeteria (if there is one), a nearby restaurant, a conference room, even outdoors under a tree have all been used as venues for these interviews and have produced the kind of helpful give and take that managers seek and value at appraisal time.

Far from being the burdensome, imposed task that some believe employee evaluations to be, they can serve as the foundation for staff growth when the process is thoughtfully and sensitively implemented.

Budgeting

Earlier it was noted that managers are required to allocate resources to accomplish the organization's purposes. One form such resource allocation takes is the budget. A budget is a fiscal plan for a given period of time, and it serves as a control against which results can be measured. Organizations and institutions vary widely in their expectations of the way budgets are developed by their managers. Characteristically, however, all budgets have two principal categories: revenue (funds available for expenditure) and expense (the manner in which it is proposed that funds be expended). Both the revenue and the expense items will be comprised of several subcategories.

Advancement offices frequently do not receive all of their funding from a single source. There is likely to be an allocation from the parent organization, often another one from the foundation (in those institutions that maintain a foundation), yet another one from funds raised (it is not uncommon for advancement offices to be required to raise at least a part of their funding in the form of contributions).* In those circumstances in which the advancement office is required to raise all or a portion of their funding from the public, planning for the manner in which funds will be expended can become difficult. Even in those institutions that have a long history of donor support and, therefore, provide the advancement manager with a degree of predictability, it remains difficult to know when contributions will be made and dollars will be available.

Depending on the budgeting practices of the institution, the expense budget is likely to contain subcategories for direct and indirect expenses. Direct expenses are those proposed expenditures over which the manager exercises control: labor (salaries, wages, benefits) and non-labor (supplies, equipment, furnishings, postage, telephone). Indirect expenses are comprised of those overhead costs that the organization charges to constituent departments, units, or divisions: occupancy, maintenance, depreciation, utilities, and so forth. Those charges are, in almost every case, beyond the control of the advancement manager.

It is understood that one of the factors contributing to the success of institutional advancement activities is the size of the advancement budget or, to express the idea as it is usually expressed, "the size of the advancement staff." The challenge facing the advancement manager is to increase the revenue side of the budget sufficient to employ the number of staff required to address the needs and opportunities of advancement in the institution. Although the president of the institution or the chairman of the board may measure his advancement manager on how much he or she can accomplish with how little, advancement staff members are likely to measure their managers on how successful they are at accumulating new, additional, or "needed" revenue.

Frequently, a few weeks prior to formal organizational budget approvals, those responsible for drawing up budgets are provided with an opportunity to make requests for revenue augmentation. The care with which such requests and their accompanying justifications are made determines the response to the augmentation request. Among the matters the advancement manager will want to convey are:

- the established relationship between advancement staff size and dollars raised
- the average amount raised by the individual staff members now in place

---

*Some large institutions have adopted a practice that requires that each dollar raised be "taxed" at a pre-agreed rate (e.g., 5 percent) with the money thus realized going to the support of the advancement operations. The remainder then goes to the intended recipient. A few institutions have instituted a more complex practice in which all contributions are invested and not released to the intended recipient until the investment has earned a certain predetermined sum. That sum is then committed to the support of advancement.

- the specific purpose to which the dollars requested will be directed, including job description(s), assignments planned, anticipated learning curve, results expected in one year, two years, three, or four

The advancement manager, anticipating delivery of a request for significant budget augmentation, will have first alerted colleagues and superior of his or her intention. Budget time is rarely a time when surprises are welcomed or approved. Some effective advancement managers make it a point to telegraph their department's needs three or four years in advance, thus preparing decision makers, including finance officers, for anticipated requests well in advance of their receipt of actual requests and justifications.

The three points identified above go to the issue of cost/benefit factors: "By providing advancement this many dollars, we will raise that much money." Cost to benefit is relatively easy to convey when referring to fund-raisers;* it is significantly more difficult, though not impossible, for other activities within advancement: public affairs, alumni relations, publications, and so forth. An illustration was used in the section titled "Management Defined and Illustrated" showing clear dollar advantages for the employment of a new part-time graphic artist in the publications department. Involvement and participation may be cited, to the degree possible, in quantitative terms to establish the benefits provided by the alumni office. Public affairs, though not simply a press release machine, may be notable for the amount of media coverage garnered and for the depth of that coverage—stories with meaning and perspective often have greater public impact than do superficial notices. In like manner, the skill of the public affairs office in defusing a potential crisis, in garnering honors for the organization's periodical, in demonstrated initiative by teasing out media-worthy stories from among the institution's staff and volunteers, all can be cited for the benefit flowing from fiscal commitments to public affairs.

One unusually effective manager goes to great lengths to personalize his requests for budget augmentation. He completes the requisite forms and fills in the blank spaces with the appropriate justifications. Then he writes an accompanying memo that, though succinct, points out the commitment and contributions of present staff—and he names them—and goes on with assurances that the new, requested staff, when hired, will be of similar importance to the organization. This manager argues, "When you personalize your request—put a face on a potential staff member—it is harder to reject the request."

---

*There have been a number of reputable studies of cost/benefit for fund raisers. Although the numbers vary greatly by types and size of organization, they show that actual dollars raised by fund-raising staffs range, on average, from $200,000 to $1,500,000 per fund raiser, per year.

Organization Culture

An organization, by its very nature, has—or is in the process of developing—a culture unique to itself. Organizational culture refers to the ground on which the organization and its employees stand. The commitments made, the beliefs held, the values shared, the unspoken understandings all contribute to the shape, form, and content of an organization's culture.

Advancement is, in all its manifestations, relationship intensive. Consider the impact of the organization's culture on the relationship that is operative between and among staff members and the employing institution. If the institution acts on a commitment to long-term employment for staff members, on promotion from within, and on continuing training for staff, that organizational culture tends to produce high levels of employee loyalty, commitment to the institution and the work, and a heavy investment in professional and personal growth. If, on the other hand, the institution makes it clear, by its actions, that it prefers to maintain an employee complement in which staff members are paid low, entry-level wages, and that it tolerates or encourages high turnover, the staff members will respond in kind: transient loyalty and lowered effort. Organizational culture shapes and defines staff responses to the several stimuli at work on and in the organization.

Similarly, the relationship of the institution to its external publics—donors, alumni, patients, students, physicians, media—is conditioned by the prevailing organizational culture. If the organization understands and acts on the reality that it exists to serve its publics and that it welcomes input on substantive issues from its publics, then the organization can expect public responsiveness in return. If the institutional attitude is, "I don't have the time to spend with that old woman (or student, or donor, or patient)," the institution can expect that it will, in like manner, receive the "brush off."

Philanthropic organizations work and live (or die) in communities. They are not isolated from the vicissitudes of human existence. Organizations are subject to the identical influences as individuals: crime, narcotics, the struggles of the family, economic uncertainty, natural disasters. Although nonprofit organizations have very specific purposes for which they were created and to which they are devoted, they divorce themselves from their communities and their problems to their considerable detriment. The pastor of a large, urban church convinced his lay leadership to make an annual voluntary contribution to the city government each year as an earnest payment on their commitment to the city. He created task forces from among the members of his congregation to address a few of the more depressing problems in the area: homelessness, elderly persons trying to survive in their tiny apartments without caregivers, children who lacked both recreational space and adult leadership. His parish came to be the linchpin that held together the many efforts for community economic development. The organization that has developed a culture of caring and practices a philosophy of involvement in the larger community will reap a harvest of involvement and support from the community. And, the organization that erects fences against the turmoil of the community will be ignored, forgotten, or the object of outright hostility and disdain.

Representing

The advancement manager is often the face the institution shows to its publics and to the larger community. The manager will embody the organization's culture, for this manager is called on to represent the institution to the world outside its own walls. He or she will attend meetings, speak on behalf of the institution, demonstrate its concern, and communicate the respect held for the values that mark the organization. The advancement manager is, frequently, the most widely known, most visible representative of the employing institution to those outside the institution. His or her words, style, good humor, dignity, and care will become, for many, the hallmark of the institution.

The same is true of the advancement manager's impact within the halls of the organization, except in that setting it is the advancement manager's responsibility to represent advancement. This is done out of a clear and detailed understanding of the importance of and the functions served by advancement operations. He or she is called on to be not just advancement's chief representative to the rest of the organization; he or she must be advancement's best, most articulate, and thoughtful spokesperson. The advancement manager should display a spirit of cooperation in relationships with colleagues, empathy for their problems, optimism in the face of difficult circumstances, and emotional equilibrium. The advancement manager will not be a huckster thrusting his or her own agenda on others, but a proponent, with compelling arguments, of the importance and value of philanthropy in twenty-first century America.

The representative role of the advancement manager is a complex and oftentimes a heavy burden to shoulder, but it is a major component of the job.

REFERENCE

1. A. Maslow, *Motivation and Personality* (New York: Harper & Row, 1954).

CHAPTER 2

The Scope of Advancement Activities

It is little more than a hundred years since advancement officers, by whatever title, began moving across the American landscape. Earlier, to be sure, volunteer efforts to secure support for institutions and organizations on the nation's social horizon had achieved remarkable success. Indeed, when the French writer and statesman Alexis de Torqueville completed his landmark study, *The American Democracy* in 1835, he gave particular praise to the citizen-initiated and supported "voluntary associations" that he felt were unique to this nation. Torqueville asserts, in his work, that the United States is the most democratic society in the world and asks the question, "Is (it) just an accident, or is there really some necessary connection between (voluntary) associations and equality?"[1] (p. 517)

HISTORICAL BACKGROUND

Educational institutions, organizations providing for the sick and the destitute, and entities to provide for the public order and safety were established in the Colonial period and served on the initiative, commitment, and support of citizen volunteers. Many important American institutions born in that era continue to thrive today. Harvard University is a prime, but not the sole, example of that fact.

The initiatives those early American "volunteers" mounted could be, and often were, haphazard; they tended to emerge in response to specific circumstances rather than as a grand design; they found their leaders from among a few who chose involvement as a way of life; and they often answered to individual conscience alone, rather than to a formal group charged with oversight. The structure of government, at every level, largely ignored community efforts in education, health and welfare, and public safety. By the early nineteenth century, the institutions of government (town, county, state) had begun to address the challenge of providing education for their young. And they began the work of establishing publicly supported institutions of higher (i.e., post-secondary) learning in several states, modeled on the voluntarily created "private" colleges of the colonial era. The effect of such efforts was to make higher education available to a wider population by providing tax monies to pay for buildings, books, equipment, and faculty, albeit with modest fees charged to enrollees. The passage of the Morril Act in 1856, which led to the creation of land-grant institutions to bring science to agriculture (Pennsylvania State University and Michigan State University are the names by which the two earliest land-grant institutions are known today), moved forward the involvement of the government in the commitment to higher education.

The history of formal involvement by the agencies of government in health and welfare issues, though different in detail, is similar to the government's involvement in education: localities, counties, and states became aware of social and health needs previously addressed solely on a voluntary basis. They created tax-supported institutions modeled on those pioneered on a voluntary basis, committing public funds to social service and the care of the sick, widows, and orphans.

In the final half of the nineteenth century, the provision of education, safety, welfare, and health services in the United States was frequently marked by confusion: Who was responsible for what services? Who paid for those services? From what sources did support come? What were the standards by which services could be measured? Who was eligible for services? Many "private" (i.e., voluntarily established institutions and organizations) found their very existence at risk. They had earlier (in some cases decades earlier) been able to depend on the largess (i.e., the gifts) of like-minded individuals to provide the funds necessary to serve their clients or students. Many also depended on fees for services (tuition in the case of colleges, board and care fees in the case of health and welfare organizations). Much, though not all, of the support necessary to provide for these private organizations came from churches, and support flowed, more or less readily, out of religious principle and conviction.

GOVERNMENT'S ROLE

The growing role of government in providing funds for public agencies threatened the life of the voluntarily established institutions. Many ceased operations. Others responded by intensifying efforts to secure financial support from their several publics. They determined it was necessary to hire persons to gather funds to support operations. *Organized* efforts to secure contributions thus were born in the United States.

The ambiguity existing between support for organizations and institutions committed to the public good depending on private contributions and those existing on public (i.e., tax) monies remains to this day. The classic question is "If an institution receives public support (a college, for example), does it also deserve voluntary contributions?" That issue has been joined in a number of ways and at a variety of points in the last hundred years. Private educational institutions called on their graduates to share a portion of their financial resources with their alma mater. Social service and youth serving agencies sought funds from the public to build facilities to deliver the services thought important by leadership. Hospitals (and tuberculosis sanitoria) and neighborhood associations looked for private dollars to sustain their efforts. All the while, these organizations sought to convince agencies of government they were worthy of tax support.

A trend became apparent among "charities": (1) to seek and secure private contributions in ever-growing amounts to support the complex of programs and services required by society and (2) to encourage the agencies of government to commit public funds in support of those services and institutions. Throughout the twentieth century the history of financing for social, health, and educational services may be seen and understood as a drama between public (i.e., tax) support and private (i.e., contributions) support. The final act of the drama remains far in the future.

PRIVATE PHILANTHROPY

Along the way, other plots have crept into the drama. For example, institutions that had their origins and their sole support in the public arena (e.g., state universities) felt a need to augment their support through private philanthropy. Those efforts at augmentation have not been free of turmoil; several years after World War II, the leadership of several public institutions of higher education in California agreed with the leadership of selected private institutions in the state that the publics would seek private support only from their graduates or their graduates' families or employers, leaving a wide universe of potential donors available solely to the nonpublic institutions. Efforts were undertaken in other states to have publicly supported institutions of higher education prohibited by law from seeking or securing gift support from the larger public. In at least one state those efforts passed into law, and have subsequently passed from the law. Such walls, thus artificially designed and erected, have, for the most part, tumbled down, and the solicitation of voluntary support has become something akin to a free market.

Designating and paying certain individuals to create the conditions for gift support and organizing to secure contributions is recent when seen against the backdrop of our nation's history. The explosive growth in the numbers of professionals employed in advancement is more recent yet. This growth in the number of advancement staff may be accounted for by several factors: (1) some institutions that, in years gone by, eschewed the search for private support, believing it to be an unreliable basis on which organizational growth could be financed, have examined giving statistics and been persuaded that philanthropy provides a vast, untapped potential for income growth; (2) nonprofit institutions in the United States have grown to phenomenal numbers in the last two decades (in 1996 the Internal Revenue Service [IRS] reported that there were over 1,100,000 organizations to which the federal government accorded nonprofit status) and many of these organizations employ advancement professionals to seek contributed support decisions*; and (3) social and political pressures and decisions have combined to cause many nonprofit organizations to expand programs and thus to require additional funds for operations.

Throughout the period of time in which the search for contributions support has been marked by staff and formal institutional involvement, the person responsible has been thought of as a fund raiser. Other terms have had their vogue: campaign director, development officer, and director of development have been, perhaps, the most common. Consistent with growth in numbers and in need, the functions clustering about private support have followed a well-known principle of social organization, namely, that operations have become highly rationalized and staff have moved toward specialization.

The current, accepted designation for the search for support is advancement. *Advancement refers to the complex of activities that seek to secure support for institutions and organizations that have been determined to be exempt from the payment of federal and state income taxes and to which contributions have been held to be tax deductible.*

Tax Exemption

A few words should be addressed on issues related to tax exemption. When the United States needed to raise additional funds in 1917 to support the nation's efforts in prosecuting the first World War, the first "permanent" federal income tax was passed by Congress, signed by President Wilson, and became the law of the land. (The nation had enacted taxes on income on earlier occasions, but they were enforced briefly or held unlawful by the courts.) The 1917 Revenue Act, as amended, provided for taxpayer deductions for the purpose of computing net income for contributions to "religious, charitable, scientific, or educational (corporations or associations) or to societies for the prevention of cruelty to children

---

*Many nonprofit organizations are very small and thus rely for support on a limited number of persons. Most of these do not employ advancement staff. The current scope of the philanthropic enterprise may be seen, however, in the ever-rising membership totals of the professional organizations related to advancement: CASE, NSFRE, AHP.

or animals." That simple provision for charitable deductions has, subsequently, been amended many times, and the current code relating to charitable gifts covers many pages and encompasses scores of conditions, exceptions, and special circumstances. Charitable deduction provisions relating to the estate tax and the gift tax were enacted as those taxes passed into law in 1921 and 1932 respectively.

The federal tax law is quite specific about organizations to which contributions may be considered tax deductible. Under Section 170 of the Internal Revenue Code, tax deductible organizations are specified for maximum deductibility (50% of a donor's base) and lesser deductibility (30% of the donor's base). The advancement manager should be conversant with the provisions of Section 170. In short (this is not to substitute for detailed legal definitions), maximum deductibility organizations include churches; educational organizations; hospitals, medical centers, and medical research organizations; governmental units; operating foundations; pass-through foundations; pooled-fund foundations; and certain other organizations whose funds are used in support of recognized charities.

Organizations held by the IRS to qualify under the tax code as exempt from taxes and whose donors are eligible to deduct contributions from their tax base are designated as 501(c) organizations. Such organizations have applied for the exempt status and supplied supporting documentation leading to the determination by the taxing authorities. There are 10 categories of 501(c) organizations, but the vast majority of exempt organizations are determined to be 501(c)(3) organizations.

> [Sec. 501(c)(3)]
> (3) Corporations, and any community chest, fund, or foundation, organized and operated exclusively for religious, charitable, scientific, testing for public safety, literary, or educational purposes, or to foster national or international amateur sports competition (but only if no part of its activities involve the provision of athletic facilities or equipment), or for the prevention of any private shareholder or individual, no substantial part of the activities of which is carrying on propaganda, or otherwise attempting, to influence legislation, (except as otherwise provided in subsection (h)), and which does not participate in, or intervene in (including the publishing or distributing of statements), any political campaign on behalf of (or in opposition to) any candidate for public office.

The IRS publishes a book annually (Publication 78) known as "The Cumulative List," which identifies all organizations qualified to receive gifts for which a charitable deduction is allowed. The publication also identifies those organizations that are 50 percent type organizations (compare above) and those that are 30 percent type organizations.

It is not sufficient for the advancement manager or for staff reporting to the manager to say simply that contributions are deductible; there are detailed and limiting provisions to deductibility, and it is a compelling managerial responsibility to be sufficiently conversant with the tax code to be able to identify those kinds of gifts or circumstances under which the limiting provisions apply. The ready availability of an attorney conversant with the provisions of the tax laws as those laws apply to charitable contributions, or of a certified public accountant (CPA), will prove invaluable to the advancement manager.

A "typical" advancement office in a large, complex institution such as a university or a major medical center will incorporate several divisions or subsets: development or fund raising, public affairs, publications, government affairs (or, perhaps, church relations), or alumni relations (in the case of educational institutions). Each of those divisions may be subdivided into several constituent parts or activities. In the case of a smaller organization, a liberal arts college, or a voluntary health agency, all or most of the activities will be undertaken by an individual or a small staff, each member of which will be responsible for a constellation of the requisite activities.

Development/Fund Raising

The acquisition of contributed or granted funds is the *sine que non* of the advancement office. Without funds to operate—funds that a public marked by greater or lesser generosity must give—the institution of which the advancement office is an integral part will cease operations. Growing understanding of the reason(s) persons give, increased sophistication in identifying and understanding potential donors, and wider appreciation for the varied sources of contributions or grants have led to remarkable levels of specialization among those charged with raising funds.

Prospect Research

As a distinct specialty within fund raising, prospect research may be seen as a relatively recent phenomenon. That is not to suggest that the activities in which prospect researchers specialize were not understood in past generations. When Booker T. Washington wrote to Andrew Carnegie requesting financial support to build a library at Tuskeegee Institute, he had searched out and discovered several important things about the philanthropist he solicited. Among them:

- where he lived
- the kinds of activities he supported

- requests with specific dollar amounts identified, which were more likely to receive favorable attention
- self-help projects were viewed in a positive light

That knowledge enabled Washington to couch his request in terms that resulted in a gift of $20,000 (the amount requested) to construct Tuskeegee's first library building.

Prospect research has informed fund raisers throughout our history and across the face of American philanthropy: when we have come to know that Mary Jones' mother was treated in our hospital; when we have learned, in conversation, that Peter Smith has a passionate commitment to young musicians; when we discovered that Roy Johnson's father attributed his financial success to the education he received in prep school, we have engaged in prospect research. Prior knowledge of a prospective donor, a program of prospect cultivation based on that knowledge, and success in securing the gift have been understood as closely related elements. That understanding has led development offices, in recent years, to formalize the search for useful information by establishing staffed prospect research offices. One well-known and successful senior-level advancement professional has commented, "The first staff member I brought with me to my present position was my director of prospect research. She is proactive, dogged, and has a clear understanding of what fund raisers need in the way of information to do their jobs. She was invaluable when we worked together earlier; she has helped to transform advancement operations in the institution which currently employs us."

Among several professional organizations for prospect researchers in the United States, the largest is the Association of Professional Researchers for Advancement (APRA).

It is informative to identify the kinds of information about potential donors that prospect researchers can provide to development officers (see Exhibit 2–1). It is not unusual for a prospect researcher to discover unexpected information in the process of searching for material to assist a development officer in making an appeal to a potential donor. Sometimes such information is of a personal or private nature. In such cases, the researcher will determine whether it is appropriate to pass along such information to the relevant fund raiser. Not all researchers are in agreement as to their responsibilities in surprise situations. Some hold that if they have discovered information, by lawful means, that information must be shared with their specific constituency (i.e., the development officer who has requested the search). Others feel that the only data to be shared must have been derived in response to queries and from public sources. Whatever the resolution to such a sensitive issue, the prospect researcher will, on conclusion of his or her information search, prepare a prospect profile for delivery to the requesting fund raiser.

Exhibit 2–1 Information about potential donors from prospect research

1. Name, address, telephone number
2. Age
3. Marital status
4. Family relationships and history
5. Memberships—clubs, churches, professional organizations
6. Education—how much, where, when
7. Real estate holdings
8. Securities holdings
9. Present and past employers and positions held
10. Giving history—how much, to whom
11. Public notice as reflected in the media

The profile, thus presented, will summarize the information uncovered in a few pages of text. The researcher may, in certain instances, ask to speak to the development officer to explain or define the information provided.

Databases

One of the reasons that prospect research has shown marked growth in recent years is the widespread availability of computers and of the databases to which researchers may refer. The growth of the Internet and the World Wide Web have made possible growing accuracy and detail in prospect information searches. When such services as Lexis/Nexis, Orca, and the various real property databases are coupled to information internally available in the institution or organization, information becomes available, to provide reasonably extensive and accurate pictures of most prospective donors.

Such a conclusion is based on the assumption that those responsible for prospect research will have been provided with appropriate hardware and a range of relevant software to support the research efforts being pursued by staff. In those organizations for which such assumptions do not hold, many are able to retrieve appropriate information from a variety of relevant, published reference directories: *Who's Who*, the several directories of the Taft Group and Knight Ridder, U.S. Census printouts, the *Foundation Directory* and companion regional or state volumes. For the expenditure of several hundred dollars annually, many small and medium-sized contribution-seeking organizations are able to acquire, maintain, and make available information derived from collections of prospect/donor data. Other organizations rely on and make use of the collections maintained in public or university libraries. It has been suggested, perhaps accurately, that much of the research data now available in print format will, within the decade, be available *only* on one or another of the electronic formats.

Prospect Management

Across the face of nonprofit America, an additional responsibility has been identified for prospect researchers: the management of prospects. The challenge associated with this responsibility may be summarized in the phrase "too many challenges, too few prospects." In brief, organizations with multiple development staff frequently find themselves facing a situation in which two, three, or more development officers have focused on the same prospect. The chief advancement officer understands that he or she can acquiesce to multiple solicitations of the prospect only at the risk of alienating this person. The problem, anxiety producing though it may be, must be addressed in ways that will meet both institutional needs and prospect desires.

In many institutions and organizations employing multiple advancement staff members, the Office of Prospect Research has been given the responsibility of "directing fund-raiser traffic." Typically, the office will hold biweekly or monthly prospect management meetings at which contact staff will be identified for prime prospective donors. The primary contact may be accorded first cultivation or solicitation rights for a period of time (three months, six months) at the end of which, failing a successful solicitation, the secondary contact person will assume responsibility and commence cultivation or solicitation efforts. Multiple requests for prospect assignment can produce significant advancement office tension and produce strain on otherwise cooperative relationships. Among the several factors that will guide prospect management efforts, these are crucial:

- the relative importance to the employing institution of the projects that the contending development officers represent
- the congruence that may be discerned between research material and the projects for which each of the development officers seek support
- the priority in time as it applies to the contending development officers that is, who first requested assignment and which project must be funded sooner

The foregoing (albeit brief) discussion of prospect management activities presupposes an institution with many fund raisers and a staff prospect operation for which prospect management is a defined responsibility. In those situations in which neither of those circumstances apply, the advancement manager will assume responsibility for managing prospects within and among staff members.

Fund Raisers

It was noted earlier that persons charged with securing contributions for their institutions go by a variety of titles. Development officer or director of development are the most common; throughout this book, those are the designations that will be used to identify the staff member charged with raising funds. Development, as a descriptor, is intended to have a meaning somewhat larger and deeper than "fund raiser." It is acknowledged that such titles have an expansive intent; still, the acquisition of contributions support for the employing institution is the *major* responsibility of the development officer, a reality that is forgotten only at major cost to other dimensions of the job.

In most advancement offices, development officers are those most exposed: they are the ones who will have been given dollar goals and who will be held accountable for reaching those goals; they will add to (or detract from) the perception within the institution of advancement office competence; they will identify, cultivate, and solicit donors; they will be part of the effort to define priority funding projects; they will be responsible for committing to words the relevant reasons for the support of projects; and they will maintain relationships, on behalf of the institution, with past donors. To employ a battlefield metaphor, development officers are on the frontline.

The advancement manager understands the responsibility to support development officers in their efforts by making provision for prospect research, training, support staff, equipment, and supplies. This manager will be available to provide advice and counsel to the individual development officer, accompany him or her on important cultivation or solicitation calls as desired, and encourage or commiserate as necessary. For all the assistance available and supplied, the development officer has primary responsibility for one-on-one relationships with prospects and donors.

The advancement manager will be most useful to fund-raisers by creating an organizational structure that makes for success. One of the requirements is that such a structure provides that the scope of the development officer's specific responsibility is both delineated and limited. Thus, in a university, a development officer may be assigned to a specific college or school within the university (the School of Physical Sciences, for example) with no responsibility, or only limited responsibility for what happens or is required in other units of the university. In a medical center, a development officer may be told that efforts should only be focused on raising funds for research, or capital efforts, or endowment efforts, while fund raising for clinical needs "belongs" to someone else. The next chapter provides extended discussion of centralized and decentralized organizational models for advancement. Whichever model is operative in the institution, the development office (as, indeed, associated staff members) will function best when specific responsibilities are defined, understood, and honored.

The advancement manager will have selected persons to serve as development officers in whom the manager has confidence. The manager will be clear, as assigned responsibilities are handed out, about *what* is to be accomplished, and scrupulously avoid the temptation to define *how* tasks are to be accomplished and responsibilities fulfilled. Unless asked for guidance about the mechanics of a contact or an "ask," the advancement manager exhibits confidence that the development staff knows how they will undertake their tasks in a fashion consistent with personal styles and commitments.

Having said that, it must also be added that the competent manager will be knowledgeable about the efforts of development officers. The manager will meet with staff, both individually and as a group. The manager will have set in place a reporting mechanism that will provide monthly information from each development officer about the personal calls made, telephone calls completed, meetings attended, materials written, and so forth. Exhibit 2–2 is a simple monthly report

Exhibit 2–2 Development officer monthly report form

ABC University   Office of University Advancement

Report for the Month of _____ Year _____

Development Director's Name _____

  Current Assignment _____

Number of contacts with prospective donors _____

Names of prospective donors contacted—Please indicate if contact was in person (P), by telephone (T), or in writing (W).

Number of stewardship contacts _____
Names of persons with whom stewardship contacts were made.

Meetings attended–specify the nature.

Writing projects in progress–identify projected completion date.

Amount of gifts received during the month _____
Amount of pledges received _____
Problems encountered or issues raised which should be addressed.

Signature _____
Date _____

Please note: The monthly report is due in the Office of the Vice President for University Advancement on the 10th of each month.

form for development officers. The information derived from the use of such a reporting device provides the advancement manager with a quick, more or less comprehensive overview of individual development officer efforts. It may serve as a useful backdrop to, or an agenda for, the manager's meetings with each development officer. The material asked of development officers, illustrated in Exhibit 2–2, will readily lend itself, where desired, to the creation of a simple computer program, thus making the filing of reports easy and quick.

Successful development officers, differing though they may be, are marked by high levels of self-motivation. The advancement manager will tune in to that trait by engaging development officers in the decision making that goes into advancement operations. Virtually every growing advancement operation has established an informal committee or task-force structure to elicit the input of staff. Such a structure may identify four or five issues of institutional importance (e.g., donor recognition, training, budget, donor stewardship) and set in place task forces to address and make counsel to the advancement manager. The task forces will be given a specific period of time in which to do their work and a date by which a report is due. A number of advantages flow from such a process: the development of quality ideas, the creation of team identity, the building of a sense of shared management, and, not least, a lessening of the manager's workload.

It is important to note that the manager will need to be conscious of the time consumed by task forces, reports, and staff meetings. Time thus expended is time taken away from the primary responsibility: the raising of funds and attendant issues. One skillful advancement manager, in a large university, limited the expenditure of time on all activities apart from the development officers' primary assignments, to eight hours per month or the equivalent of one working day in each 30-day cycle. That manager was not only clear in his own mind about that parameter, he spoke about it to staff, faculty, and deans for the sake of making clear his priority for development officers: the raising of funds.

Planned Giving

Those who are charged with assisting prospective donors to structure their assets in ways that will benefit both the institution and the donor are typically referred to as planned giving officers. Advantaging themselves by responses shaped by the relevant provisions of the federal tax code, such prospective donors are able to take advantage of giving vehicles that range from the simple (bequests) to the complicated (charitable remainder unitrusts, annuities, charitable lead trusts, pooled income funds, etc.). In the case of bequests, the donor is enabled, by will, to benefit a nonprofit institution or charity and create circumstances that will reduce or eliminate taxes potentially owing by the donor's estate. The other cited giving vehicles provide current tax advantages (based on the donor's age at the time the planned giving contract is executed) and income flow. It has been estimated that trillions of dollars will pass from one generation to the next in the decade ending 2010; federal and state taxes are likely to take significant percentages of the intergenerational transfer of funds through inheritance and estate taxes. To the degree that funds are transferred to nonprofit organizations or institutions, estate and gift taxes may be reduced or eliminated, and provide other lifetime benefits to the donor.

Advancement staff members with responsibilities directed to asset-related or estate-related issues have provided services to the advancement functions of nonprofit organizations and institutions over the course of several decades. As donor asset bases have grown by leaps and bounds (in part as a result of real property inflation), as taxes have come to appear more confiscatory (capital gains as a partisan issue), and as institutions of the third (nonprofit) sector have grown in sophistication, the advantages of financial planning have become greater and more apparent and suggest a larger role—one that advantages donors—for charitable giving.

Those employed by nonprofit organizations as planned giving officers may be (or may have been) practicing attorneys. Many will have attended or graduated from law school. Others will have taken courses or completed course work designed to make participants expert in the arcana of U.S. tax laws as they relate to the assignment of assets. Many organizations, including CASE and NSFRE, offer instruction in planned giving. Similarly, course work provided by such vendors as Conrad Teitel, the Robert Sharpe Co. of Tennessee, and other firms has enjoyed wide support and produced successful planned giving officers. Among the institutions employing planned giving specialists are colleges and universities, hospitals and medical centers, national offices of health, social service and youth-serving agencies, and the headquarters of established religious organizations.

Having been assured in the employment process that a planned giving officer is technically competent, the advancement manager will understand that growing institutional resources from planned gifts tends to be painfully slow. While the typical fund raiser (development officer) is likely to raise funds in the first year on the job that are equal to a multiple of the officer's annual salary, the planned giving officer will, not infrequently, require three to five years to produce a positive cash flow. On the positive side, when dollars for the institution from planned gifts start to flow, they tend to be significant (i.e. large), often unrestricted, and certain. The employment of staff in planned giving represents an investment in the future. The availability of large resources for intergenerational transfer suggests that planned giving is a certain, if delayed, path to philanthropic success.

Foundations and Corporations

As planned giving officers, those charged with responsibility for seeking and securing funds from foundations and corporations are development officers with a difference: their job is defined by the potential source of money for the employing institution rather than by the subunit seeking funds. Foundation and corporate giving officers appeared on the scene in many advancement offices some years before prospect researchers began showing up in numbers. They are, as their titles indicate, responsible, in degrees that vary by institution, for securing philanthropic support from organizations.

In small organizations, foundation and corporate fund raising may be the responsibility of the mainstream development officers(s). To the degree that a staff member is specifically assigned the foundation/corporate solicitation responsibility, the foundation/corporate assignment may have fallen to a development officer who has demonstrated (or is expected to demonstrate) particular skill in dealing with funding agencies. In medium-sized organizations, the director of foundation and corporate giving will research and identify prospective donor organizations, write and submit proposals, and negotiate the terms of grants. In larger fund-raising operations, the foundation/corporate giving officer may manage solicitations, working with decentralized fund-raising staff to plan requests, writing proposals, and involving several staff in determining which of several possible asks should be set before which funding entity. In large fund-raising staffs, there may be several foundation and corporate giving officers, and they may have assigned specialties. Most foundation and corporate giving directors have succeeded to their positions from generalist fund-raising responsibilities. Perhaps they experienced some noteworthy success in the grants field; perhaps there was a vacancy to which they were assigned.

Understanding that grants writing may be the least important element in a successful foundation or corporate solicitation, the foundation or corporate officer will spend much of the time building relationships of mutual interest and trust with program officers or corporate executives. Efforts will be expended on creating a proper match between requests and the commitments of the funding entity. Courses in grants writing may be found in the extension or regular offerings of a majority of community colleges and universities in the country. Instruction on the larger issues of strategizing for foundation and corporate grants is one of the marks of the courses offered through the Grantsmanship Center, a Los Angeles organization offering instruction in classes scheduled throughout the country.

Database Directors

Staff members responsible for overseeing and maintaining the integrity of advancement databases are to be found in most of the institutions and organizations in the nonprofit world. Their titles differ widely. Once thought to be "only" a clerical function—and still understood in that fashion in many smaller organizations—the work of keeping track of prospect and donor names, addresses and telephone numbers, gift history, pledge payments, and important supporting data is one of the critical functions of every organization depending on gift support. On the one hand, the job has been made infinitely easier, in recent years, by the wide availability of computer hardware and sophisticated software. (We have come a long way from the days where constituent records were maintained on file cards in the proverbial "shoebox.") On the other hand, records maintenance and accessibility have become complex due to the volume of material it is now possible to keep, manipulate, and use. The following example illustrates the contribution that can be made by a database director.

Brian, a highly competent advancement records director, has made his services virtually indispensable to his institution by becoming the advancement staffs' computer guru. He makes certain that each member of the advancement staff has a functioning, late-model computer and the availability, close at hand, of fast, letter-quality printers. He assures that all of the staff know how and when to use the several software packages available to them. He provides regular training to his colleague advancement staff members and ensures that they are able to take advantage of relevant information available on the Internet.

Simultaneous with the provision of such valuable in-house service, the database records manager will maintain all of the organization's advancement records of relevance. The single most valuable asset of every nonprofit organization is its list. The database manager knows and understands that fact and provides the staff of the institution for which he or she works with the lists—and supporting data—necessary for them to accomplish their work. The records will be brought to currency on a continuing basis, new information being added to existing data as it becomes available. The database manager will interface easily and frequently with colleague advancement staff members, regularly filing the information discovered. This manager may be charged with overseeing the process of acknowledging gifts or, if another staff member is assigned that responsibility, will work in close cooperation to assure that the "thank-you" process is both prompt and accurate.

Among the major responsibilities of the database manager is learning about, evaluating, and making recommendations regarding advancement software packages. The field changes rapidly; software that was adequate last year may be obsolescent this year. The firms that design, test, and market advancement-related software are innovative and aggressive; as they "push the envelope," it falls to the database manager to determine if the new products available will serve the institution's advancement needs more appropriately than those previously in use. Both the hardware and software available and in service for advancement operations require significant investments on the part of nonprofit institutions; it is not uncommon for a "conversion" to new software for a major institution to require the expenditure of several hundreds of thousands of dollars and the commitment of vast amounts of staff time. Though the costs may be less for smaller institutions, they will still represent a significant dollar commitment in relative terms. Cost/benefit ratios must be thoughtfully calculated and weighed. The effective database manager earns the confidence of the advancement manager by sensitivity to institutional budget realities.

Annual Fund

A baseline activity for most nonprofit organizations, the annual fund is the effort to secure gifts, usually unrestricted, that may be applied to the ongoing operations of the organization. It is referred to as an annual fund because, unlike program grants or planned gifts, the efforts to secure gifts must be repeated each year. In most institutions, the annual fund not only raises money, but it serves the important purpose of identifying potential future major gift donors. "Before a donor will give $50,000, he will first have given $100" the advancement aphorism instructs. Thus, the advancement office scans the annual donor list for the names of persons who may, by cultivation and solicitation, be moved up the giving pyramid.

Techniques in use to secure annual gifts fall into three primary categories: direct mail, the telefund, and special events. In most, though not all institutions, the annual fund director will engage in activities associated with all three techniques. Staff reporting to the annual fund director are, by and large, focused on providing efforts in support of one or another of the strategies.

Direct mail. Direct mail solicitations are well known to most Americans. A mailing package, typically consisting of a number 10 carrier envelope, a letter, a brochure, and a business reply envelope, is received by the addressee. In the letter and brochure, an appeal is made for funds to support an organization or a cause. The letter is often signed by a person known to the addressee, sometimes a celebrity. The message contained in the letter and brochure states a need (often in story format), a solution (the services provided by the organization making the appeal), and urgency ("please write and send your check today"). That direct mail solicitations are and can be effective in raising funds may be deduced from the volume of such mail. Mail specialists identify three factors impacting on a mail appeal's success: the list, the package, and the message or appeal.

The use of direct mail can be expensive. The cost of supplies (paper), labor (printing), and postage have driven up the cost per letter mailed (sometimes abbreviated as CPLM) to a level at which its efficacy is in question. Competition, compounded by the multiplicity of appeals received by the average householder, has driven down the returns per letter mailed (RPLM). Many nonprofit organizations report that prospect mailings rarely result in a response rate greater than one quarter to one half of 1 percent. Letters to previous donors, however, typically result in much higher returns. As a consequence, increasing numbers of organizations using the mail to raise money focus their efforts on appealing to previous donors, reserving prospecting for other techniques (e.g., the telephone or special events). Other nonprofits use direct mail only as a supplement to their telefund: sending mail or postcards announcing that a recipient is to be called on a particular night or indicating that a call was attempted without success and a response by mail will be valued. Recent improvisations on the direct mail theme (the use of e-mail, fax messages, overnight mail) may be seen as efforts to retain the principal advantages of mail: making contact, on behalf of the institution, with many potential or actual supporters at one time, with a minimal expenditure of staff time, while minimizing the disadvantages (large amounts of competitive mail, low-levels of readership, etc.).

Utilization of segmentation techniques by many organizations utilizing direct mail similarly are attempts to maximize both numeric and dollar response to mail appeals. With segmentation, addressees are grouped by known or presumed interests for receipt of letters written and designed to appeal to those specific interests. Thus, instead of sending a single, all-purpose appeal letter to everyone on the list, an institution committed to prospect segmentation may create eight, ten, or more versions of the appeal letter, sending a given version only to those whose profile closely corresponds to the content of the letter.

Telefund. The telefund (sometimes referred to as a phonathon or a telethon) is, at its simplest and most direct, the organized effort to solicit, by telephone, prospects or previous donors on behalf of the organization. The use of the phone for fund-raising purposes is several decades old, but its widespread use in the telefund format grew most rapidly in the 1980s and 1990s. A distinguishing mark of the telefund is that many persons are engaged in making fund-raising calls from one location at the same time. It is felt that the group spirit, thus created and maintained, is useful in counteracting the gloom that may accompany negative responses to the appeal and in communicating a high level of vitality and enthusiasm to those called.

Some organizations making use of the telephone for the annual fund campaign rely solely on volunteer callers. Others hire persons with ties to the organization (students, for example, in the case of colleges) to do the telephoning. Still others enter into a contract with a telemarketing firm to do their telephone fund raising for them. A few organizations use some combination of these identified mechanisms. In whatever fashion the telefund is staffed, the standard arrangements call for a large room with many desks (or tables), chairs, and telephones. In some cases in which callers are paid, each station is furnished with a computer on the screen of which appear the names, addresses, and telephone numbers of persons to be called. Where a computer is available to the callers, responses to a call (financial commitment, rejection, equivocation) can be immediately recorded on the prospect's/

donor's record. Where computers are not available, the callers are provided with lists of persons to be called. Record-keeping is accomplished by hand for input to the database at a later time. A relatively recent electronic development affecting the telefund is the implementation of predictive dialing equipment, which automatically dials numbers on the list, thus accomplishing contact rapidly and predictably.

Virtually all organizations provide telefund callers with a script that provides for self-introduction, identification of the organization sponsoring the call, reasons to support the organization, the appeal, and the ask. (Some telemarketing specialists encourage callers to ask questions of the prospects and to record questions and concerns for later use by advancement staff. Others stress brevity for the sake of maximizing the number of calls per telephone minute.)

Also provided to callers are pledge forms that are to be completed as a prospect agrees to contribute. (See Exhibit 2–3 for a reproduction of a telefund pledge form.) Callers are encouraged to check the accuracy of records at the time the pledge is recorded: spelling of name, correct address, correct ZIP code. Some telefunds encourage the use of credit cards on the basis that the pledge commitment is sure to be fulfilled within a brief time; others avoid asking for credit card information, recognizing the negative publicity associated with various telephone credit card frauds. Effective telefund managers are agreed that the completed form, together with the business reply envelope, should be mailed to the donor on the same day or evening the pledge has been secured.

Virtually all enduring and successful telefunds have a manager in the phone room at all times to answer questions, deal with problems as they arise, replenish supplies or refreshments, and encourage callers. Many telefunds have a policy in place that calls for all pledges in excess of a predetermined amount (perhaps $500 or $1,000) to be verified by return phone call, initiated by the manager, to the pledger.

The fund-raising effectiveness of the telephone campaign is demonstrated by the fact that affirmative responses to a phone request for a contribution often are in the 30 percent plus range when the list is comprised of persons with an identified relationship to the calling organization. The reverse side of those highly encouraging statistics is that many persons, including some who have a solid and continuing relationship to the calling organization, resent the intrusion that a fund-raising phone call represents to them. That resentment may be lessened when the caller is a volunteer, a fellow alumnus, or a student.

Special events. A special event is one to which members of the public are invited, for which they typically pay an inflated price to participate, and from which the sponsoring organization benefits as a result of the excess of revenue over costs. Thus, the Acme Neighborhood Association, a tax-exempt organiza-

Exhibit 2–3 Telefund pledge form

Trulygreat Medical Center
7890 High Street
Best City, U.S.A.

Donor Name
xxx Main Street
City, State 12345

Dear Mr. Name:

Thank you for the generous pledge you made to Trulygreat Medical Center when ___(name of telefund worker)___ spoke with you last evening, ___(date)___.

Your pledge of ___(inserted pledge amount)___ will enable us to continue to provide high quality medical care to the citizens of Best City and to do so at the lowest possible cost.

We note that you expressed the desire that your contribution be directed to ___(insert special interest identified by donor)___. At Trulygreat we are committed to abiding by the instructions of all our donors.

I have enclosed an envelope you may use to mail your check in support of your pledge. The envelope requires no postage. I want to express the appreciation of the Board, the entire staff, and the patients at Trulygreat for your support of our efforts.

Sincerely,

John Smith, M.D.
Chairman of the Board

P.S. Your prompt response to this pledge confirmation will enable us to put your gift to work at once. Thanks again.

---

tion, sponsors a black-tie dinner dance at the Truly Ritzy Hotel. Friends and neighbors are invited to attend with tickets selling for $250 a couple. Two hundred couples attend, producing a gross revenue of $50,000. As a result of careful negotiation, the annual fund director of Acme Neighborhood Association is able to hold expenses to $92.20 per couple or $18,440. The special event thus nets the association $31,560 (the difference between the $50,000 revenue and the $18,440 expense), which is immediately incorporated into the organization's operating budget.

Among the characteristics of successful events are:

- identification of events that have broad appeal
- enlistment of an event committee comprised of persons who are prepared to recruit their family, friends, and neighbors to attend
- a ticket price that will be deemed "reasonable" by the invited public but will, at the same time, maximize revenue for the sponsoring organization
- recruitment of financial support from individual or corporate underwriters to pay for some or all of the expenses
- creation of a device that will capture the names and addresses of attendees for potential future use by the sponsoring organization
- exploitation of other means to maximize event income (selling ads in the program book, silent auction, raffle, etc.)

Special events are, as a rule, staff intensive even when a solid committee is in place and operational. The difference between expense and income frequently appears small when compared to effort. The tie-in between the nature of the event (a dinner dance) and the purpose of the organization (feeding the hungry) is frequently weak and often tortured, in which case the sponsor runs the risk of appearing inconsistent or even ridiculous. On the positive side, special events often focus attention on the sponsoring organization and bring public recognition. They can be, both in the planning and implementation phases, a lot of fun, serving to galvanize volunteers and cement relations between staff and volunteers. They may also be useful in identifying affluent future supporters for the organization.

Perhaps the most useful function served by a special event is that the funds realized are usually unrestricted and, assuming the event is successful, can be replicated in a year. Many social service and health agencies depend, in large degree, on special events income to provide the principal support for their organizations. In such cases, it is not unusual for the agency to sponsor eight to twelve events a year ranging from large (hundreds of attendees) to small (dozens), from big ticket events (several hundreds of dollars or more) to inexpensive events ($30 or $40).

The IRS has held that the entire price of an event ticket may not be deducted for income tax purposes; only that portion of the price that is in excess of the cost of the benefits received by the ticket buyer may be considered a charitable gift and thus eligible for deduction. Volunteers, in their enthusiasm, often exclaim ". . . and your ticket price is tax deductible." The advancement manager and staff will be on guard against such over promising, prepared to demonstrate, when necessary, that donors have been well and fully informed on the deductibility issue (i.e., that portion of the ticket that truly represents a charitable contribution). Where special events are involved, it is no longer sufficient for the sponsoring organization to say ". . . deductible to the full extent authorized by law." The organization is required, by federal regulation, to identify for donors the portion of the ticket price that may be construed as a contribution.

Special events staff bear many titles in America's nonprofit community, and their reporting relationships vary from one institution or organization to another. Because special events is often seen as an entry-level position that may lead to another advancement position, the manager will, in providing direction to special events staff, help them to understand that the "fun and games" dimension is not the purpose of their jobs; rather, the staff are a means to acquiring income that the organization seeks in order to accomplish its mission.

Major Gifts

It is safe to say that every advancement manager wants and values major gifts. There is, however, no single definition of a major gift in the nonprofit world. For some organizations, any gift of $500 or more constitutes a significant—a major—commitment; for others even a $100,000 contribution fails to earn major gift status. Every gift-seeking institution defines "major" for itself, taking into consideration the size of the total budget of the organization, the magnitude of the need, the history of gift giving, and the affluence of the prospect/donor pool.

As the definition of major gift varies, so too does the organizational structure put in place to cultivate donors and solicit major gifts. It has been common for medium-sized and large organizations to employ one or more persons who are given specific responsibility for working with the affluent and acquiring large contributions from them to benefit the organization. Often these staff members, titled major gift officers, were persons who were well along on their advancement careers. Major gift officers tended to have an air of self-confidence, a businesslike mien and wardrobe, and extraordinary communication skills. In recent years, many institutions have taken the position that all development officers are or should be major gift officers. They have looked for smaller gifts to flow from the efforts of the well-organized and implemented annual fund effort. In such circumstances, the staff employed to serve the subunits (schools or colleges in a university) have been expected to spend time and energy cultivating and soliciting gifts, contributions, and grants that are of substantial proportions—major gifts. When assistance may be needed or desired in support of a major solicitation, the senior advancement manager has been available to become involved. The part to be played by the chief executive officer of the institution (president, administrator, executive director) is not to be ignored; many such high-level administrators play active roles in the resource acquisition process, especially as that process focuses on the affluent donor who has been cultivated to make a large financial commitment.

Although the concept that "every development officer is a major gifts officer" has gained wide acceptance in advancement offices, large institutions with rich fund-raising histories continue explicitly to name staff to major gift responsibilities, sometimes defining the responsibilities of such officers as the solicitation of gifts in the $500,000+ range.

PUBLIC AFFAIRS

As development constitutes one primary activity within an institution's advancement function, so does public affairs. The offices assigned such responsibilities are variously designated as public affairs, public relations, external relations, and so forth. The officers to which such assignments are made are concerned with the complex of activities that cluster about communication with the institution's many publics.

One focus of the public affairs communications efforts is the internal audience. Depending on the nature of the institution's activities (education, health, welfare), the internal publics vary and tend to include persons in such groups as students, parents, alumni, faculty, staff, administration, volunteers, patients, doctors, other clinical staff, advocates, service recipients, or counselors. Any organization that needs to ensure accurate communication with its internal publics must commence by defining those who comprise the internal public. It has become apparent, with the rapid changes in American society and the polarization that often results from those changes, that careful and continuous communication with those closest to the organization must be undertaken to provide for their sustained and supportive involvement. The communications vehicles utilized will vary by institution but will almost always include group meetings (convocations, retreats), one-on-one encounters (the "open door" policy), print (newsletters, memos), and electronic media (video, e-mail). Scrupulous and regular efforts to inform the internal constituency of institutional activities, policy changes, staff changes or additions, program initiatives, and financial status are crucial to securing and maintaining the support from within, on which every institution depends for organizational health and well-being.

The members of our internal publics live in the community. They relate to friends and neighbors on a regular, ongoing basis. They are, not infrequently, asked questions by friends and neighbors about their work and their employer. Nothing so damages institutional reputation as much as disaffection in the ranks of those closest to the organization. Unexplained changes and inaccurate or incomplete communication are major contributing factors to such disaffection.

A few words must be addressed to the subject of printed communication for the internal constituencies. Most nonprofit organizations will institute some print means of telling the facts of institutional life to their internal publics, most often in the form of a newspaper, newsletter, or newsmagazine. Long, and sometimes sad, experience has established that the form taken by the internal communication vehicle is of less significance than that (1) the material printed is trustworthy, (2) the issues addressed are covered in timely fashion, (3) the material is readable and relatively brief, and (4) the publication is reproduced and distributed on a predictable schedule.

Those charged with staffing public affairs activities are responsible, along with the institutional leadership, for identifying the internal publics with which communications must be maintained; with overseeing the writing, reproduction, and distribution of the print vehicle; and with determining what will be communicated. It has become an axiom of management as we come to the end of the twentieth century and enter on the twenty-first century, that it is difficult in the extreme to keep secrets in organizations. Despite that, some executives prefer to hold back information from their internal constituencies or to dole it out in small, presumably digestible chunks. The public affairs staff will seek out information relating to the organization with a passion for truth and will commit to the disclosure of relevant information as fully as possible. To that end, they will encourage institutional leadership to be frank and forthcoming and will earn respect for their doggedness and their judgment.

Much of the foregoing relates as well to communications with external publics. The public affairs director and staff have major responsibility for creating or maintaining the institutional image. *Image may be defined as the perceptions a person or a group has of an institution, organization, group, or person.* Though many activities go into the building of institutional image—athletic events, plays, concerts, workshops, continuing education, clinics, special events, etc.—the public affairs office involved in most or all such activities. The content in the public media (print and electronic), as that content relates to institutional life, is of great importance.

Thus, the work of public affairs is often seen as comprised almost wholly of writing and sending out press releases. Effective public affairs officers understand, however, that their work and their responsibility is both broader and more complicated than such an attitude suggests. They must "dig out" stories as a reporter searches out the news: this quiet and unassuming physician played an important role in developing a new treatment protocol for diabetes; that social science faculty member is an award-winning grower of orchids; one of the sophomore students has spent his summer vacation working with a missionary team in the slums of Sao Paulo. Such "reporting" of the news through the media to the wider public of the employing institution builds institutional image in important and positive ways.

Of course, the public affairs officer will create and send releases about the ongoing business of the institution and thus place the public on notice about that business: the health fair, the well-baby clinic, the senior recital, the staff promotions. All have a level of importance attached to them, and it is necessary that they find their way into the media. But the step beyond—the identification and distribution of the unexpected news that contributes to readership or viewership interest—is the point at which the merely competent public affairs officer becomes the extraordinary one.

The public affairs office is frequently evaluated on the amount of press coverage received each year by the institution. Although space has a measure of significance, of even greater significance is the depth of coverage secured, that is, how important are the issues addressed, the stories placed, on behalf of the institution? In what detail are issues covered? There are institutional public affairs offices that secure little media coverage and place relatively few stories that are, nonetheless, impressive because of the quality of the reportage their efforts represent. "Not the pounds of ink consumed, but the significance of the coverage our institution receives, is the standard by which my work should be measured," one public affairs director stated. Such a commitment—for depth rather than simply volume—requires the public affairs officer to understand the employing institution in such detail and with such scope that he or she can design and plan the flow and content of the materials made available to the media. The perception behind an approach to an organization's external publics based upon the delivery of comprehensive information of important issues depends upon the cultivation of close, trusting relationships with media professionals. The public affairs office will have built a basis for confidence that major issues will not be trivialized and that complex concerns will not be simplified, in the media, to the point of meaninglessness. The nature of the content communicated to the external public is closely linked to the media relationships nurtured and the trust levels established (organization to media, public affairs officer to reporter).

The advancement manager will expect that the public affairs staff will nurture internal and external contacts, will develop plans for the content of information made available to the media, and will insist that, in addition to routine material, the public affairs staff offer material that is:

- important
- truthful/accurate
- supportive of organizational objectives
- consistent with the institutional mission
- aligned to the interests of the community

It is noted that the requirements of a public affairs office in large institutions are of such nature and complexity that many create and operate a news bureau for dealing with the media.

Yet another issue of moment for the advancement manager is that he or she will expect the public affairs office to set in place a crisis plan. It has been well and accurately said that if any organization exists long enough, it will face a crisis that impacts on the public. The crisis may involve an untimely death, scandal, dereliction on the part of well-known staff, accident, earthquake, fire, or any of a myriad of other untoward events. Every year, countless organizations in the United States are damaged by media coverage of such crises; too often the causes of the damage may be attributed to a lack of preparedness on the part of the institution involved for dealing with crisis. When media representatives descend on an institution in the wake of tragedy, they tend to seek information and attitudes (statements) that are quickly communicated to the public from the first persons they encounter.

A professionally conceived and developed crisis plan will accomplish several goals. It will

- identify a single spokesperson for the institution
- communicate on a continuing basis, to the internal constituency that there is but one official spokesperson
- identify roles to be played by all persons and offices that may be required in crisis situations (the chief executive officer [CEO], police, fire, medical center) with contact persons for each
- be committed to accuracy, even when unpleasant
- be rehearsed, at least annually, by key persons making use of realistic scenarios

In the event of a crisis, the public affairs director (characteristically designated as the organizational spokesperson) will typically be expected to be placed on 24-hour duty. The advancement manager will articulate the crisis plan in formal institutional policies and procedures, will assure that those policies and procedures are endorsed by the institution's highest policy-making body (the board of trustees), and will distribute the approved policies and procedures to key staff and volunteers.

GOVERNMENT OR CHURCH RELATIONS

Government

Staff charged with responsibility for government relations are to be found in publicly supported colleges and universities, some private institutions of higher education, large medical centers, national offices of health, welfare and youth-serving agencies, and in the national professional associations relating to such groups. Sometimes structured as part of the public affairs office, government relations is, more frequently, an independent function whose staff reports directly to the senior advancement manager or the CEO of the employing institution.

Government relations, as that term applies to the organizations of the nonprofit sector, moves in two directions. First, staff members are charged with understanding the details of what is transpiring at the various levels of government (city, county, state, federal) that are of concern or interest to the institution and with communicating those details to the leadership of the institution. Second, those assigned with responsibility for government relations are tasked with representing institutional concerns to both elected officials and governmental staff.

As government relations personnel seek knowledge and understanding, they will read the bulletins, releases, notices, and other published materials made available by the public authorities identifying those arenas of action (or potential action) that might impact on institutional priorities. They will also meet with elected and appointed public officials in both formal and informal settings to understand their agendas and the arguments mustered in support of their positions. The availability of public funds for institutional use, the imposition (real or proposed) of regulatory provisions impacting on the institution, or legislation charting new or modified courses of action in the public sector are all of interest to the government relations staff member. Making certain that institutional leaders are thoroughly and accurately briefed on present and future governmental directions is the highest order of priority for the staff committed to government relations.

Presenting the interests and needs of the employing organization to arms of government is often defined as "lobbying." That term has become, in recent years, one of opprobrium. Representing organizational interests to elected and appointed officials, however, does not necessarily or primarily mean "arm-twisting" of reluctant public servants. In many cases, legislators and regulators do not know but want to be informed of ways in which legislation or regulations may affect specific institutions in the nonprofit sector. Government relations officers are called on to serve a helpful role in the formation and implementation of public policy decisions by helping government officials understand the impact of proposed legislation or regulatory action. As government relations officers are made aware of specific institutional needs for government action (or, on some occasions, inaction), they will inform elected and appointed officials of those needs and contend for them. The government relations staff members of nonprofit institutions will not, as a general rule, participate with institutional funds to the financial support of electoral campaigns of specific candidates or to policies as reflected by ballot initiatives or referenda. Under federal law nonprofit organizations operate under specific strictures relative to organizational funds committed to public policy issues. (They are not forbidden to engage in lobbying or electoral politics; they are limited and thus subject to government review and sanction.)

Among the guidelines observed by advancement managers with reference to staff in government relations is that such staff will stringently avoid representing themselves (i.e., their social/political positions are their own and they have a right to those positions), but when acting in their assigned roles will represent the employing organization and its commitments. Their efforts will be on behalf of the institution, its mission and vision, its strategy and tactics, its program and constituency. In short, institutional commitments will guide the actions of government relations officers.

Church Relations

In those institutions that have a religious tradition (colleges, universities, hospitals, and advocacy groups), the institution's church relations office often occupies the organizational place reserved for the government relations office as identified above. Church relations officers will listen and communicate, and they will represent the employing institution and contend for it in a manner similar to their colleagues in more secular organizations. Their audiences will differ, however, from those addressed by their government relations colleagues: these will be congregations and synods, conferences or dioceses, clergy and laity at local and national levels. Church relations officers' activities also will differ from government relations colleagues in that they will often understand their constituencies (i.e., ecclesiastical agencies) as donor prospects and will develop plans that will result in efforts to secure fiscal support from the religious institution from which they seek to learn and to which they seek to communicate their institutional message. Church relations officers who are often clergy or clergy wives will travel, speak, preach, and solicit as they represent their institutions.

PUBLICATIONS

Even in an age of electronics, the printed word remains a standby of advancement office operations. Compelling messages, presented in appealing graphic formats, reproduced in appropriate numbers, and delivered to relevant audiences in a timely fashion continue to be vital to advancement operations. As with government relations, publications is sometimes structurally resident within the public affairs office; more frequently, it is a stand-alone operation with its staff director reporting in a direct line to the chief advancement officer.

Among the personnel to be found in an institutional publications office are writers, artists, contract (i.e., bidding) officers, or production specialists. The scope of material written, designed, and published ranges from newsletters, tabloids, newsmagazines, brochures, view-books, and case statements to letterhead, envelopes, and labels. In a typical institutionally-related publications office, staff members will be available to respond to assignments. Thus, the staff may be asked to prepare a brochure aimed at recruiting female students for the Engineering College. They will not, under typical circumstances, have identified the need or the purpose of their work. Having received such an assignment, however, they will designate a writer, create a time line for design and production, identify a designer or design team, and outline the work needed to complete the project within overall publications demands.

Among important factors impacting on the efforts of publications offices are the following:

- availability of writer
- time demands imposed by internal customer's needs
- approval requirements of internal customer
- availability of artist
- institutional graphics standards and their applicability to the specific assignment
- customer/institutional budget for the subject project
- publication specifications as agreed to by customer, writer, and artist
- reproduction source (external, internal)
- means of distribution of subject publication
- relationship of subject piece to other institutional publications

The advancement manager will provide leadership and direction for the publications office around such issues as the conformity of publications to institutional objectives, the consistency of design with the institutional "look," the accommodation of delivery schedules to customer needs and desires, and the maintenance of the "tone" of the copy with institutional standards. It is common for publications offices to require all material written, designed, and reproduced for outside distribution to be approved by the publications office for the purpose of maintaining quality control.

A host of additional issues faces effective publications offices and the advancement manager. Among them are in-house printing versus the use of external vendors, bidding of print jobs, internal or external designers, print quantities, use of mail houses, and so forth. As electronic communication expands to encompass growing numbers of the public, the future of institutional publications is sure to see growth in the utilization of e-mail, CD ROM, the Internet and its many permutations, interactive television, video conferencing, and others. It may be anticipated that the publications office as it exists in the year 2000 will have metamorphosed by 2010 to an office that continues to provide services for print communications, but to an increasing degree meets institutional communications needs through electronic means.

ALUMNI RELATIONS

Largely found in educational institutions (colleges, universities, professional schools, community colleges, independent schools), examples of the alumni office are also to be found in some hospitals (especially teaching centers), youth-serving agencies, a few occupationally related groups, and even some athletic and cultural groups. The common pattern has been for alumni offices or alumni groups to be related to or a part of the advancement office and to report to the senior advancement manager. In a limited number of institutions, primarily those with a large alumni base, the alumni office is a stand-alone operation, related (sometimes tenuously) to the CEO of the institution.

It is important to distinguish two sometimes conflicting dimensions of alumni work: (1) activities that are initiated, directed, and financed by and for institutional alumni, and (2) activities that are initiated, directed, and financed by the institution for the benefit of alumni relationships with the supporting institution. Those two dimensions usually exist happily side by side; occasionally they do not.

Alumni-initiated activities typically take shape in a structured alumni association, often incorporated as a separate, nonprofit organization. Dependent on the payment of membership dues and other fund-generating devices, the independent alumni association is characterized by a representative board of directors, an association-determined mission and program, staff, and, often, a facility.*

Independent alumni associations are sometimes accused of "going their own way," of disregarding institutional priorities and directions. Advocates of independent alumni associations insist that the needs of their members do not always or necessarily coincide with interests of the institution and that the association's first and primary responsibility is to the membership or to those who are eligible for membership. Over the years, there have been some well-publicized, albeit rare, occasions when independent alumni associations have taken courses so distasteful to the institution that they have been "disaffiliated" from the institution. As noted, such instances are rare, but when they have occurred, they have represented major problems for both the association and the institution.

The other model, the creation and support of alumni activities by and for the institution, is clearly the dominant pattern throughout the country. In the imple-

---

*I am aware as I write these words of the use of many modifiers (typically, usually, often). Alumni organizations are characterized by many differences; each seems to have a distinctive "window on the world." The effort here is to be as descriptive as possible without implying that one or another alumni approach is normative. Even the definition of alumni differs among and between institutions: some institutions insist that anyone who ever attended the institution as a student (or otherwise participated in organizational life) is an alumnus; some use a length of time determinant (anyone who attended for one year); others insist that alumni are those who completed a course of study. It is characteristic of work with alumni that each institution sets its own standards, and each alumni association develops its own operational style.

mentation of this model, the institution employs alumni relations staff, mounts activities presumed to be of interest and value to alumni, makes available alumni databases and services them, and solicits the assistance and financial support of alumni. In institutions whose alumni activities are so structured, an alumni board will be created and maintained, the members of which may be designated by election or appointment.

An interesting and important development recently has been the growth of departmental alumni associations (e.g., The Political Science Alumni Association) or the school or college association (e.g., The Association of Graduates of the School of Humanities). Of even more recent origin is the trend toward the creation of ethnically defined alumni groups (e.g., The Association of African American Graduates). Such discipline specific or ethnically determined clustering of alumni seems to be a clear response to the sheer size and consequent lack of involvement on the part of students or graduates with the contemporary mega-university. The manner in which these alumni "fragments" relate to the larger (official) association and to alma mater herself varies by institution and by group, but, in general, it can be said that cooperative relationships are maintained at varying levels of intensity and satisfaction.

Opportunities for institutional service afforded to graduates include:

- mentoring current students
- assisting in student recruitment and admissions
- providing "person power" for the speakers bureau
- career counseling
- utilizing their expertise in classroom lectures
- lobbying agencies of government on behalf of the institution
- introducing the CEO or advancement office personnel to potential donors
- serving on institutional boards and committees

Advancement managers value these contributions made to an alma mater. They see such contributions by graduates, former students, and recent participants as important buttresses to the institutional agenda. They also understand and appreciate that alumni are among those most likely to contribute to the support of the institution. Studies have shown, over a period of years and among institutions of all types, that involved alumni (i.e., members of associations) are the persons most likely to participate in voluntary financial support of the institution: this group has more givers, givers at higher levels, and givers with fewer "strings" attached (i.e., givers with a lesser commitment to restricted areas of support).

Advancement managers might be most familiar with and even prefer a donor flowchart that looks similar to this:

Prospect ➡ Cultivation ➡ Contribution

Many prospective donors fall into such a pattern.

With alumni, the flow more closely resembles:

Alumnus ➡ Alumnus Involvement ➡ Contribution

In the first instance above, the advancement staff will be responsible for cultivation and will anticipate developing the institutional gift as a result of (or in consequence to) the cultivation. In the second, the involvement of the graduate or former student mediates the gift; the fact of that person's continuing participation in institutional life, through alumni involvement, is the factor that leads to commitment. The contribution results from a satisfactory alumni experience.

A wide variety of factors come to bear on the issue of alumni support as shown in Exhibit 2–4. The advancement manager will become aware of the ethos of the institution with respect to its alumni; will be knowledgeable of the extant practices of former students in the institution served; will seek on a continuing basis to know and understand the issues of importance to graduates as they relate to the institution; will represent, fairly and honestly, institutional commitments in a timely fashion; will value organized alumni opinion but not be "cowed" by such;

Exhibit 2–4 Independent associations and the institutional program

Independent alumni associations
- membership dues—yes? no?
- size of membership dues
- affinity credit cards
- insurance programs
- travel programs
- other commercially related ventures (phone cards, dinner programs, purchasing alliances, etc.)

Institutional alumni program
- membership dues—yes? no?
- the annual campaign
  1. mail
  2. telephone
  3. special events
- major gifts—campaign-oriented
- planned gifts
- commercial ventures (credit cards, travel)
- special events

and will act out of the understanding that his or her own commitment is to the institution and its mission for which support is sought.

Advancement operations in the American third sector have evolved from volunteer staff to limited staff, to growing staff, to specialized staff in rationalized structures. The contemporary advancement manager, mobilizing and utilizing resources, focuses efforts in an ever more complex environment on securing support. Activities and decisions, plans and structures, goals and fiscal commitments are directed to and focused on institutional health and well being. Functions and staffs must serve that end.

REFERENCES

1. A. de Torqueville, *Democracy in America*. Vol. II, Book II (New York: Harper Perennial, 1988).

CHAPTER 3

Structuring Advancement Activities

Organizational structure represents the definition and delineation of relationships within an institution: who reports to whom and for what, what staff member interfaces with what other and to what end. Organizational charts are not, therefore, sterile boxes on a page, but formal and intentional displays of the internal institutional dynamic. There are at least three dimensions of structural relationships having to do with advancement in charitable institutions:

1. the position of the advancement manager to the CEO or the board of the organization
2. the position of advancement staff vis à vis the units that comprise the organization
3. the internal relationships within advancement and the consequent management imperatives

These dimensions are discussed in sequence.

ADVANCEMENT MANAGER AND CEO OR BOARD

The advancement function, in most contemporary organizations seeking and depending on contributions, exists in close relationship to the leadership of the organization: the senior advancement manager reports to the organization's CEO and, in some cases, to the board; advancement staff reports, directly or through an intermediary, to the senior advancement manager. Authority/responsibility lines are clear and definitive (see Figure 3–1). The reasoning that rests behind this position for advancement and advancement professionals is simple and compelling—a contributions-reliant institution is dependent for its overall success on

72   THE EFFECTIVE ADVANCEMENT PROFESSIONAL

```
┌─────────────────────────────┐
│    The Board of Directors   │
└─────────────────────────────┘
              ↕
┌─────────────────────────────┐
│        The President        │
└─────────────────────────────┘
              ↕
┌─────────────────────────────┐
│ The Vice President Advancement │
└─────────────────────────────┘
              ↕
┌─────────────────────────────┐
│      Advancement Staff      │
└─────────────────────────────┘
```

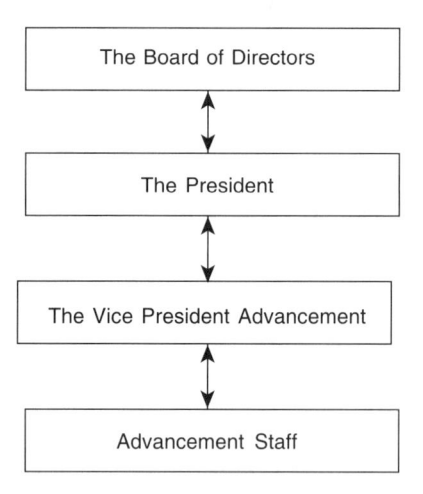

Figure 3–1 Authority/responsibility lines in a typical nonprofit organization

securing and retaining the financial or psychological support of the community, however that community is defined. Given the level of importance attaching to advancement, it is to be expected that the senior-most leader of the organization (the CEO) will want to relate immediately and directly to advancement and its designated leader. Such a reporting relationship permits the CEO to exercise immediate influence and control over advancement, to express needs with clarity, to identify priorities, to provide direction, and to evaluate efforts.

Vice president Herb, who is also the chief operating officer of the foundation supporting the medical center for which he works, arrives on Tuesday afternoon for his regular meeting with his boss, the CEO of the hospital, ancillary operations, and the foundation. In hand, Herb carries the agenda he has prepared, to focus the meeting. As he sits, the CEO says, "Put away your agenda. We have some new—and major—issues to address." In the next few minutes, Herb learns of a major capital need identified by the board: the design, construction, and utilization of a new community outreach facility in a nearby housing development. Herb's boss describes the reasons this project has priority status, the time line that the board feels must be met, and the approximate amount of money to be raised from the public. Herb leaves the meeting with a focused understanding of this new institutional priority and of the challenges he and his staff must address.

Susan, who has recently been retained as the senior advancement manager in her employing institution, responds to a call from the university's president. When she arrives in the president's office, he says. "Susan, we have been 'stalled' at about $500,000 per year in our annual fund. This institution needs greater flexibility in budgeting contributed dollars. Simply put, we need more unrestricted dollars. Maybe we should have told you this when you were hired, but the honest reality of our current situation is this: there must be more freely flowing dollars, ones which are unrestricted. I'm prepared, today, to tell you how much and why." Susan asks questions and receives direct answers. When Susan leaves the meeting an hour later, she feels energized by the clear definition she has received of her immediate objectives.

Those scenes are not unfamiliar to advancement managers; but they can be enacted, and responded to, only in circumstances in which the advancement manager and the institutional leader have direct, immediate, and open communication. Both Herb and Susan have received their marching orders firsthand. They have had the opportunity to ask questions and to receive answers. Most institutions, owning a measure of dependence on contributions, are organized so that the advancement manager and the CEO have a direct-line reporting relationship. There are exceptions. Those exceptions sort themselves out into two major categories: (1) some institutions, based on history, lack of faith in advancement staff or donor loyalty, or insecurity about advancement demands of the CEO, design structures in which advancement managers are assigned to and report to other senior managers with unrelated responsibilities: administration, finance, student services (see Figure 3–2); (2) many organizations, already tax-exempt by definition and by law, create separate philanthropic (i.e., 501(c)(3)) organizations (usually called foundations), assign advancement staff to those organizations, and expect those organizations to pay advancement staff in order to stand at arms length from fund raising, fund-raisers, and donors (see Figure 3–3). In some cases, often health care institutions, the foundation is the employing entity for the entire advancement staff or for key members of the staff. The exception to the rule that advancement managers and CEOs are directly related (as in the first category

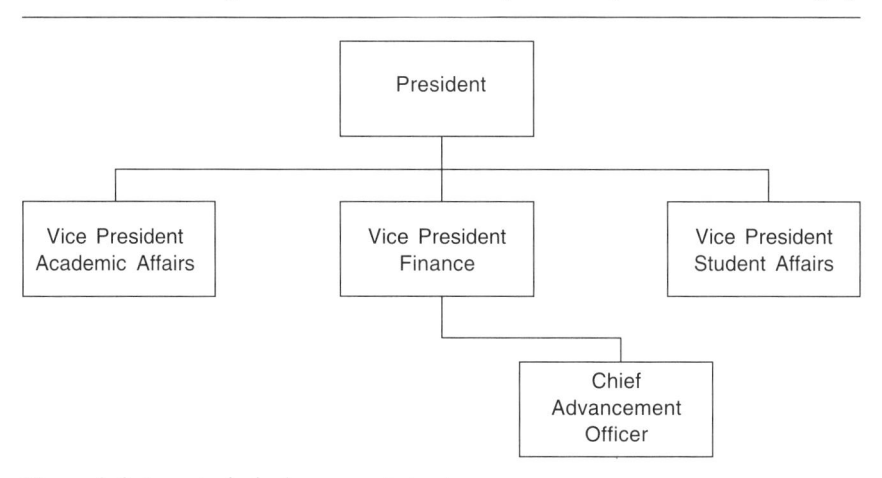

Figure 3–2 An untypical advancement structure

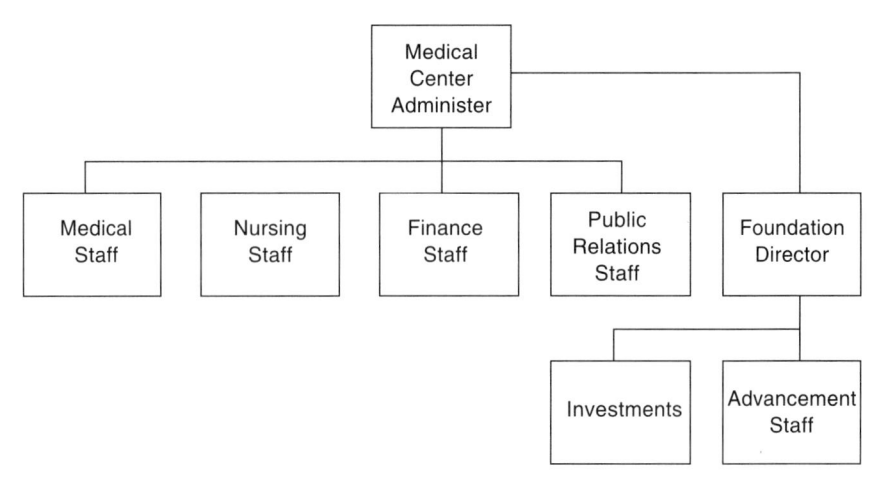

```
                        ┌─────────────┐
                        │   Medical   │
                        │   Center    │
                        │  Administer │
                        └─────────────┘
   ┌─────────┬─────────┬─────┴───┬──────────────┬──────────────┐
┌──────┐ ┌───────┐ ┌───────┐ ┌─────────┐ ┌────────────┐
│Medical│ │Nursing│ │Finance│ │ Public  │ │ Foundation │
│ Staff │ │ Staff │ │ Staff │ │Relations│ │  Director  │
└──────┘ └───────┘ └───────┘ │  Staff  │ └────────────┘
                              └─────────┘       │
                                     ┌──────────┴──────────┐
                                 ┌───────────┐     ┌─────────────┐
                                 │Investments│     │ Advancement │
                                 │           │     │    Staff    │
                                 └───────────┘     └─────────────┘
```

Figure 3–3 Foundation-focused advancement structure

---

above) often reflects institutional disquietude about philanthropy and the staff whose task it is to encourage contributions.

The second organizational idiosyncrasy (the nominally distant foundation) permits an institution to maintain that it is only marginally dependent on donors and has little responsibility for advancement personnel. (Organizations that have established and maintain foundations often report greater flexibility in disbursing foundation funds than they have experienced with funds incorporated in the institutional budget.) Some organizations create and maintain nonprofit foundations to serve as a "bank" for funds realized from contributions or earned by auxiliary operations. In such cases, the foundation receives and disburses funds according to policies and procedures set by the board, employing only financial staff. Where this organizational model operates, advancement staff are employed by and exist within the structure of the "parent" organization.

Having identified the exceptions above, the prevailing organizational structure for advancement (i.e., immediate reporting relationships and direct, ongoing, and open/honest communication between advancement manager and CEO) is one that not only allows for but encourages frequent and candid interchange among advancement personnel and other institutional leaders.

It is a truism that support is sought by institutions of the third sector (whether emotional commitment or financial) to accomplish purposes. "We're raising funds to do something important, dammit," I heard a frustrated, but gifted development officer say to a prospective donor one day. And she was right; in the best of circumstances, dollars are not gathered for their own sake in American nonprofit organizations. The dollars solicited and secured, the media enlisted, the alumni mobilized, all are to an end. The specific ends vary from one project and one institution to another—as do the amounts sought and given, the purposes served, the staffs at work—but the philanthropic endeavor (and the advancement staff supporting that endeavor) has, as its overarching purpose, the betterment of the human condition. The organizational imperative for advancement, therefore, is to create a structure that will maximize potential for community support. Direct reporting relationships (advancement manager to CEO) are responsive to such an imperative.

In a structure marked by a direct reporting relationship, the CEO will:

- meet with the advancement manager on a regular and continuing basis
- promote a relationship characterized by trust and honesty
- withhold judgments until the senior advancement manager has been consulted for information and counsel
- share dreams and visions, needs, and problems with the advancement manager with candor
- make himself or herself available to support advancement activities, solicitations, media relations, and so forth
- solicit information about philanthropic potential and include such information in the institutional planning process
- measure advancement activities and achievements against institutional goals and objectives
- hold advancement staff responsible for shortcomings and reward advancement staff for successes

The chief advancement officer, in a direct reporting relationship to the CEO, will:

- have direct access to the institution's senior decision maker and utilize that access judiciously
- be prepared to discuss problems, present plans, and engage in continuing conversation about advancement challenges
- grasp the opportunity afforded to understand institutional priorities and the reasons for specific decisions by the CEO and other colleagues
- have gathered information sufficient to develop informed plans
- engage the CEO in the most important advancement objectives (e.g., a major donor solicitation, media initiative)
- represent community interests within the institution and the institution to the community
- provide the CEO and other institutional leaders with counsel based on past experience and knowledge, even when such counsel may be uncomfortable or controversial

ADVANCEMENT MANAGER AND ORGANIZATIONAL UNITS

Setting the advancement function in a direct reporting relationship to the organization's CEO is but one dimension of structuring advancement operations. Also at issue is the relationship of advancement staff to the senior advancement manager and to the units that are constituent parts of the institution. Such issues and the manner in which they are addressed are frequently identified, in complex nonprofit institutions, as either centralized or decentralized issues.

Centralized Operation

The organization chart shown in Figure 3–4 schematically represents a centralized advancement operation in a large university. Note that all members of the advancement staff are responsible, in most cases through intermediaries, to the vice-president for advancement. Many are assigned to units of the university for their day-to-day work, but all are ultimately responsible to the vice-president. In a fully centralized advancement operation, staff are recruited, hired, assigned, compensated, and evaluated by the senior advancement manager or a designee. The advancement office provides budgeted funds to pay each staff member and to provide for all necessary support services, program funds, equipment, and supplies. Frequently, though assigned to a unit of the institution, advancement staff members in a centralized operation will be housed in a single advancement office suite.

The marks of a fully centralized advancement operation include:

- a defined reporting line, for all staff, to the senior advancement manager or his or her designee(s)
- budget for all advancement operations and staff resident in the advancement office
- advancement strategies and tactics (therefore all activities) subject to the approval of the senior advancement manager
- assignments of advancement personnel understood to be the prerogative and responsibility of the manager alone

In a centralized advancement structure, when a dean or other unit manager serviced by advancement staff becomes unhappy or dissatisfied with the staff member assigned to the unit, that dissatisfaction must be taken to, and resolution sought, through the efforts and actions of the senior advancement manager.

Well-defined advantages flow from rigorous application of the centralized advancement model.

Structuring Advancement Activities 77

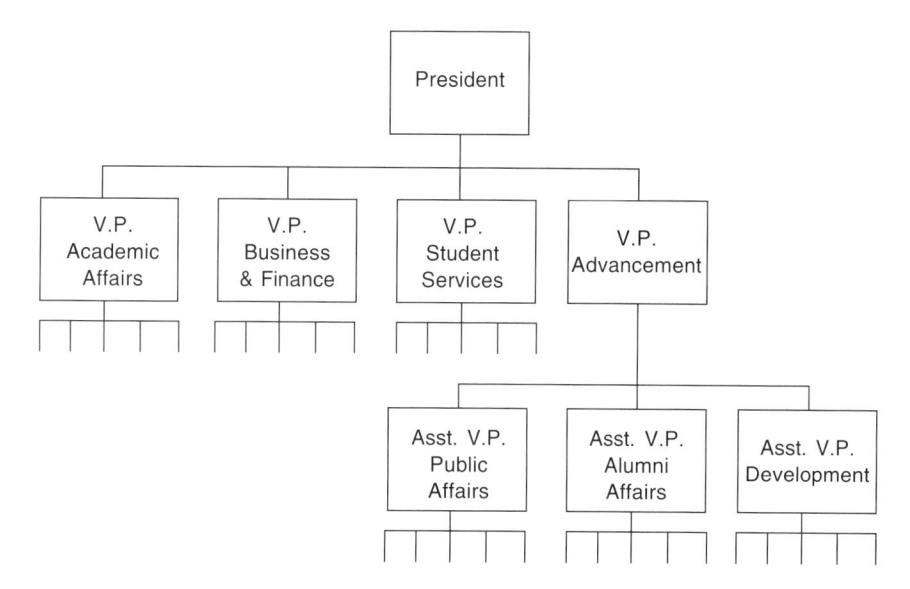

```
                          ┌───────────┐
                          │ President │
                          └─────┬─────┘
        ┌──────────┬───────────┼───────────┐
   ┌────┴────┐ ┌───┴────┐ ┌────┴────┐ ┌────┴────┐
   │  V.P.   │ │  V.P.  │ │  V.P.   │ │  V.P.   │
   │Academic │ │Business│ │ Student │ │Advance- │
   │ Affairs │ │&Finance│ │ Services│ │  ment   │
   └─────────┘ └────────┘ └─────────┘ └────┬────┘
                                           │
                        ┌──────────────────┼──────────────┐
                   ┌────┴────┐        ┌────┴────┐    ┌────┴────┐
                   │Asst. V.P│        │Asst. V.P│    │Asst. V.P│
                   │ Public  │        │ Alumni  │    │Develop- │
                   │ Affairs │        │ Affairs │    │  ment   │
                   └─────────┘        └─────────┘    └─────────┘
```

Figure 3–4 Centralized advancement model for a university

- A single manager is responsible for results.
- Institutional/organizational priorities can be built into advancement strategies and thus diminish the impact on advancement activities of lesser, transient unit concerns.
- Each advancement staff member understands whose instructions (the senior advancement manager) must be followed, and that clarity results in purposeful, focused behavior.
- Advancement expenditures are closely monitored so that personnel and programs can be effectively evaluated.

The fully centralized structure carries with it some important disadvantages.

- Unit managers (e.g., deans) to whom advancement personnel are assigned may see such staff as outsiders, related to but not a core part of the unit's efforts.
- Unit managers may feel that their specific needs or wants are dealt with as secondary (or tertiary) concerns.
- A sense of separation may develop between the unit manager and the assigned advancement staff member (the unit manager is not able to instruct or direct).
- Immediate, presenting concerns, as they may relate to advancement activities, are apt to be set aside (ignored) in favor of larger institutional issues.

- "Ownership" of advancement activities may be lacking: "The program belongs to the vice-president for advancement . . . not to me."
- The existence of a centralized advancement office—and the power that flows from that reality—tends to set advancement over, against, and separate from other, important organizational activities.
- The unit administrator is likely to feel that his or her insights can be or are ignored in a centralized structure, leaving him or her with ineffective or inappropriate advancement staff.
- Unit-assigned personnel may resent the central advancement staff.

Decentralized Operation

Figure 3–5 charts relationships in a national volunteer health agency. The organization depicted may be described as a decentralized organization. (Although the chart represents operational relationships in an organization of national scope, it also depicts the broad outlines of the decentralized structure that sometimes exist in a single, locally based, educational institution or health care delivery entity.) A review of the relationships schematically represented in the figure reveals that the central advancement office provides prescribed, limited services to advancement personnel, even as advancement staff members are most directly related to subunits of the organization. The units are responsible for identifying, hiring, assigning, paying, supervising, and evaluating advancement staff. The unit budgets provide for the financial support required of advancement staff and operations. They make available office space, requisite equipment, and supplies. The unit identifies priority needs and sets goals.

It falls to the unit manager to determine, in a decentralized structure, if and when staff are to address organizational needs as opposed to unit needs. The unit determines the arenas of activity, ideally consistent with overall organizational needs. Where a decentralized structure is operational, the prevailing sense is that advancement personnel "belong" to the unit. Goals are set, strategies and tactics determined, and activities and programs mounted in response to unit needs and unit managers' directives.

Decentralized advancement operations are characterized by:

- advancement staff set in a structure in which reporting relationships are close to hand (i.e., to the nearest manager)
- budget for local advancement operations is in the control of the unit manager
- success or failure in advancement operations is determined by the degree to which they serve local/unit goals and objectives
- relationships with other institutional/organizational advancement staff are held "at arms length"

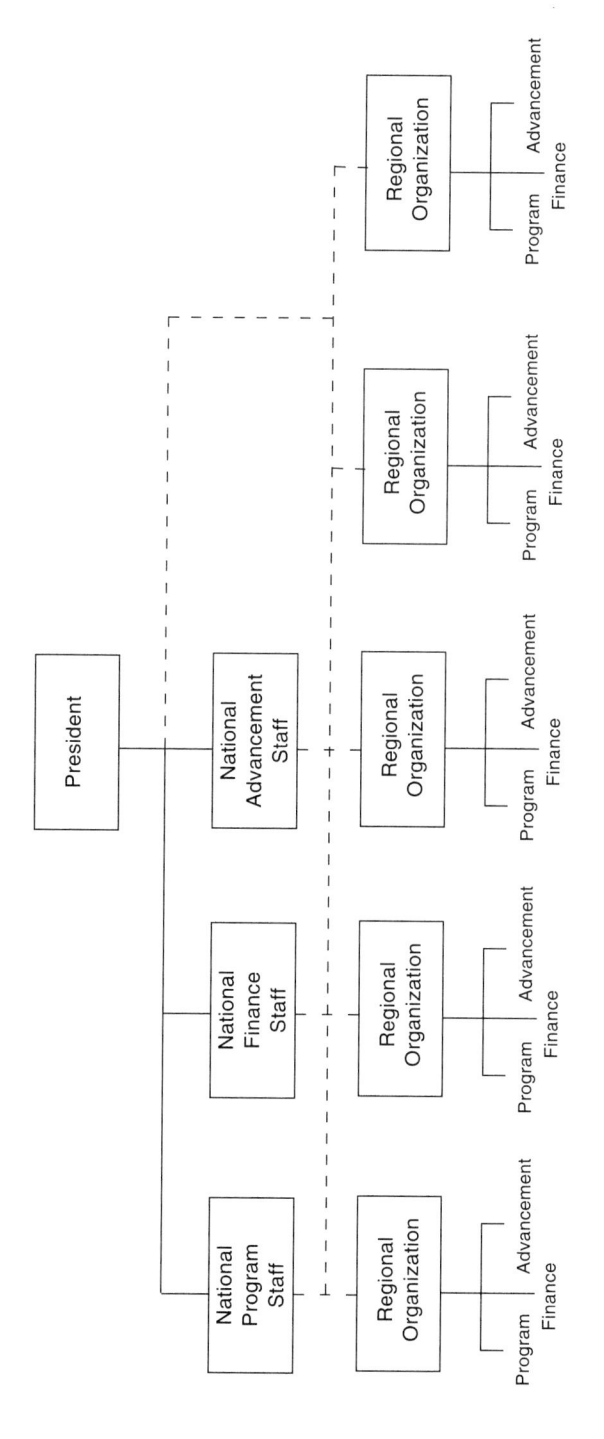

Figure 3–5 Decentralized advancement model for a national health agency

- overall involvement in the advancement activities of the parent organization is focused on inspiration, motivation, and training

The advantages attaching to advancement activities in a decentralized structure are clearly defined:

- The unit, which needs and determines the uses for support, is the context in which the specific advancement staff person lives his or her professional life and pursues responsibilities.
- Needs for which the advancement staff member seeks community support are close at hand and immediately observable. The advancement staff member, in a decentralized structure, learns "the talk" and is motivated to "walk the walk" of the unit to which he or she is assigned.
- The unit manager is physically positioned to observe advancement staff members, to weigh activity against achievement, and to evaluate the effectiveness of advancement efforts.
- The time commitments of advancement personnel are focused more readily on unit challenges rather than on institutional housekeeping chores.

Among the negative factors attaching to decentralized operations are:

- Advancement effort and resources are dissipated due to the widely varied interests and concerns of the units within the institution.
- There is unevenness in knowledge about and commitment to advancement activities among unit managers: some value the contributions advancement can make to the institution; others deny the importance or worth of advancement.
- The varying standards for advancement activities that may be set by unit managers make for widely varying performance by advancement staff.
- A lack of team consciousness and loyalty among those assigned to mount advancement initiatives may result from the commitments and behaviors of unit managers.
- Competition for prospective donors inevitably arises where advancement staff "belong" to units and are supervised by unit managers.
- Advancement staff morale tends to suffer in circumstances in which priorities, activities, and standards are subject to wide variation.

The issue of structuring advancement operations within the institution can be of profound importance to institutional success, it is not an exercise divorced from reality. The author once served as a consultant to an academic institution in which the dean of one of the important schools in the university "ran his own show." He was charismatic and hard working; he was deemed to be highly successful and, thus, had accumulated considerable power within the university. Because of his perceived success, the president allowed the dean to operate with few institutional strictures. The dean admitted that he saw his efforts as the equivalent of serving as president of his own, free-standing college. As his efforts related to advancement, the dean hired his own staff without consultation, set the unit's fund-raising priorities, identified and kept confidential the school's prospects for gifts, had media releases written and distributed as he decreed, even determined which all-university advancement staff meetings "his" advancement staff members could or could not attend, and the ones they were allowed to attend were few.

The results of these behaviors were such that his fund-raising totals were good, if not excellent; his media relationships were of high quality; student recruitment was highly successful. The university as a whole, however, suffered: institutional priorities were effectively thwarted by the dean's go-it-alone behavior. In an interesting but perhaps inevitable twist, the dean had trouble retaining advancement staff, they felt separated from and even looked-down on by their advancement colleagues.

Mixed Model Operation

The experiences resulting from the dean's behavior in the above illustration speak to the importance of implementing a structure that serves the entire organization as well as its constituent parts. Organizational structure is a means by which institutional and unit needs can be defined, understood, and communicated. Even a cursory review of the material presented on the centralized and decentralized models makes clear that there are valid arguments for both models. Advantages and disadvantages attach to each, which is why most third sector institutions adopt what might be called a mixed model, one that seeks to combine the advantages of both the centralized and decentralized models while minimizing or avoiding the disadvantages of each. One successful and well-known senior advancement manager confounds audiences of advancement professionals by proclaiming solemnly that he believes in a highly "centralized/decentralized approach": he's talking, of course, of his belief in a mixed model.

The nature and dimensions of the effective mixed model vary widely according to the distinctives of the specific institution involved. Figure 3–6 represents the operative institutional structure for advancement in one institution of higher education. The paragraphs that follow detail the issues involved in creating a structure that will maintain both institutional integrity with reference to advancement and, at the same time, allow for unit prerogatives and distinctives.

82   THE EFFECTIVE ADVANCEMENT PROFESSIONAL

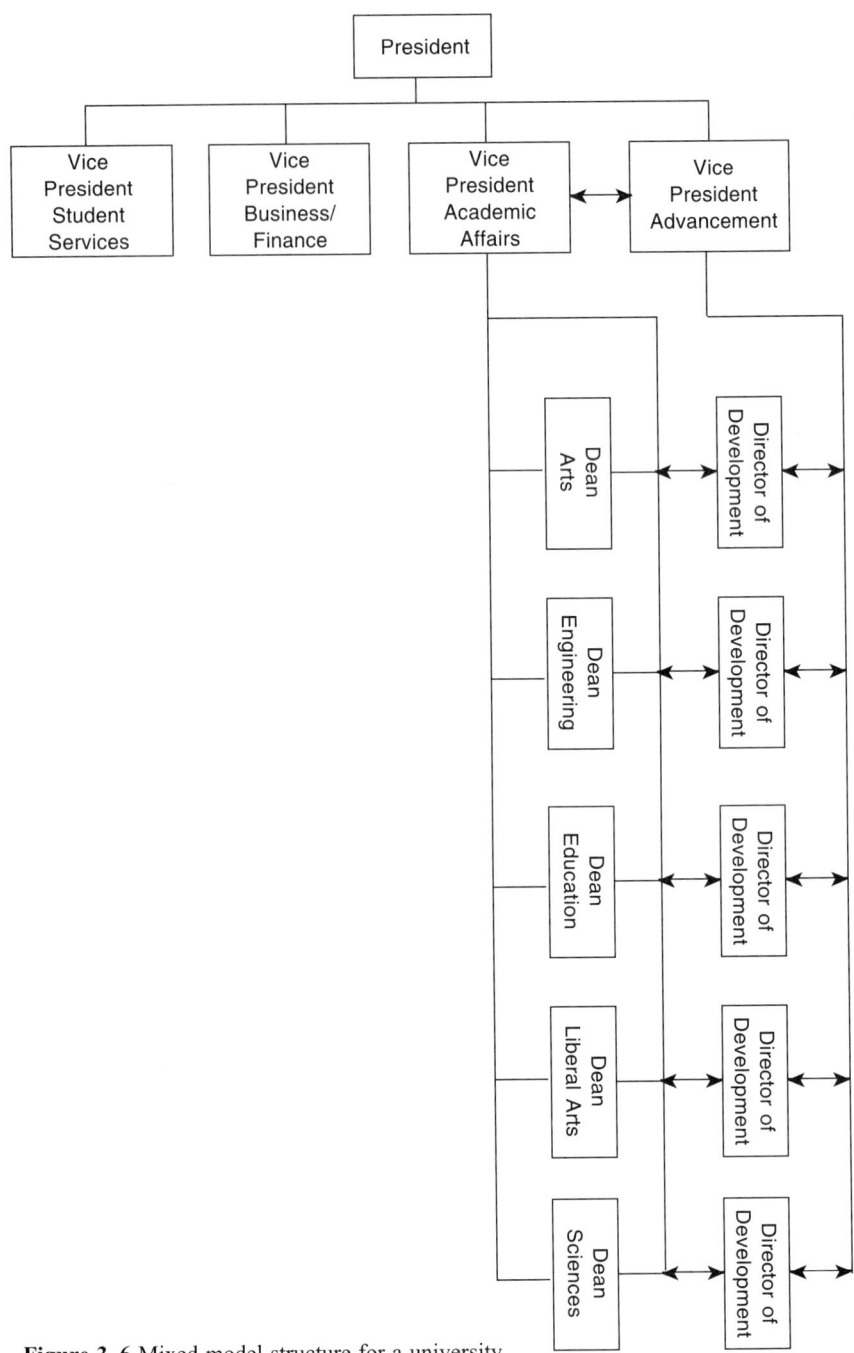

Figure 3–6 Mixed model structure for a university

Areas of Cooperation

Hiring advancement staff in a complex institution and operating with a mixed structure is a shared responsibility. The senior advancement manager or a designee is part of the process for what that person can offer of a technical nature about advancement. The manager's responsibility is to determine if a given candidate for employment has accumulated experiences and incorporated them into professional life to assure that the candidate can meet the demands of the position in question. The unit manager will be part of the hiring process because he or she has an existential understanding of the needs and challenges attendant to the specific position. The unit manager knows and works with the persons with whom the newly employed advancement staff member must work and, as a consequence, can measure and evaluate the match.

An effective hire based on both technical and existential qualifications is not an accident but the happy result of a plan effectively implemented. This is illustrated in the search for and employment of a public affairs director for a state affiliate of a national voluntary health agency. The state organization recruited persons for the position of director of public affairs. When the candidate pool had been gathered, screening interviews were conducted by a panel of staff and volunteers from that state affiliate. Five candidates were identified as finalists. At this point, the national director of public affairs flew into town, reviewed the paperwork of each of the finalists, and participated in the final interviews. As a result of the interviews, an offer was tendered to and accepted by one of the candidates. It was a successful hire; both the organization as a whole and the unit were represented in the process. Six years later that candidate, having served the state organization with distinction, applied for and was named to the position of national director of public affairs.

Many potential problems are vitiated when both the unit manager and the senior advancement manager are represented in the selection process: problems of assignment, of relationships of the staff member to the unit and to the core advancement operation, and of responsibilities (staff meetings, training) to each.

Budget is another area in which cooperation between unit and central advancement must be pursued in the mixed model of organization. Wide variations in fiscal practices exist where the mixed model is practiced. In some institutions, staff salaries are shared (i.e., the unit pays a portion of the salary and the central advancement office pays the remainder). In others, salaries of advancement personnel assigned to units are paid out of the central advancement budget, but units with advancement staff are "taxed" a specified amount to assist in support of advancement operations. Similarly, variations may be observed in financial arrangements for equipment, supplies, and support personnel as those necessities relate to unit-assigned advancement staff.

Because budgets (and the funds of which they are comprised) are power and influence issues in virtually all organizations, it is at the point of financial operations that mixed organizational structures have the greatest potential for breakdown. Rarely does a manager—advancement or unit—believe he or she has sufficient financial resources to accomplish what has been assigned. As a consequence, few are willing, without struggle, to surrender what they feel they already have or that is rightfully theirs.

Vivian had assumed her position as vice-president for advancement in an institution that had operated with a decentralized structure. At the time she was selected, she convinced the selection committee and the CEO that a mixed structure would better serve the university. Faced with implementing her commitment, she spent time with the vice-president for finance discussing the financial needs implicit in the model she sought to set in place. He said, "If the president approves, I'll simply tell the deans and other unit managers, at the start of the next budget year, that I am taking the funds I have been allocating to them for advancement activities and assigning them to you. They are going to complain, though." Vivian proposed to accomplish her purpose another way than through fiat. She scheduled herself on the agenda of two meetings, a month apart, of the Council of Deans. At the first meeting she told the deans about the structure she intended to implement. She spoke of the president's support for the new structure. Vivian also told them of the advantages she saw in the mixed model and of the manner in which she proposed to work with and through them to implement advancement operations and results. She spoke directly of the financial implications. At the subsequent meeting, she answered the questions put to her by the deans, stressing again the advantages her model afforded and of her commitment to cooperating with the purposes of the deans and the several units. In the end, the council endorsed her approach, although some members grumbled about their budget reductions. The vice-president was able to allocate Vivian the funds necessary for the new operational mode from funds previously assigned the units. The manner in which Vivian approached the delicate financial issues spoke more loudly than her words about the cooperation the unit managers could expect from the advancement officer under her leadership.

Evaluation of advancement personnel is yet another area in which institutions committed to the mixed structure create areas of shared responsibility between the unit manager and the advancement office. Although not common, it is sometimes true that one party to the shared enterprise is totally happy with a staff member while the other is seriously discontent. Establishing a mechanism that provides for joint input to performance reviews is an important ingredient of successful implementation of the mixed structure. One institution meets the needs for shared input to employee evaluations this way: the unit manager prepares the performance review and sends it to the advancement manager; the advancement manager either accepts the review or revises as necessary; the two meet to accommodate any differences between them; both conduct the evaluation interview with the advancement staff member. Although this process appears, on the surface, to be more cumbersome than the typical performance review process (four steps rather than two), the practical reality is that it makes for significant unit/advancement office cooperation and more effective evaluations. Both factors, over the long haul, contribute to time and energy saved in the pursuit of community support.

The identification of those priority projects on which unit-assigned advancement staff expend their efforts is another arena in which activity must be shared between the unit manager and the advancement manager. In the decentralized model, the unit manager is enabled to pursue his or her own advancement-related priorities; in the centralized model, the senior advancement manager determines priority efforts, with or without consultation. Where a mixed model is operative, both will look to have their needs met, their own points of view prevail. Once again, consultation is the key to fruitful implementation, although in the area of priority setting, others than just the two managers are involved.

A procedure that has proven useful in determining priority emphases for fundraising initiatives in universities has involved the unit-assigned advancement staff member, the faculty, the unit manager (or dean), and the senior advancement manager. The procedure has five steps:

1. The advancement staff member develops a "wish list" of all the projects faculty feel are suitable for contributions support.
2. The list is given to the dean who utilizes a review process (often involving department chairs).
3. A unit-defined priority project list is developed as a product of the review.
4. The priority list is shared with the senior advancement manager who incorporates the identified projects into the overall program of advancement initiatives (or revises as deemed appropriate and consults with the unit manager).
5. The president and cabinet or board is engaged in final decision making to the degree that any of the items in the program of advancement initiatives involve or require a major institutional commitment (for example, a capital campaign).

This characteristic mixed model procedure does not depend, at any point, on edict. Wide participation is sought and valued. Opportunity is provided for extensive involvement in the priority-creating process. Where differences of opinion or emphasis occur, there is provision for consultation. The process, though detailed, is far from tedious; it provides for group "buy-in" as decisions are shaped and, therefore, saves the time that might otherwise have to be spent on "selling" a project, program, or priority.

Finally among the distinctives that characterize the mixed model is the goal-setting process. In both the centralized and decentralized models, advancement goals are determined by a limited number of persons (often only one or two). In institutions that have committed to the mixed structure, the setting of advancement goals involves many persons. It is simply no longer adequate (and it never really was) to define fund-raising goals by saying, "What you raised last year plus ten percent"; it is not appropriate to determine public affairs goals by spelling out the number of column inches expected in the local newspaper on the subject of the institution. Difficult as it is for those in fields other than advancement to understand, not all of the goals associated with our work can be defined in terms of total dollars raised, or total media coverage garnered, or total alumni involvement secured. Other factors go into overall advancement success: new donors, gifted additional advancement professionals attracted to the institution, expenses reduced, new subjects introduced to the media, favorable secondary references, lost alumni found, and so forth. Having said that, it remains a fact that in a society in which costs increase, due not only to inflation but also to higher salaries and wages and to our demand for products and services of growing sophistication, the pressure on advancement professionals to be more productive (raise more money, add to our circles of support) grows with each passing year. If "raise what you did last year plus 10 percent" isn't appropriate, what is?

In the eyes of the advancement professional, goals make demands on performance. Hundreds, indeed thousands of advancement staff, perfectly decent and honorable people, leave the field each year because of the stress resulting from performance demands. Others who are also negatively impacted by results-driven expectations may react in other ways. Unit managers and CEOs (deans and presidents in universities and colleges, executive directors in agencies, administrators in hospitals and medical centers) face the need to answer to their bosses and their peers for advancement results.

For many years, managers and administrators of many types in privately supported educational institutions have understood that their job descriptions (whether written or unwritten) include the responsibility to add to the support flowing to the institution. In publicly supported institutions, deans have, in recent years, come face to face with their responsibility to engage others in support of their institutions. More recently, presidents of publicly supported universities have found private support added to their already bulging portfolios. (In the late 1990s, the campus presidents in the nation's largest system of senior higher education learned that future evaluations of job performance would include elements related to advancement and to the acquisition of contributed support. This in a system that five years previously had made no formal provision for the existence of fund-raising activities and only minimal provisions for public affairs, publications, and alumni activities.) In the face of such trends, which are sure to quicken and increase, it is a matter of importance that goals for advancement be set in a context that takes account of the interests and concerns of the many whose professional lives are now entwined with advancement performance. This is especially true in those institutions organized in what we have called a mixed structure.

It follows that goals must be arrived at in consultation. Indeed, in most institutions of the third sector, goals—and their achievability—are matters of considerable sensitivity. Deans, directors, and others are no more eager to "miss the target," that is, to fail to achieve their goals, than are development staff. Meaningful goals are related to identified institutional and unit priority needs. As noted earlier, funds are not raised as ends in themselves; rather support—financial or psychological—is sought so that worthwhile efforts may be realized, efforts that depend on, and await, gift support.

The identification of dollar goals to be reached through contributions and gifts, for the manager, is made reasonable through the understanding and application of two formulas, the second flowing from the first:

1. $PN + Pr + Qpr + CH = CP$

    (Priority Need + Preparation + Qualified Prospects + Contributions History = Contribution Potential)

2. $CP + TS + SpR = DG$

    (Contribution Potential + Trained Staff + Support Resources = Dollar Goal)

It may be argued persuasively that the acquisition of contributed income depends on relationships—and so it does. However, the elements comprising these simple formulas, when fairly gathered and weighed, provide the advancement manager with the information on which he or she can base realistic unit and institutional goals.

The ideas represented by the formulas for the goal-setting advancement manager are: (1) funds are raised to address institutional and/or unit needs, which are agreed-upon priorities; (2) challenges set before prospective donors are expressed in terms that are compelling and that in reality require written or visual preparation,* which are then placed at the disposal of potential givers; (3) the clustering

---

*Preparation associated with major fund-raising efforts includes the writing, design, and reproduction of written materials such as case statements and brochures and/or the development of pertinent audiovisual materials; the identification and recruitment of a volunteer leadership cadre; the commitment of budget for activities associated with fund raising, etc. In identifying achievable goals, the advancement manager will factor in the current status of preparation and the time, staff, or funds required to complete preparation.

or gathering of gifts to accomplish the purposes envisioned in identified priority needs depends on the identification of a "critical mass" of qualified prospects*; and (4) an understanding of the institutional or unit gifts' history will suggest the level of responses to the appeals set forth to secure funds necessary to support the priority need.

As the four items discussed above and identified in formula 1 are considered and weighed (along with the comments in the footnotes), the contributions' potential or goal for the identified priority project begins to emerge. As the contributions' potential is seen, for advancement purposes, in the context of trained staff available to "work" the project and the availability of supporting resources (clerical personnel, prospect research, travel funds, expense money for cultivation), the project dollar goal begins to come clear. That is, the expression of a goal in dollar or numeric terms emerges as a responsible projection.

These formulas are not mathematically certain equations. Rather, they incorporate the elements that are present in successful dollar-focused advancement initiatives and then adhere to them, producing, if not certainty, something approaching likelihood. Our contentions—that advancement goals will be determined in contexts that are responsive to institutional or unit needs and that many have a stake in the goals process—have bases in hard, philanthropic realities when the elements represented in the formulas are carefully brought together, considered, and weighed. From such a process, performance expectations may be quantified and announced.

ADVANCEMENT STAFF RELATIONSHIPS

The third dimension of advancement structure has to do with the manner in which internal advancement operations are ordered, that is, defined advancement staff relationships. Because professional advancement staff, by whatever name they are called, represent a relatively recent development in the voluntary sector, institutions have little tradition or history from which to take instruction about

---

*The term "qualified prospects" refers to the identification of an appropriate number of those who are deemed to have the means to give at the levels required to reach the dollar goal associated with the priority need. The usual starting place in determining this number is the creation of a gift table that projects requisite contributions at specific levels. Although "rules of thumb" can deceive, experience suggests that, in good economic times, three to four qualified prospects will be identified for every gift required. In bad times, the qualified prospect cohort will need to reach six or seven. Thus, a gift table that projects a need for 10 gifts of $100,000 or more will require 30 to 70 qualified prospects (depending on the economic climate), persons who have the means to gift the institution at that level. If the gift table anticipates 100 gifts at $10,000, then 300 to 700 qualified prospects will be required. Goal setting leads, inexorably, to prospect identification; without qualified prospects, goals are no more substantial than wishes.

organization and structure. A common growth pattern has emerged in the sector: as needs became clear and budget was made available, more persons were employed to seek community support in its several manifestations: fund raising, public affairs, database management, and so forth. Characteristically, each person hired to perform advancement functions was expected to have some sort of reporting relationship to the senior advancement manager. Even in those instances in which unit managers played prominent roles in setting priorities, in providing budget, and in evaluating effort, the advancement manager served a more or less prominent role in the relationships created.

Over the course of several years (approximately 1955 to 1980), advancement staff numbers in many institutions grew to a level practically beyond the control of and outside the effective management range of a single manager. Simultaneous to this numeric growth in advancement staff was the development of highly rationalized job descriptions for advancement staff members and focused/specialized assignments (the arena of specialization is discussed in Chapter 2).

The more than 20 years of these trends—growth in numbers of advancement staff and the assignment of staff to specialized responsibilities—were also the years in which much management literature discussed and defined "span of effective control." Managers were cautioned that they could not expect to provide effective leadership to more than a limited number of persons; although the authors varied in prescribing the appropriate number to report to a given manager (5, 8, or 12), most of them called for intermediaries to be set between the "doers" and the "leaders." The prevailing circumstances included greater numbers of advancement staff members; advancement staff assigned, increasingly, to specialized tasks; and management "experts" calling for limits on the numbers reporting to the manager.

These factors came together at a time and in such a fashion that advancement staffs across the country set in place a growing number of secondary advancement managers (assistant directors reporting to directors, directors reporting to senior directors or executive directors, executive directors reporting to an assistant vice-president, and so forth). That system made for staff control and oversight. It protected the time and energy of managers "up the ladder." It assured the scheduling of many meetings. But it did not always provide for the time or the human power necessary to achieve advancement objectives.

Recent years have seen the "flattening" of management structures in most American industries. Middle managers, though not extinct, have become fewer in number and have been expected, in their job descriptions, to mix "doing" with "managing." If manufacturing, banking, and retailing are currently marked by flatter management structures, so, too, is advancement. "Span of effective control" has given way, as a management principle, to such factors as goal attainment, cost/benefit ratios, and market responsiveness. As these trends impact advancement management, they result in fewer middle managers and managers—at all levels—with cognate performance expectations in one or another of the advancement arenas.

This is not to suggest that in large, complex, nonprofit organizations the senior advancement manager should have 50 or 100 staff members reporting directly to him or her. Rational decisions regarding the internal structure of advancement staffs will take into account the total number of staff involved, their specialties (i.e., the nature of their job assignments), the tasks to which they have been assigned, the level of readiness possessed by staff to fulfill their assignments, and the readiness within the institution for advancement initiatives. As a general rule, staffs with low levels of experience or training require a more intensive management structure. Advancement characterized by a very high community profile, similarly will argue for more rather than less management.

As the senior advancement manager shapes internal staff relationships into a management structure, these principles will be defining:

- Like will be grouped with like (i.e., all persons with public affairs responsibilities will report on a similar organizational path, fund raisers will exist in similar relationships to other fund raisers, etc.).
- Subordinate managers will have technical knowledge of and demonstrated skills in the areas of those persons they are assigned to manage.
- Communication—upward, lateral, and downward—will be encouraged, and both formal and informal means will be employed to assure such an unfettered flow.
- Specific advancement-related assignments will be present in the portfolios of all advancement managers.
- Lines defining authority and responsibility will be clear and definitive but will not be so rigid as to preclude change or the potential for collaborative efforts among advancement staff members.

After Vivian, described above, had instituted her mixed model structure, she set out to delineate relationships within the advancement staffs. She recruited for, and hired from within, an associate vice-president, who was given supervisory authority over fund raisers, a total of 26 persons. She named an assistant vice-president with responsibility for leadership of all public affairs and publications personnel. Another assistant vice-president was designated to exercise authority, on behalf of the institution, over alumni activities and special events. A support services manager was designated to direct all clerical staff activities. Vivian reserved, for herself, the supervision of the small number of staff who did not readily fall into one or another of the four categories she had created.

When the new structure was announced, Vivian also gave each of her managers specific activity assignments consistent with the areas over which they exercised leadership. The new management team, under Vivian's leadership, soon fell into a collaborative pattern: each met with "the boss" on a one-to-one basis every other week; all of the managers met, as a group, on alternate weeks. Internal communication was thus assured; cooperation among and between the managers and with Vivian reached high levels and produced growing job satisfaction; performance levels showed quick and steady growth.

In this discussion we have shown that structure has to do with defining relationships within the institution and its several parts. We have argued for and identified the advantages of a direct reporting line to the CEO for the senior advancement manager. Three models were explored for structuring relationships of the advancement function to constituent units of an organization, and the advantages and disadvantages of each were identified. The internal organization of advancement activities was addressed in terms that take account of current management trends and elements central to the work of advancement.

CHAPTER 4

The Language of Management

Language—spoken and written—is a means by which persons communicate. It is not the only means; meanings are also conveyed by expressions, tone, posture, dress, setting, and so forth. Music, art, and dance all communicate in sure, if sometimes ambiguous ways. Chapter 5 on communication explores the nature, function, and scope of communication for the advancement manager. Here, we examine some of the words that have currency in the management setting, the concepts those words represent, and their implications for the advancement manager.

Words may convey meaning. They do not, in and of themselves, have meaning; the knowledge and experiences of persons combine to assign particular meanings to peculiar combinations of letters and syllables, and those meanings may vary significantly depending on the context in which they are spoken or written and depending on their audience.

The word "yellow" is not, itself, yellow. Moreover, that word stands for one thing when applied to the color of the hair of a child, another when used to describe a sunrise, yet another when conveying meaning about an engagement ring, and something else altogether when the category is courage. Yellow conjures up one image in the mind of a blind person, another in a color-blind man, and another in a lover. Humans have long sought precision in language: note the vast number of words in the English language, a clear indication of the efforts of those who speak and write this language to assign a word to every circumstance, every distinction, every nuance. Despite the fact that ours is the richest language in human history, at least in the size of our vocabulary, we find that in some fields of human endeavor, we must fall back on words from other tongues, even other ages. It wasn't long ago that physicians, in the name of precision, utilized words, phrases, and abbreviations from the Latin. Members of the legal profession routinely employ phrases from that language. Certain branches of science utilize words from other tongues—German, Russian, French—because those who practice the disciplines of science have agreed that a particular foreign word conveys meaning with a specificity that words in our own language may not capture. Social scientists, theologians, and cultural commentators frequently fall back on words from the native tongues of the theorists who first proposed or promulgated an idea. In disciplines from art to zoology, practitioners have reached agreement on defined meanings for words important to and widely used in the several disciplines. Trouble develops, meanings are lost, and ideas are miscommunicated when important words, meant to convey precise meanings, are poorly understood or inaccurately used.

Such is the case in the practice of management. When the meaning of a "management" word such as "procedure" is well understood and correctly used, managers in a variety of settings, giving leadership to persons in differing fields, know what is meant and how procedures can regularize management functions. They can communicate because they have a common understanding. When one or another party to the process does not understand the meaning of the word, communication ceases to flow. Those who work for managers similarly must hold, in common with their managers, definitions of frequently used terms if ideas are to circulate and communication is to occur. Many words, common in management practice, are ordinary words, that is, they are frequently used in conversations outside of management where they convey something quite different from what they mean in management. Persons think they know or "have an idea" of what the word is intended to convey, when, in fact, their understanding is skewed or partial insofar as the word is used in a management context. In the material that follows, we identify management terms important for the ideas they represent and define and illustrate their meaning in the setting of advancement management.

MISSION

An organizational/institutional mission is a statement of purpose. In relatively short form, the mission statement conveys what it is an organization commits itself to do. The mission may seem startlingly prosaic, but it is not intended to be a clarion call to action. It sets before staff, board, and the public the reason the organization was brought into being and exists today. By its nature, mission is limiting; if the organization is going to do one thing, or a particular group of things, it follows that it is not going to do other things.

An organizational mission tends not to be subject to rapid or substantial change, even over a period of many years. By its enduring quality, the mission provides organizational focus and, thus, serves to shape program and advancement efforts.

A community hospital might state its mission thusly: "ABC Hospital provides high quality health care services, primarily to citizens living on the east side of

Cleveland, Ohio, utilizing state-of-the-art equipment, and employing procedures that meet or surpass community standards of medical practice. Services are provided at prices that are as low as possible consistent with the economic well-being of the institution." This statement sets out the basic commitments of the hospital for persons in and out of the institutional setting:

- providing quality health care services
- serving a primary patient base that is geographically limited
- acquiring and using contemporary equipment
- meeting current medical standards
- providing for the continuing life of the institution through its pricing practices

The mission statement also makes clear that there are many things that this hospital is *not*:

- a research center
- a teaching hospital
- an institution with a nationwide (or even citywide) patient base
- a charity institution

It is apparent, in the illustration, that the mission of this community-based institution will not change very much over the years. Indeed, it was noted above that mission statements are resistant to change. There are exceptions: with the effective conquest of polio, the March of Dimes redirected its organizational purpose to addressing the problem(s) of birth defects; many institutions that were founded to provide teacher education enlarged their purposes following World War II to provide comprehensive, higher education; some baccalaureate degree–granting institutions expanded their offerings to include master's degree and doctoral programs. Where those changes have occurred, it became necessary and appropriate to modify or enlarge the institutional mission.

The organizational mission has relevance for the advancement manager because it is the ground on which the case for support of the organization stands. Often, as seen in the community hospital illustration above, the mission helps to define those who are prospective supporters of the organization.

Sally, who was the advancement manager for a residential facility serving abused children, was instructed by her executive director to seek support from a grants-making foundation with special interest in the needs of homeless and immigrant children. She told her executive director, "I know there is a real need to serve homeless children, and kids from other countries, too. But that isn't our mission. That's not what we tell our publics we do. We may not even know how to service that client population." Sally's boss was exasperated by her response. "You just get me the money. We'll put a program together and provide the services." Over the next few days, the relations between Sally and the executive director were tense. He repeatedly pressed his charge on Sally, and she repeatedly spoke of the organization's obligation to donors to remain "on mission." The executive director was unwilling to take the mission issue to his board. In the end, Sally left her employing organization.

Some may find fault with the firmness of Sally's stand. She, however, took seriously the mission of her organization and felt that if the organization were to move toward a new and expanded program, it was necessary for the board to be involved in that decision, and, thus, in re-thinking organizational purpose.

The parameters set by mission, if not sacred, are clear and compelling: advancement efforts must grow from the institutional mission. The small hospital that tries to raise money by invoking the value of medical research, even when the hospital asking for funds is not engaged in such research, is sailing under a false flag. The small liberal arts college that trumpets, in its advancement efforts, the major international impact of American higher education, even though the college has few or no international students and offers only two courses in international relations, is engaged in activity that is, at root, fraudulent. Organizational purpose, made explicit and public in the statement of mission, provides the rationale for the organization's appeal to its publics.

VISION

Institutions, through their leaders and supporters, have dreams; they harbor hopes and aspirations. The institutional vision is the organized expression of the dreams regarding the future to which the institution is committed. One man or one woman may have a firmly held aspiration for future developments in an institution's life, but until a significant number of those important to the life of the institution have claimed those aspirations as their own, there is no institutional vision. To be sure, those who see a particular future with a clarity informed by passion may exercise major influence in charting an institutional vision, but if leaders are people with followers, institutional visionaries are people whose dreams are claimed by others.

This fact has led, in recent years, to the creation in institutions and organizations of the third sector of vision task forces or vision committees. Characteristically, vision activities, by whatever name, comprise a number of representative persons in the organization who are charged with shaping organizational aspirations and with developing a mechanism by which those aspirations are spread throughout the organization. Activities related to charting organizational mission often, but not always, are incorporated in a strategic planning process.

The president of one public, comprehensive university appointed a senior faculty member to serve as the director of a vision task force for the institution. The faculty member was given assigned time for the activity. Over the course of the next year, the director of the vision task force engaged in the following activities:

- Identified, with the president, and appointed members to the vision task force—9 persons;
- Met with members of the task force a total of 18 times;
- Met with selected members of the university administration—27 persons—to elicit their views on appropriate aspirations for the university;
- Initiated a quarterly newsletter about task force activities and the institutional aspirations that were surfacing—mailed to over 800 persons;
- Held group meetings with faculty members of the constituent schools of the university—over 220 attended;
- Sent a draft "Vision" to the entire university community for comment, nine months into the project—mailed to over 1,200 persons;
- Reviewed comments received and incorporated some of those comments into the final draft;
- Held six group meetings for the university community—one each on consecutive work days—to present the "Vision" and to answer questions.

Through the entire process, the director met regularly (once a month) with the president to keep him informed of the process, its problems, and its promise. A review of the eight steps in the director's process reveals that the director took great care systematically to widen the circle of those involved in creating the vision: from 1 to 9 to 27 to 800, etc. When the vision report was formally received by the president and made available to the media and, thereby, to the public, not all in the university community were wholly satisfied with the future that was charted, but all had to admit that they had been kept informed and provided opportunity to hear and be heard.

It is critical to an understanding of the creation and adoption of an institutional vision to see that formalized aspirations result in the development of an action plan: dreams of this kind are intended to lead to deeds. It is not enough to aspire to having 60 percent of all alumni be donors to the institution. Rather, efforts must be initiated to bring to pass that happy circumstance: the case written, literature prepared, staff assigned, and so forth. In short, the elements of the vision must be activated in the goals, objectives, procedures, and priorities, which are identified and discussed later in this chapter.

If it is the nature of institutional mission that it is slow to change, it is the nature of organizational vision to admit to the evolutionary impulse and, thus, to modification. The rapidity of change in the social environment dictates that institutional posture vis à vis the future exists in a dynamic mode. What we hoped for last year may be ours next year; what we aspired to in the recent past may soon be irrelevant. As a consequence, some organizations have created structures to assure that the institutional vision receives continuing attention. That is not to suggest that the intense involvement characterizing the efforts of the public, comprehensive university cited above should be extended year after endless year. It is to say that, perhaps as part of the president's annual retreat with his cabinet officers, time should be allotted on the agenda to review the institutional vision, to evaluate it for relevance, and to examine the progress of the action plans that flow from the vision. Every five years (or four or six) the institution will find it valuable to repeat the process leading to the articulation of a "new" vision and a fresh take on the future.

Diedre was the director of a small, independent, secondary day school. She was a "take-charge" person who, over the course of several years, had dreamed great dreams for her school. Her dreams had been incorporated into and served as a vital part of a business plan the school had promulgated. Only a limited number of faculty, parents, or board had shared in drafting the plan or shaping the vision. When Diedre's school retained advancement counsel, the firm asked questions about the commitment of the school community to elements of the vision. She admitted that most knew little about it. When counsel sought to learn about the plans that had been implemented to reach the aspirations, Diedre could point to only one or two minor undertakings. And, when the content of the vision was evaluated for current relevance, it became clear that events had passed by two of the key components of the vision. The school was trying to assure its future by coping with yesterday's problems.

Rather than declaring defeat, however, Diedre eagerly embraced the opportunity offered by the consultants to craft a new vision, one to which the school community could give ready assent. Faculty, board members, and parents were brought together in a joint visioning process for the school, agreements about the shape of a desirable future were reached, and an action plan was charted. Diedre and her school community have ceased being victims of an unknown and frightening future and have, instead, determined to shape themselves to prevail in that future.

POLICY

A policy statement spells out, in definitive terms, what an organization will do or how it may be expected to respond when certain circumstances, problems, or opportunities arise. A policy is always oriented to the future: if that happens, this is how the organization will react. Ideally, policies are written, adopted, and distributed in times free of turmoil or crisis. They are the product of a clear, consistent, and comprehensive thought process that has carefully considered what might happen to or in the organization and how to respond in a fashion that serves best the organization, its employees, its clients, its constituency, and the community.

Allen, a director of development for a young but promising arts organization, was accused of sexual harassment by a secretary working in the organization. Fortunately, a sexual harassment policy had been written by staff and adopted by the board. The policy provided: (1) that a person alleging harassment was, first, to discuss the charge(s) with the immediate supervisor who would (2) gather facts from both parties and from such others as might be privy to the facts, and (3) render a decision about actions to be taken. The possible actions ranged from dismissal of the allegation to dismissal of the offending employee with intermediate steps from lesser to greater severity. Subsequent elements in the sexual harassment policy addressed such issues as appeals when the accuser fails to be satisfied by the supervisorial action(s), monetary settlements and the amounts authorized, and legal representation in the event of a lawsuit.

In Allen's case, the charge against him was, after investigation, set aside by the secretary's supervisor. The accuser was not satisfied by that decision and went to the next step outlined in the policy: appeal to a higher level supervisor. At that stage, the charge was, again, disallowed. The secretary continued to be dissatisfied and threatened to file a lawsuit against the organization, its officers, and Allen. A human resources officer counseled her about her options and, though continuing to threaten legal action, the secretary found employment elsewhere and left the organization. No lawsuit was ever filed.

The sexual harassment policy was followed precisely. An apparently nonoffending staff member and the reputation of that employee was saved. The organization acted responsibly and sensitively. The departure of the secretary resolved the internal discomfort. And, though the secretary failed to get what she sought, she was provided the opportunity to have her charges heard and a decision rendered.

A small, private airplane, trying to return to the field from which the pilot had just taken off, crashed into the roof of a hospital. The pilot was killed in the crash. In the fire that resulted, several patients suffered minor burns and one patient was burned severely. Jessica, the director of public affairs, had written a media policy to be invoked in the event a crisis occurred that affected the hospital. The board had adopted the policy and declared it in force. The policy had been delivered to all management and supervisory staff.

While the fire department was still on site, Jessica contacted every supervisor on duty at the time of the event and reminded them that the crisis media policy existed and that it provided that there would be only one spokesperson for the hospital, the director of public affairs. She returned to her office and wrote a brief two-paragraph statement setting forth the facts of the accident as she knew them, expressing her own and the hospital's sympathy for the family of the flier and for the injured patients and their loved ones. She assured the public that the hospital was open and continuing to care for patients.

Thirty minutes after the accident, just moments after the members of the media had arrived on site, Jessica met them, read and distributed her statement, and answered questions. When the media departed, she made certain that all supervisors not on duty at the time of the crash were called, told of the event, and reminded of the media policy.

In both of these illustrations, there is a presenting circumstance—a sexual harassment charge in the one case, a tragic accident in the other—and a carefully conceived, written approach to address the event: a policy that had been written and adopted by the highest organizational authority, the board.

Although the above cases have negative characteristics, policies do not deal exclusively with problems. Organizations have purchasing policies (the triggering event is the need to acquire supplies, equipment, etc.); employment policies; personnel policies; and, specifically of interest to the advancement manager, gift acceptance policies, donor recognition policies, planned gift policies, and financial reporting policies. All of them have been written to define how the organization will respond when prescribed circumstances are present.

In the nonprofit world—indeed, in organizations of all kinds—it is frequently declared that the board is responsible for policies while staff is responsible for operations. The distinction is useful and, in the main, accurate: it defines, for board and staff alike, a reasonable separation of roles. (I know of no nonprofit manager who wants to have a board comprised of members who insist on involving themselves in day-to-day operations, demanding to approve the payment of every bill or evaluating all the employees on a daily or hourly basis.) On the other hand, in many large organizations in the independent sector, it is common for the CEO to have been granted the authority, by the board, to set forth, approve, and promulgate operational policies. Usually, in cases where such policy-making authority has been so delegated, board members will require that they be informed, in detail, of the content of new policies, the reasons for them, and the reasoning in them.

The advancement manager plays a role of major importance in formulating, writing, and implementing policy. He or she must identify areas in which clear-cut policies related to advancement are needed. Although policy needs vary widely from one institution to another, any listing of advancement-related policy requirements would include gift acceptance, planned giving, in-kind gifts, donor-recognition and naming, pledges and pledge payments, use of contract employees or consultants, capital campaign(s), and conflicts of interest.

It falls to the advancement manager to write (or cause to have written) policies that impact on advancement and to provide the rationale for such policy recommendations to the members of the board or the CEO. The preparation of written policies for adoption by others implies disciplined thought about what we have referred to as the trigger, the circumstance that develops in advancement operations that calls for the existence and application of a specific policy. No advancement manager, of course, will be able to conceive everything that *might* impact the organization; he or she should reflect on operations in detail and assure that the common and consistent events related to advancement operations are understood and that relevant institutional policies are in place to address those events as needs present.

PROCEDURE

Effectuating policy is the aim of organizational procedures. A procedure is a statement that details the activities to be taken, in order, in accomplishing an identified task. Procedures have the force of institutional authority behind them and are more than simple instructions about how a task may be done. Rather, they specify how that task will be done. The training of an employee to undertake a specific task will frequently involve the use of a relevant procedure. However, in circumstances and for tasks for which approved procedures have been adopted, the assigned employee is not intended to have options about the use of the procedure. For those job assignments for which procedures exist, the advancement manager or supervisor may not take the position that "when you get really good at it, you will find your own way to do it." An organizational procedure is prescriptive.

In the community college for which Kathleen worked, much of the fund raising was done by direct mail, sometimes in conjunction with a "phone-a-thon" and sometimes not. Kathleen was eager to assure the college's publics of the integrity of the institution's money-handling process. She wrote a procedure for opening envelopes and counting funds, which included the following steps:

- handling of mail receipts requires the involvement of two persons;
- both persons sign and date the tally sheet before envelopes are opened;
- every envelope is date-stamped before opening;
- during the counting of receipts, every check is copied;
- copies of checks are attached to the tally sheet on conclusion of the counting process;
- funds reported received each day are required to reflect exactly the checks or cash accompanying the day's tally sheet;
- both of the persons involved in counting should sign and date the tally sheets attest to the accuracy of the report.

The issue here is not whether the above procedure is complete in every detail (it's not) or whether it will be effective in eliminating the potential for pilferage (it would appear to make petty theft considerably more difficult). The issue is that, by virtue of the procedure, no one in the organization—not Kathleen nor any member of her staff—is free to handle funds in any manner other than that prescribed in the procedure. Even on those days in which only one or two envelopes arrive in the office, the procedure is operative: two persons, signatures, dates, stamps, copies, accurate balance, and so forth.

Procedures provide consistency; tasks are performed in specific ways, and performance is not dependent on the skill, wisdom, or whim of a particular staff member. Procedures allow for comparing institutional accomplishments, like to like; when everything is done in the same way, at more or less the same time, there is a likelihood that records will be complete and contain identical (or at least similar) relevant detail.

Procedures can appear to be—and often are—rigid. Rigidities within organizations have a way of stifling creative thought and initiative. Consequently, many experienced advancement managers work to minimize the number of tasks to which formal procedures apply. Such tasks that require following procedure often are of a clerical nature—money handling, travel and entertainment expenses, purchasing, gift acknowledgment, and database record changes. Where formal procedures apply, they serve to assure the advancement manager, the leadership of the institution, and the wider public that tasks are performed in a thorough, appropriate, consistent, and workmanlike manner.

GOALS AND OBJECTIVES*

Goals and objectives are concepts that move in at least two directions for the advancement manager. They may refer, first, to programmatic targets that are demanding of focused effort. They may also be used to describe desired monetary or percentage achievements.

Goals

When goal is utilized to describe programmatic targets, the word focuses on large, overarching emphases. "This is the year of the alumni," declares a large poster on the bulletin board in the vice-president's office, and the subject of alumni is a recurring theme of brochures and letters emanating from her office. That thrust reveals something: there will be targeted efforts toward alums in that particular advancement shop in this specific year. It does not reveal everything, however. Will alumni be the principal subject of the media releases this year? Will they be solicited for larger contributions than in the past? What will spell success for this alumni emphasis?

---

*The words goal and objective and the concepts that rest behind them are curiously confused in management literature. Some writers use the word objective to describe the ultimate destination—note text above—while others, as here, utilize goal. When objective designates the larger target, goal is utilized as the word referring to the proximate target. The usage in this text corresponds to the dominant usage in the literature.

The goal may be seen as the destination at which an organization is committed to arrive. It is, however, useful in the context of advancement management to see the goal as the ultimate or final destination. To reach that final destination there are many stops along the way that, taken together, assure that progress is being made. To these intermediate or proximate destinations the word objective is applied. Continuing with the trip image, reaching each objective helps the organization along, moving it a little bit closer to its goal.

Objectives

The emphasis on alumni in the earlier illustration is based on some assumptions: alumni are important to institutional well-being, their professional and personal accomplishments reflect favorably on the institution, and they are a valuable resource in student recruitment. Strengthening alumni ties, thus, is a goal of the institution, a destination, if you will. How to do that and what constitutes strengthened alumni ties is another matter. As program is developed to that end, objectives are identified:

- a 20 percent increase, this year, in alumni contributions
- the location, in the next six months, of 2,000 alumni currently "lost" to the institution
- the placement in the media this year of stories about 24 graduates of the institution
- a homecoming celebration next fall for which 50 percent more alumns are registered than have been registered in past years

The relationship of objectives to goals is schematically represented in Figure 4–1.

Objectives are characterized by two realities: (1) they are time-specific, and (2) they are measurable. Rigorous applications of these principles means that the advancement manager will not be content with objectives that are of the "more and better" variety. Objectives are designed to answer the questions "how much" and "when." It is as such questions are asked and answered, explicitly, that objectives become an effective management tool.

Inevitably, then, the quantifiable and time-specific nature of objectives leads to and impacts on the advancement manager's fiscal concerns. Advancement offices, wherever they exist in the nonprofit world, are measured by their responses to the "how much" and "when" questions. They are expected to perform in a variety of arenas—press, record keeping, relations with governmental entities, etc.—but, above all, in most institutions the advancement manager is required to secure contributions, to raise money. Although there are exceptions, advancement

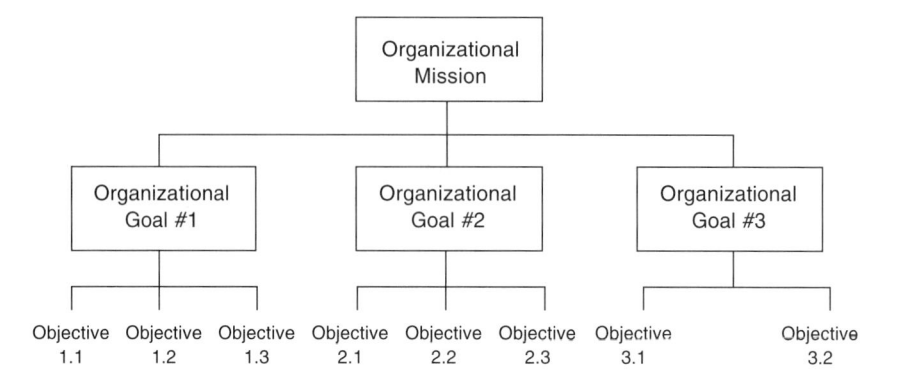

```
                    ┌─────────────────┐
                    │  Organizational │
                    │     Mission     │
                    └─────────────────┘
         ┌───────────────────┼───────────────────┐
 ┌───────────────┐   ┌───────────────┐   ┌───────────────┐
 │ Organizational│   │ Organizational│   │ Organizational│
 │    Goal #1    │   │    Goal #2    │   │    Goal #3    │
 └───────────────┘   └───────────────┘   └───────────────┘
   ┌───┬───┐           ┌───┬───┐           ┌───┐
Objective Objective Objective Objective Objective Objective Objective  Objective
   1.1    1.2    1.3    2.1    2.2    2.3    3.1                3.2
```

Figure 4–1 Relationship of goals and objectives

offices have dollar goals they are expected to reach, and, within those goals, objectives to help reach the total for which they are striving. Earlier, the manner of setting achievable goals was discussed; goals are a natural outcome of priority projects of the institution, prospects, and so forth. There are many ways to express the means to goal achievement or, to say it another way, there are many ways of breaking out the objectives that lead to the goal. One way is to divide the goal into income strategies.

ABC Hospital—Goal $5,000,000	
grant proposals	$550,000
major gifts	2,000,000
annual fund	1,150,000
special events	800,000
in-kind gifts	500,000
Total	$5,000,000

Another way is to identify sources of potential gifts and set objectives for each source.

XYZ private school—Goal $3,000,000	
alumni	$1,100,000
parents	450,000
parents of former students	900,000
foundations	550,000
Total	$3,000,000

Perhaps the method used most frequently to identify means by which the overall, institutional dollar goal will be achieved is for the senior advancement manager to set objectives for contributions on behalf of the subunits to which advancement staff is assigned.

LMN University—Goal $7,850,000
Liberal Arts	$715,000
Education	390,000
Engineering	2,620,000
Physical Sciences	1,400,000
Fine Arts	640,000
Business Administration	2,085,000
Total	$7,850,000

Where this methodology is employed, advancement staff will understand the contributions their unit is tasked with raising as a goal and will design objectives to meet and surpass the expectation placed on their efforts.

Useful Benchmarks

Goals and objectives are not meant to be kept as secrets. One of the important reasons for identifying goals and objectives is the motivation they provide to staff and supporters alike. To identify a goal privately and to hold that goal in confidence is to play a fruitless mind game. Clearly, goals and their concomitant (evaluation of success) can be frightening. "What happens if I don't make the goal? Will I be fired?" Still, for all the threat that follows from public knowledge of goals and objectives, it is important to recognize that most staff members function most effectively when they know how their efforts will be evaluated and what is judged to be acceptable performance.

The achievement of a goal is not, however, necessarily a sign of superior performance. I once had a young staff member who said to my assistant in August, "I've reached my goal now. What do I do? Am I done for the year?" The goal attainment was the result of the arrival of two gifts that had been cultivated and solicited by the staff member who had previously served the unit in question. The naive staff member had done little to reach her goal.

Nor is the failure to reach a goal necessarily a function of poor job performance. Many factors beyond the control of staff may contribute: donor tax woes, donor emergencies, bad press, or stock losses, to name a few. It is only when failure to reach one's goal is repeated two or more years that falling short of the goal may suggest a need for a staff change.

Dollar goals, appropriately and equitably assigned, serve as useful benchmarks for all engaged in the advancement enterprise from the senior-most manager to the new hire on his or her first job. Rarely is there an advancement staff more aimless and disheartened, more diffuse and unfocused, than the staff without goals and objectives. It falls to the advancement manager to determine realistic dollar goals, to set those goals within a framework of achievable objectives, to get agreement to the goals and objectives from those involved, and to inform institutional leadership and the constituencies of the goals and the purposes to which contributed income will be committed.

PRIORITY

As with other words common to advancement management, priority is a word used frequently, if not carefully, in ordinary conversation. Priority refers to the rank ordering of importance of programs, plans, and efforts. It says *this* before *that* and *that* before *something else*. To identify the priority attaching to something is also to identify the level of urgency with which that thing is invested.

By itself, the concept of priority is readily apprehended. Problems occur, however, when the word priority is used without an appropriate modifier. If a particular program is declared by the appropriate authoritative person as a *top* priority, staff and others know that program is intended to have first call on the time and resources available. If, on the other hand, it is identified as *a* priority, staff are not altogether certain where it ranks on the urgency scale. Still, the word priority may imply, and may be taken to mean, importance of the first order.

The newly arrived president of the community college asked to see his vice-president for advancement. "Here is a program I used in the raising of discretionary funds in the college from which I came. It was very effective." After describing the program in some detail, the president announced, "Get going on it. Make it a priority." The vice-president already had in place a program to serve the identical purpose. Moreover, his overall advancement effort had been extraordinarily successful, producing record-shattering results. Twice he tried to talk with his new boss about the dislocation that would be caused if he were to mount the president's initiative. Each time the president, listening to his vice-president with diminishing patience, declared that the program he wanted initiated was a "priority."

With no staff to spare and wishing to please the boss, the vice-president pulled one of his most productive staff members from her existing assignment and charged her with mounting the president's initiative. Was the president's transplanted program really his top advancement priority? Was it only one among the many existing? The president, though asked, never explained.

Most advancement offices are faced with a plethora of items of major importance, all of them ranking someplace on the scale of importance, all of them priorities (high, low, intermediate) of some sort. The concept of priority can be invaluable because a clear understanding of relative importance is a vital component of the process of assigning resources.

One of the mechanisms used by long-time advancement managers is to visit the issue of priorities at least annually: to identify and list all of the ongoing and new projects for which the manager is responsible, to weigh one against another for overall importance to the institution and for urgency, to evaluate the potential worth of each, and to assign a numeric value to each on scales of importance, urgency, and potential. One manager who engages in this discipline keeps his list very private but uses it to inform staff of his decisions regarding resource allocations; another shares her ranking with selected staff and with her respective president, accepting counsel and varied opinions. A chart, prepared by one who committed his priority-setting efforts to writing, could look similar to that in Table 4-1. The manager, in his judgment, identified the ongoing efforts in the School of Engineering as his first advancement priority. Other activities trailed, although the planned giving program and the program in the School of Business were close behind. Interestingly, the capital campaign for the new Humanities Center rated no higher than priority 6. It is clear that priority determination in this fashion may be criticized for subjectivity. Still, the advancement manager is held accountable for results and must allocate resources among many projects. This "subjective" evaluation is the most pertinent priority list the institution is likely to develop. In the scenario described above of the newly arrived president imposing his plan on the vice-president, such a priority evaluation might have proven useful in the efforts to cope.

"A rose by any other name would have smelt as sweet," Shakespeare wrote of the meaning of words. The meaning is not in the word itself but in the reality to which it points. The language of management is one in which certain words point to specific and detailed meanings. When managers use words such as mission, vision, policy, procedure, goal, objective, and priority, they use words laden with a cargo rich with meaning and nuance. Correct usage of such words informs; incorrect usage confuses.

Table 4-1 Priority projects

Project description	Importance	Urgency	Potential	Overall
Capital campaign—Humanities Center	2	1	3	2.0
Annual fund	1	3	4	2.6
School of Liberal Arts	2	2	3	2.3
School of Education	3	4	4	3.6
School of Engineering	1	1	1	1.0
School of Physical Science	2	2	1	1.6
School of Fine Arts	3	3	3	3.0
School of Business	1	2	1	1.3
Planned giving	1	1	1	1.3
Foundations and corporations	2	2	1	1.6

CHAPTER 5

The Manager and Communications

Success in performing the complex of activities associated with advancement is dependent, almost wholly, on relationships: public affairs officer to media representative, development director to potential donor, alumni staff to graduate. Relationships between and among advancement staff and with others in and out of the organization are significant for information garnered and provided, knowledge acquired and shared, and the support offered and received. All such elements of advancement operations depend on skill in communicating.

Relationships are created and sustained by the quality of the communication flowing from, to, and among the parties to a relationship. People communicate all the time; they can't *not communicate.* The person who remains silent, whose visage is impassive, who appears not to hear or comprehend or care is, in fact, sending a multitude of potent messages. He or she is, by nature of the apparent separation from people and events, communicating, and that which is communicated may not be what is intended. At its simplest, most basic level, communication is the process by which information is exchanged. Although spoken and written language is the obvious means utilized in the information exchange, countless nonverbal channels also serve as elements in the communications process.

The bulk of the advancement manager's work has to do with communication. The manager is constantly in the mode of sending and receiving messages: "Do this," he says, but also "Keep me informed about that" and "Let's see if we can work together to. . . ." Quite literally, nothing is more important to the work of the advancement manager than skill in the exchange of information—communication.

MODELS OF COMMUNICATION

The process of communicating seems, as first blush, simple and ordinary. It would appear to be as common, and as uncomplicated, as breathing.

The headmaster expresses a measure of dismay to Kevin, his development director, because all of Kevin's direct mail solicitation letters conclude with a postscript. Concluding an exchange that registered disagreement, the headmaster says, "Change it!"

A lot of things may happen in such a moment.

Kevin is caught off guard. His mind races. Doesn't the headmaster like his letters? Aren't the contribution responses sufficient to meet the headmaster's expectations? Is Kevin's knowledge of advancement being brought into question? Is his job at stake?

Kevin expresses his willingness to forgo the P.S., in response to his headmaster's concern, but he explains that studies have shown that the postscript is the element in the letter that is read most frequently. He goes on to assert that, in his use of the P.S., he tries to restate one or more of the salient and compelling arguments in the body of the letter. It is, Kevin says, "our last chance to persuade the reader to support the school."

The opportunity may now have been created, in the exchange, for greater understanding and the building of a deeper relationship.

The headmaster says, "I thought it likely that you had your reasons . . . I just didn't know what they were." Inwardly, Kevin breathes a sigh of relief. His headmaster continues, "You are aware that good writing, the proper use of language and the construction of persuasive statements, is one of our school's basic commitments. I feel that a letter with a P.S. suggests—unintentionally, mind you—that the letter, as originally written, wasn't well constructed. I sure don't want our graduates and our other supporters to think we don't know how to write a cogent letter."

The exchange has moved to a new level: the headmaster has explained the reason he dislikes the postscript, the value he places on the uses of language, and his concern that others may judge him or the school harshly if a letter they receive over his signature appears to be poorly constructed.

Although sensitive to the implied criticism in the headmaster's comments, Kevin responds readily, "It would be hard for me to imagine that our graduates and friends would conclude, after reading this letter, that it wasn't well constructed. More likely, they will focus their attention on our request for a contribution—'Should we send $100 or $200?' At least that's how I hope they will respond. The letter can, of course, be written and sent without a postscript, and I'll do that if you think it best."

New elements have found their way into the conversation: a focus on the purpose that gave rise to the letter in the first place and the acknowledgment that one of the parties to the exchange, the headmaster, possesses powers of office.

The headmaster's response is warm, "Good for you, Kevin. You reminded me that this letter is about raising money. Perhaps I forgot that fact. Let's do this: split the mailing in half. Send the letter without a postscript to half the list; and one with the P.S. to the other half. Keep a careful record of responses. In a couple of months when all the responses are in, and you share responses with me, we can figure out, together, the power of the P.S."

Kevin smiled, "I think that's a good idea. I've always wanted to test the P.S., but was reluctant to run the risk of diminished contributions if the postscript were of great importance. After our test, we should have some solid information. Thanks."

The several elements in this exchange between the headmaster and Kevin reveal three models of communication: linear, interactional, and transactional.*

Linear

In the initial interaction—understood as the *linear* model—the headmaster told Kevin that the repeated use of a postscript in solicitation letters caused him dismay. He said, "Change it!" The headmaster knew Kevin, perhaps valued Kevin as a development director, but gave no sign that he was interested in his director's response to the message the headmaster had to deliver. Presumably, he wanted Kevin to change his ways, to modify this and all subsequent letters.

Interactional

After dealing with the fear and threat implicit in the message he received, Kevin ventures an explanation of the reasons for concluding the contributions appeal with a postscript, and his explanation seems reasonable. The headmaster responds by specifying the nature of his concern about the letter, and he reveals, somewhat tentatively, his own insecurity. This part of the exchange is characteristic of *interactional* communication. Marked by efforts to clarify the message or to adapt the message to the recipient's understanding, interaction in communication is marked by the reality that two parties are involved in both sending and receiving messages (unlike the linear model where only one party is sending and the other party has the sole responsibility of receiving).

---

*Many models or ways of understanding communication have been proposed by communications theorists. The three here noted—linear, interactional, and transactional—were agreed to by participants in a conference held at the University of Maryland in the mid 1970s. Subsequently presented to the Speech Communication Association, these models represent a standard view of models of basic speech communication as currently understood and accepted by theorists and practitioners.

Transactional

As the exchange continues in our illustration, the level of understanding deepens as both parties—Kevin and the headmaster—*transact*, that is, they become involved in a process in which both are sending and receiving messages simultaneously. One can imagine Kevin nodding his head and saying "uh huh" at appropriate places. We see the smile on the headmaster's face and value his acknowledgment that Kevin has his priorities straight: the purpose of the letter, after all, is to raise money.

Many communication exchanges in advancement follow this path: first we tell; then we engage, seeking clearer understanding; finally, we transact, attempting to find ground on which both parties can stand in accomplishing a common purpose. It is the bias of this author that linear communication almost always stops short of achieving the purpose resting behind the message sent. Albeit that interaction in communication is an improvement on the "tell" quality of linear communication (it provides for questioning and message adaptation), it falls short of mutual involvement. Transactional communication is the model pertinent to the work of the advancement manager, because, at best, it is marked by mutuality and agreement and shared purpose.

Had the exchange between the headmaster and Kevin concluded when Kevin was told to drop the postscript, the development director would have, after acquiescing, nurtured the belief that his headmaster knew nothing about raising contributed funds or at least about raising funds by mail. And Kevin might well have felt professionally abused. Had the exchange concluded after the two separate explanations been offered, the relationship between Kevin and his headmaster would have been damaged, but not destroyed, for the power of the headmaster's office and not his reasoning or his commitments would have been determinative. But, because the exchange continued to the level marked by mutuality of purpose—not a compromise—both headmaster and development director felt that the communication had been successful. Indeed, it was.

Although our illustration focuses on communication between two staff members in an institution, the principles involved in the operative models apply to all communications: wife to husband, advancement manager to volunteer, development director to donor, and so forth. Communication is most effective and most certain to build sound, effective relationships when the messages exchanged go beyond telling, beyond assuring understanding, to involvement in common purposes.

QUALITY OF COMMUNICATION

Noise

Earlier it was noted that factors other than words impact on the quality of communication. One such factor is referred to as *noise*. Noise, in communication, is anything external to a specific communication exchange that impedes understanding or flow of information. It may, in fact, refer to actual noise: the chattering of a jackhammer outside the office window can make effective communication difficult or impossible; loud conversation or extended laughter from the next office renders quality exchange daunting in the extreme; constant ringing of the telephone creates distractions hard or impossible to overcome.

Noise takes many forms: the temperature of the office, inappropriate attire, past exchanges that have been unproductive or unhappy, the time of day or week at which the exchange takes place, unfinished business from other meetings, illness or other problems in the family of one of the parties to the exchange, weariness of one or more of the participants, the physical setting of the meeting; all can create noise in the communications process. And that may be, regrettably, the case even when both parties to the exchange have the best of intentions.

It falls to the advancement manager, intent on assuring the quality flow of communication, to create a setting in which noise is held to a minimum. Among questions asked in that regard are:

- Do the papers on the desk have the potential to prove distracting?
- Have I scheduled this meeting at a time that is convenient, or at least acceptable, to my communications partner?
- Is the person(s) with whom I am meeting aware of the meeting topic?
- What has been the quality of my past exchanges with this person?
- Have I set an appropriate place for this meeting?
- Has the other person been made aware, ahead of time, how long this exchange is scheduled to last?
- Is the setting in which this exchange is to occur conducive to the focus required of the subject at hand?

Nonverbal Communication

The matter of noise may be understood as a nonverbal element in communication. There are many others. Nonverbal communication refers to those acts or circumstances, intentional or unintentional, in which messages are sent and received without, or in addition to, words.

On a recent flight, the passenger in the seat next to me began to sniffle and wipe her eyes with tissue. After a time, she commenced crying, openly. I was uncomfortable and unsure of an appropriate response to her. Should I inquire about the cause of her distress? Should I offer a hand? Should I pretend to be asleep? As I pondered my response, my seatmate made a brief comment about the snow on

Mt. Shasta, which we could see through the windows of the airliner. After responding, I asked if I could be of assistance to her. She took my hand and held it tightly and explained that the reason for her distress was that the plane was late, and she was going to "disappoint my stepson, again." In explanation she told me that she had recently married a man with three children whose mother had abandoned them. Her stepson was ten years old and was playing in a basketball game that afternoon; she had promised him that she would attend—and now she was not going to make it. I hope that my words of counsel provided some surcease from her agony.

In terms of nonverbal communication, one would notice that her tears indicated, clearly and without words, that she was in distress. Taking my hand suggested that she sought and needed comforting. But to that point in our exchange, I had no knowledge of the content of her distress or the events that gave rise to her desire for comfort. Only after her words did I learn of the reason for her pain. That is one of the characteristics of nonverbal communication: it can be and often is ambiguous.

Nonverbal communication takes many forms:

- body language (rigid, slouching)
- the sounds we impart to words (harsh, warm, soft, loud)
- the use made of space
- physical characteristics (attractiveness, size, color)
- clothing, makeup, jewelry
- the use made of light or color
- time

Perhaps the most important consideration for the advancement manager's use and understanding of nonverbal communication is *congruence*. Congruence refers to the appropriate matching of nonverbal cues to circumstances. Creating and maintaining congruence between nonverbal and verbal language may seem to be easy but prove to be difficult to accomplish: we know, most of us, to refrain from laughing aloud at someone's tragedy; it is rather more difficult to determine where to sit at the conference table for an important meeting or what to wear to the lead donor's barbecue. Yet both require that our nonverbal cues be consistent with our words.

The concept of congruence means that both the nonverbal language and the verbal language we use convey similar messages. If the advancement manager is a serious professional working for an important organization that is addressing vital issues, and if he or she takes seriously the lead donor, then the attire chosen for the barbecue will be consistent with the verbal messages: not a clown suit certainly but also not formal garb. Rather, the advancement manager will have learned what "casual" attire is accepted in the community in which the barbecue will take place and will be clothed in that fashion. (Note: appropriateness in clothing varies from one region of the country to another and may also vary within regions.)

As written and spoken languages have rules to assure understanding (e.g., a plural subject always requires the plural form of the verb), so too does nonverbal language have rules that may minimize ambiguity (happy subjects are accompanied by frowns and grimaces only at the risk of serious misunderstanding and the consequences flowing from misunderstanding).

In passing it may be noted that congruence is an issue involved when the male advancement manager makes unwanted advances to female staff or volunteers. He expects to be seen and dealt with as the boss and followed as the leader doing work of significance. Expressions of unwelcomed affection or lust directed to female staff are not consistent or congruent with the role claimed. Small wonder, then, that harassment charges are the too-frequent and always unhappy consequence.

Listening

Both verbal and nonverbal communications are commonly understood as active; *listening* is too often perceived as purely passive. "When I listen, I sit quietly and take in what someone else is saying." Not quite so. To listen effectively is not simply to receive auditory stimuli. Listening requires active involvement: paying attention to the messages sent, both verbal and nonverbal; relating to those messages; and responding.

Although the word listening implies the use of auditory receptors alone, active listening involves attending to the nonverbal cues, many of which are visual, that accompany words. Paying attention is a trait that many never master. It is characteristic of these persons, in their interaction with others, that they listen with only part of their consciousness while, with the rest, they work at formulating responses and listening for pauses they can fill with their own words.

How many messages get short-circuited by responders who intrude on thoughts and ideas with unwanted interruptions? Such persons use a word, an image, or part of an idea, as a jumping-off place for the intrusion of questions or comments, and those questions or comments are pressed whether or not they are germane to the thoughts of the one who had held the floor. Worse, these nonlisteners, failing to locate a pause long enough to commence "contributing," often talk over the other person, producing a babel of sound in which no thoughts are communicated and no feelings are sent or received.

Actively attending to the thoughts of another implies hearing out that person, listening until the case is made or the argument completed. Even when it seems to the listener that the one holding the floor is taking a disproportionate time to shape an idea, the active listener waits, searching for the thrust of the contribution. The active listener poses questions of the speaker to ascertain meanings when they seem unclear or obscure. An active listener understands and shows by the nature of his or her contributions that communication is not a contest but a cooperative undertaking.

A second component of active listening is formulating a relationship to the ideas expressed. The ideas, when heard and understood, will be set, for the active listener, in a personal context. The listener asks, "How does this thought or suggestion involve me and my work?" "How will my department be impacted?" "When will these ideas affect my staff? My volunteers?" "What does this direction mean for the projects on which I am now working?"

In the work of advancement, proposals, suggestions, and ideas have power; they are "put out there" because someone believes they may make a difference. Because that is true, the manager who is listening will try to fit ideas or requests into the framework of ongoing work and responsibilities. The quick and dismissive response is utilized in the communications of the professional advancement manager only to the manager's detriment. Whether he or she is dealing with a simple request for a day off or a plan to restructure all advancement activities, the attentive manager will listen to what is said and relate to the words, feelings, and ideas sent in terms that are marked by his or her engagement with the sender and the institution.

Responding

Then the advancement manager will be prepared to respond. Speakers seek responses to the messages they send. Perhaps the response is simply to file away information as background data with greater or lesser potential for later use. A far more likely circumstance, however, because of the nature of the issues brought to advancement managers, is that the manager will be expected to give a "yes" or "no," to indicate that the matter discussed will be given consideration, to suggest some modifications or accommodations to the speaker's suggestions, or to offer counsel or advice. The manager's response may take the form of a request for more detailed information, for clarification, or for illustration. It may involve encouragement of the speaker, or the response may be the expression of clear disagreement with the speaker's ideas, suggestions, or requests.

Persons enter into communication with advancement managers expecting and hoping that the manager may make a difference. To be sure, some persons, especially staff, tend to believe the manager has more power than he or she really possesses. It is difficult for them to see or understand the degree to which power and authority are limited by the realities of organizational life. So they come to the manager seeking responses, answers to questions, and a willingness to intrude into the present circumstances to create a differing, presumably better, outcome in the future. When the advancement manager has paid attention and integrated the information provided or ideas offered into the realities of his or her responsibilities, only then is the manager prepared to respond.

It is not within the purview of this book to delve into the advancement manager's psyche. However, it is clear that the way in which the advancement manager evaluates self has a profound impact on the way in which he or she relates to others. The advancement manager whose self-concept is basically positive is positioned to communicate openly, honestly, confidently, and from a position of authority with others. Many pieces go into making and realizing a positive self-concept; among them:

- knowledge of the job
- appreciation of the employing organization
- belief in the work undertaken by the employing organization
- personal life that provides general satisfaction
- a measure of contentment with personal income level
- recognition from friends, family, neighbors, and employer
- overall consistency between belief systems and actions
- job challenges sufficient to provide for a sense of "reach"
- the regard of fellow professionals and other colleagues

Most of us do not possess all of these re-enforcers all of the time; there are times our boss ignores us, entire months when we seem mired in routine, periods when compensation appears woefully inadequate. We are not, however, doomed to the "slough of despond" by the occasional circumstance when one or another of these factors seems beyond our grasp. In general, when such factors characterize our lives, basic optimism and the sense of self-worth enable us to function from a position of personal strength.

The manager, however, who doubts his or her efforts or the ability to do the job, who insists on validation from others, who dislikes a member of his or her family, who hates the boss, or who lives life in a way that is inconsistent with his or her belief system is one who operates from a position of weakness that is sure to find expression in the nature and content of communication with others.

Striving, that is, wanting more and better, is an ingredient of contemporary life, and that ingredient is especially characteristic of the work of advancement professionals: higher goals, more ambitious projects, greater media recognition, larger gifts. Communications and the relationships flowing from quality communications are enhanced for the advancement manager who, from time to time, administers a self-inventory and recognizes, with appreciation, the satisfiers that exist in life. From such a base, the manager is enabled to meet and relate to others with strength and confidence.

STAYING IN TOUCH

Tom Peters and Nancy Austin in *A Passion for Excellence* have written, "The number one managerial productivity problem in America is, quite simply, managers who are out of touch with their people...."[1 (p.8)] Advancement managers cannot afford to be out of touch with their people, whether their people are staff, volunteers, donors, or the men and women of the media. The demands placed on advancement managers, already large, grow larger year after year. The work of advancement is accomplished through people, and it is in the interest of answering those demands that the advancement manager gets in touch and stays in touch with all of those who enter into or have influence on his or her work.

Negatives

That is not an easy accomplishment in an era in which organizations and institutions change their goals, their philosophy, their audiences, their programs, and their leadership with unnerving regularity. The advancement manager is often called on to seek support for the institution in a climate of organizational tumult.

The advancement work force similarly is being shaped into a new creation: more women, more members of ethnic minority groups, increasing specialization, and larger staffs with better educated employees mark contemporary advancement staffs. Recently the profession was largely comprised of males, who were almost exclusively white; however, members today represent growing diversity. Gone with the white-dominated male profession is the world view shared by development practitioners in those bygone days: styles, values, belief systems, and even dress once were held in common. No more.

Personal and family problems, including divorce, teen pregnancy, drug and alcohol abuse, and street violence, though clearly outside the purview of the advancement manager's assigned responsibilities, are not outside his or her orbit of concern. Valued staff members going through marital dissolution are almost certain to bring their personal circumstances with them when they come to work. So will those whose children are acting out in ways that are causing them anxiety and grief or those who have an elderly parent now dependent on them for 24-hour care or prospective donors wrestling with the demons of chemical abuse. In short, the institutional and larger world context within which it is required that the advancement manager get in touch and stay in touch has grown increasingly complicated. But relate the manager must, whether organizational policies make it difficult or societal disintegration looms or leisure-time activities take precedence with some on whom one depends.

A recent television commercial for a major airline focused attention on the manager of a company telling his staff that they had lost their oldest and best customer because they had allowed themselves to get out of touch. The manager distributes airline tickets (it is an airline commercial, after all) to his staff and instructs them to go and reestablish personal contact with the firm's customers across the nation. When asked where he is going, the owner says, "I'm going back to see that old friend I just lost."

Contemporary technology—e-mail, cellular or digital telephone systems, pagers, electronic information networks—though providing near limitless opportunity for contact is no substitute for personal interaction. It is the relationships found and cultivated one to one and face to face on which the advancement manager depends to accomplish his or her work and meet responsibilities.

Positives

What does the manager have to offer as such relationships are building?

Time

Relationships are planted and nurtured in shared experiences. Such experiences require time. And time commitments, once made, must be honored. Changes and postponements, admittedly unavoidable on occasion, should be held to a minimum. Interruptions for telephone calls or quickie walk-in conferences should be tolerated only with the greatest reluctance. Partners to a relationship are willing and prepared to commit and to expend time lavishly.

Attention

The building of a vital relationship with another implies honest focus. Patronizing is transparent and plays no part in quality relationships. Active listening efforts are critical as ideas and information are shared and to which concrete response is made. Minds rarely wander in the nurtured relationship.

Interests

"If you want a friend, be a friend," children are taught. And the homily is relevant for the advancement manager. Some of the interests others hold important will be outside the range of the interests of the advancement manager, but not all of them will be. The relationship builder will explore the range of interests of his or her companion and will find those to which both are drawn. Time together will focus on common interests. Enthusiasm for that which is shared will be unfeigned.

Informality

Large formal meetings have their purposes, but easy, informal exchange often serves better when bonding is the purpose. Even sessions involving several people with carefully defined purposes can have an informal air about them: the setting of the meeting, a loosened tie, shoes kicked off, and casual asides revealing affect serve to put participants at ease, even when task-focused. Relationships are cemented in gracious and easy social intercourse.

Honesty

Effective and mutually satisfying relationships are grounded in honesty. Each party to such a relationship understands and values the other for their trustworthiness. Words are bonds, and veracity is never at question. Of course, the honesty on which supportive relationships rest is not the variety that is merely an excuse for insult; it is, rather, one in which facts are stated as facts, opinions are identified as such, commitments are honored. Honesty in lasting relationships does not trade in gossip nor does it betray confidences. It is rather a mutually understood condition of the relationship.

Self-Disclosure

As persons move to the level at which the relationship takes on meaning, some measure of self-disclosure is always involved. As one finds oneself at ease with another, the impulse is to reveal more of the self: What is held dear? What is embarrassing? What is disliked? What goal is important? Self-disclosure, when proffered at the appropriate moment, tends to elicit similar disclosure from the other party to the relationship, which in turn implies that both are co-conspirators in the business of life.

Humor

Warm, good humor marks effective relationships. The humor in substantive relationships is not the joke-telling, back-slapping bonhomie of the neighborhood bar or the contrived silliness of the situation comedy. It is, rather, characterized by the gentle, often self-deprecating quip or observation that brings a smile. Such humor does not seek an object to be held to derision. When offered, it is comfortable and comforting, both creating and reflecting the sense of ease that exists between and among the parties to the relationship.

CONFLICT

As the course of true love never runs smooth, so, too, relationships—rich and meaningful though they may be—often become conflicted. Conflict need not destroy a relationship; it is sure, however, to try the relationship. The manner in which conflict is addressed and resolved, the inner strengths and commitments of the parties involved, and the solidity of the established relationship all contribute to the enduring quality of a relationship, even one in conflict.

Vice President Jerry had gone to work at the college 11 years earlier, some weeks after his old friend, Douglas, had made him aware of an opening at the institution for which Douglas worked. At that time, both Douglas and Jerry were well down the organizational structure—"worker bees" they called themselves.

Douglas was promoted first and Jerry reported to his buddy for a time. Later Jerry received a promotion to the same level as Douglas. Their friendship was real; each helped the other, and both enjoyed social relationships, outside of work, in which their respective families were included. After a couple of years it became clear that Jerry's star was on the rise. He clearly had a zest for his work and real talent at meeting the obligations assigned him. Douglas was less engaged in his career. He found excuses to avoid fulfilling obligations. He arrived late for work and left early. He missed meetings and fell short of reaching his goals.

Five years after he came to work at the college, Jerry was named a vice-president. Old friend Douglas worked for him, and Douglas had become a problem employee. Jerry spoke with his buddy repeatedly about job performance, attitude, and potential, all to no avail. At last, Jerry had to terminate his friend's employment. That responsibility was agony for Jerry. The relationship was put at risk. Douglas was devastated; Jerry was personally dismayed, though convinced he had acted in the best interests of the institution.

Four years later, their relationship has returned to its old level of vitality and meaning: Jerry continues to serve as a vice-president of the college and maintains his old zest for his work; Douglas is the successful operator of a retail business he opened after he left the college.

CONFLICT RESOLUTION

How did the conflict between Jerry and Douglas come to be resolved so satisfactorily? Conflict occurs when the interests or behaviors of individuals or groups are incompatible. Conflict situations often result in negative emotional states in the parties to the conflict. It is important to recognize that there are many degrees of conflict, from the severe to the trivial. At the most devastating level, that is between or among nations, it can result in war with the accompanying agony and suffering. At a lesser level, conflict may represent little more than a passing annoyance. The intermediate levels often produce the greatest angst in the parties to the conflict. The ability to evaluate conflict situations for their significance and impact is among the advancement manager's most important challenges.

Persons deal with conflict in a variety of ways: some run from it, others deny it exists, a few revel in it, the committed work to resolve or diminish its impact. There are seven steps that, when taken in sequence, may prove useful to the advancement manager seeking to find resolution to conflict.

Step 1

The reality of the conflict is faced frankly. When conflict is denied or ignored, the emotions associated with it take root in the parties to the conflict; those emotions tend to deepen and metastacize.

The baseline requisite of efforts at conflict resolution is an open admission of the conflict—the apparent incompatability of interests involved. The definition must be honestly set forth; that is, the position of both parties to the conflict will be faced fairly and sensitively. If the advancement manager is playing a mediating role and the parties to the conflict have sought his or her assistance or decision, the manager ascertains the accuracy of the conflict definition. If the manager is party to the conflict, he or she should identify the nature of the conflict with scrupulous fairness and offer his or her statement of definition as an earnest of the commitment to find resolution.

Step 2

Both parties to the conflict seek agreement to the proposition for which both want resolution. As interpersonal relationships can't flower when only one party is involved, so conflicts are not resolved when but one party seeks resolution. And that sometimes happens; not infrequently, the only satisfactory conclusion to a conflict for one of the parties is domination: he or she prevails. Under those circumstances, the only option is for an outside party, someone with power, to impose a decision.

When both parties agree that they want a mutually satisfactory resolution, however, hope exists for finding a way out of the conflict. Two committed problem solvers, facing a difficult circumstance with little in the way of ready solutions on the horizon, are ones who are likely to find or create a solution.

Step 3

The resolution process firmly focuses on the nature of the conflict and the facts associated with the conflict. Because emotional states typically accompany conflict, it is common for attempts at resolution to get bogged down in personality issues: "He said . . .," "She said . . .," "Last year, you . . .," "When we tried to close that gift, I . . . ."

When hurts or slights, real or imagined, creep into efforts at resolution, the promise of identifying a conclusion acceptable to the parties grows dim. To the extent that there is a time and place for airing personal grievances, the time and place is clearly not in the midst of resolution efforts.

"Just the facts, ma'am," said Sergeant Joe Friday years ago, and so says the resolution seeker. Facts and circumstances laid out with painstaking care and clarity have a way of suggesting solutions.

Step 4

The facts associated with the conflict are checked for accuracy and precision. Are the facts as they seem? Have circumstances been skewed as tempers flared and emotions rose? Are the numbers correct? Do the projected consequences follow from the facts? And do the conclusions drawn from the facts reflect sound reasoning?

Many conflicts commence and move on to a bubbling roil based on inaccurate information, implausibly interpreted and incorrectly extrapolated. Having said that, however, many conflicts are the result of apparent or real incompatibility between (or among) two (or more) proposed courses of action.

Step 5

The resolution process moves toward identifying potential resolutions. The list that emerges encompasses both poles to the conflict, but also identifies other potential handles, other means of resolving the conflict. Although compromise is not to be ignored as a possible solution, neither is it to be rushed to as the inevitable and easiest way out. "Half a loaf is better than none," the compromiser crows; but that is not necessarily, or even very often, the case. Sometimes the midway position, the compromise, results in mounting an organizational initiative that is timid when a bold initiative might have proved transforming for the organization. (This is frequently the case with the allocation of budget resources.) Often compromise results in a circumstance in which all parties to the conflict situation feel dissatisfied, as though they were abused in the resolution.

When a series of possible solutions is identified, the potential exists that one or another of those solutions will suggest an answer that serves well the purposes of the organization and offers mutual rewards sufficient for the parties to the conflict to find satisfaction.

Step 6

On examining the potential solutions, it remains for one to be selected *and agreed to* by the parties to the conflict. Throughout this process, negotiation has been going on; with this step decisions are made. The conflicted parties will, of course, seek to maximize their own advantage. The remarkable experience associated with the conflict resolution process, however, is that once the parties have come off their original positions (or at least have recognized that their original positions are no longer likely to prevail), other positions may be examined dispassionately, the merits of each weighed, and assent given more or less readily.

If the process has been employed fairly, the parties—once conflicted and probably angry—can move away from the process with a decision in which their recent adversary has become a collaborator in finding and accepting resolution.

Step 7

The resolution to the conflict will be revisited—perhaps more than once—in the weeks following the agreed-upon actions to determine if the decisions made are effectively serving the circumstance that originally gave rise to the conflict. Further, the advancement manager will give attention to the potential for lingering negative effects on job performance, morale, or teamwork stemming from the conflict.

Options

The imperative for the advancement manager in conflict resolution is to understand that conflict among staff, with colleagues in the organization outside the field of advancement, or with donors is a circumstance that requires, and often retreats before, management. The existence of conflict does not require the manager to leap into the fray and render a Solomonic judgment. Conflict rarely yields to charisma and only grudgingly does it give way before the exercise of power. It can be met and resolution can be found through the application of systematic and thoughtful management.

It has been rightly said that the options available to the parties to a conflict are win-lose (one party prevails, the other gives way), lose-lose (a solution is found and implemented that satisfies neither of the contenders, a compromise, for example), and win-win (effort produces a resolution in which at least the major needs of both parties are integrated). It is toward the win-win option that the advancement manager commits his or her energy.

ORGANIZATIONAL COMMUNICATION

The communications concepts addressed to this point—communications as a necessity for relationships, communication models, noise, nonverbal language, self concept, interpersonal communications and relationship building, and conflict and conflict resolution—have applicability to the interpersonal dimension of communication. It remains for us to look at communication as an organizational phenomenon.

More than 60 years ago, one of the pioneer organization theorists observed, ". . . in any exhaustive theory of organization, communication would occupy a central place, because the structure, extensiveness, and scope of organizations are almost entirely determined by communication technique."[2 (p.8)] Twenty years later, another prominent organization scholar noted, "The question to be asked of any administrative process is: How does it influence the decisions of the individual? Without communication, the answer must be: It does not influence them at all."[3 (p.109)]

The indisputable fact is that organizations and institutions of all types, both nonprofit and public sector, have a stake in creating, providing for, and benefiting from effective communications directed toward and benefiting from the actions of their publics. It should be added that, from a contemporary perspective, the importance of communication goes beyond technique[4] and that the "individual,"[5] as the term relates to the management of organization includes many in addition to those who are integrally involved in "administrative process."

The means by which organizations communicate and encourage communication among their widest constituencies are well known: letters, memoranda, proposals, electronic networks, telephones, newsletters, magazines, meetings, retreats, conferences, training sessions, and the like. It is not our purpose to belabor such media, individually or in their totality, except to observe that the variety of means employed in the interest of better organizational communication underscores the widespread recognition of the need to "tell the institutional story."

Management theorists and practitioners alike agree that successful organizations require communications to accomplish their purposes. But that insight is akin to a recognition of the importance of motherhood. What is being said by the experts is rather more specific:

- The organization must keep its internal publics informed to assure the support of those within the organization for the organization's purposes.
- The organization must engage in dialogue with its publics—their ideas, attitudes, and feelings—in order to maximize effectiveness.
- The organization must encourage relationships within and among its publics in the interest of building and maintaining loyalty.

Comunication Flow

The concern and end purposes of organizational communications have to do with communications flow. To the degree that the organizational structure is viewed as a flow chart—and it may usefully serve such a purpose—we may speak of the downward flow of communication, the upward flow, and the lateral flow.

Downward Flow

Most, though not all, of the means of organizational communication are representative of the downward flow. The managers of the organization write, or cause to be written, materials that are reproduced and sent downward and outward, informing staff, stakeholders, and community of information they are thought to need to know. Typically, some effort is made to inform those closest to the organization of "breaking" news before that news is made available to the wider public. In the advancement world that scenario might be enacted in the following fashion.

The senior administrators of the community college district have prepared a detailed plan to open a branch campus in an underserved area some distance from the main campus. The leadership has met individually and informally with each member of the district's board and is assured that, when the branch campus proposal is presented at the Tuesday evening meeting, it will be endorsed. The community college leadership has the public affairs office prepare a detailed article on the new campus and on the way in which the proposed initiative will impact the main campus and its operations. The article is printed as the lead in the campus publication, which is delivered to faculty, staff, administrators, trustees, alumni leaders, key donors, and selected political office-holders. The editor of the student newspaper is invited to interview the president of the community college about the branch campus.

On Tuesday, hours before the board members are to vote on the proposal in open meeting with media representatives present, the internal audience receives the publication in which the story is printed. On the same day, the student newspaper carries the branch campus story as its lead.

In such a circumstance, downward communication serves a vital purpose: those closest to the institution have been made aware of a leadership initiative, they have been informed of the presumed impact on the organization and on their own interests, and they have learned of these things with an emphasis consistent with management's desires. In theory, at least, such communication decreases or eliminates rumors and prepares internal publics to answer such questions as may be put to them by friends and neighbors who comprise the wider public.

As valuable as downward communication flow is or may be, it is one-way communication or, to use a category discussed earlier in this chapter, it is an exemplar of the linear model of communication. The receivers are being *told*. Channels of communication that are downward or one way are relatively easy to create and to set in motion. They tend not to provide for interaction or transaction and thus do not assure that messages sent are understood, believed, or supported.

Upward Flow

Upward flowing communication within organizations is considerably more difficult to assure in a steady and regularized fashion. Senior-level managers need to know and, for the most part, want to know what those at lower levels in the organization are thinking, how they are responding, and what organizational issues are receiving what kind of attention.

Although the announcement of the plan for the branch campus should have put an end to rumors, it was not to be the case. The board voted favorably on the proposal as projected. The story on the proposed new campus was run in the local press and on radio and television. Public response was generally favorable.

On campus, though, word spread that the financial needs of the branch campus would exact a toll on funds needed to fund operations on the main campus. Other rumors gained currency about the way in which the new venture would impact teaching loads and teaching assignments. Somehow, the new campus was said to threaten tenure and its prerogatives, although it wasn't at all clear how or why. When the president was made aware that his campus was rife with rumors, virtually all of them negative about the branch campus initiative, he told his vice-president for advancement, "Let's hash it out in faculty council . . . we'll tell them our story." "I'm not sure that's going to be enough," the vice-president responded. "I suggest we do two more things—let's create a survey instrument that we send to all of those who received our original announcement. We won't be asking for their approval of the project; rather, we'll try to design the instrument so that we can identify specific fears. When the forms are returned and tabulated, we can arrange for a series of meetings in which we'll address concerns directly and openly."

"I like that," the president said in assent. "If you really think things are that stirred up, get your plan in gear."

Assuredly, the upward communication flow is difficult, even cumbersome. Whereas the organizational initiative may originate with a limited number of leaders, no more than 10—the negative responses to it may emanate from hundreds, each representing potentially a different perspective on the issues and, prospectively, many constituencies. Although downward flowing communication can be and usually is controlled by the senior leadership as to content, timing, and circulation, the upward channels are often out of the control of management. Once it begins to flow, the content of upward communication is shaped by circumstances and attitude and, in the main, uncontrollable except as misstatements of fact may be challenged and corrected. The manager who wants to hear what those at lower levels in the organizational structure have to say must be prepared to hear things that may not be pleasant. Pleasant or not, upward flow of communication within the organization is valuable for the information and ideas made available to those in the senior levels of management and for the creation of an atmosphere in which staff and others believe that they can be—and, in fact, are—heard.

The events related to the community college campus—managerial initiatives, communication, and faculty rumor—do not provide for the role that should be played by mid-level managers in learning about staff anxiety and discontent and communicating this to senior managers. Such intermediate managers will always number among their roles, even when the responsibility is undefined, the communication of staff responses to senior management proposals and actions.

Lateral Flow

A third dimension of communication flow is lateral. Different in content from the downward and upward channels (which tend to be policy/program intensive), lateral flow often is operations intensive or personally focused. Lateral flow has reference to the channels between and among those with like assignments within the organization. The prospect research office provides information to the development officer, the public affairs staff seeks the details related to a compelling story from the representative in the southeast, and the database manager incorporates new data made available by colleagues in the alumni office.

As individuals cannot fail to communicate, advancement staff, in the fulfillment of their several and specific job responsibilities, engage in the sending and receiving of messages, marked by greater or lesser detail, on a regular and continuing basis. Such interchange of information is the *sine qua non* of advancement operations. And such interchange, to be effective, rests on a consistent flow of frank, honest, accurate information among those engaged in the advancement enterprise; to the degree that the advancement manager inhibits the flow of information among staff or tolerates or initiates trade in inaccurate information, he or she is party to the creation of circumstances that may place strictures on organizational success.

The existence and importance of yet another kind of lateral communication must be acknowledged: the informal communication that takes place between and among advancement staff personnel. The advancement manager will know that staff communicate with one another about all manner of things: their work, their relationships, their respective levels of compensation, their attitudes toward one another and the "boss," their support, and the organization and its direction. Such unstructured, but inevitable, communication may contribute to institutional purposes even though it is spontaneous and shaped largely by self-interest. It is incumbent on the advancement manager, therefore, to be *open* and not given to keeping or suggesting secrets, *accurate* in reporting information relating to operations, *timely* in passing along relevant data and plans, and *careful* in making evaluations.

In both interpersonal and organizational communications, the effective advancement manager will have developed an understanding that communications is an operative system to which he or she is party. A system is a set of interdependent parts. A system, as it relates to communication, means that the communicating manager cannot lie here, tell the truth there, suggest something on this occasion, and something else on another. A system implies wholeness, integrity; it does not focus on the constituent parts of an idea or an action. Rather, a system stands for totality and completeness.

As communication is based on a systems commitment—whole, complete, integral—both internal and external publics can believe, can have confidence, and can plan and commit to the person and the organization. When, on the other hand, communication is conceived to be a negotiable commodity—now forthcoming, then withholding—staff and publics will behave as ones standing on shifting sand. The organization and its purposes will suffer.

REFERENCES

1. T. Peters and N. Austin, *A Passion for Excellence* (New York: Random House, 1985).
2. C. Barnard, *The Function of the Executive* (Cambridge, MA: Harvard University Press, 1938).
3. H. Simon, *Administrative Behavior* (New York: MacMillan, 1957).
4. C. Barnard, *The Function of the Executive*.
5. H. Simon, *Adminstrative Behavior*.

CHAPTER 6

The Manager and Technology

Judie had accepted her new position as the senior advancement manager at a midwestern university after almost 11 years in her previous job at a similar institution in a neighboring state. When she took up her responsibilities, she professed to be shocked that day-to-day operations in her new office were, as she put it, "in a shambles." She couldn't get all of the information on donors that she needed and what she got took hours longer than it should have. The systems—from phones to computer hardware and software—were old or slow. They were limited, in the extreme, in what they could provide by way of reports and past giving records.

When she brought the problems to the attention of her boss, the president of the university, the president acknowledged the need to undertake an upgrade of equipment and systems. Judie met with her staff and shared her frustration with the equipment and the systems in place and announced her intention to improve and update advancement office technology.

To her surprise, her staff seemed lukewarm to her plans. "We're getting along okay with what we've got, even if it isn't the latest." "Conversions are such a pain—they disrupt everything, and they take so long." "What about cost? We haven't had a raise in two years, and if we spend a ton of money on equipment, we won't get a raise for another two years." Judie listened to all the comments, promised to consider them, and recessed the meeting for several days.

When the staff reconvened a week later, Judie thanked her staff for the honest expression of their concerns. She pointed out that her objective was to make the work of her staff easier and more effective. She acknowledged that systems conversions could be difficult and time consuming but also could support efforts to achieve significantly improved fund-raising results, something that would surely enhance institutional appreciation for advancement operations. And she promised to seek funds for salary enhancements immediately and totally apart from the funds required to improve the technology available to support the work of advancement. Judie's staff left the meeting unconvinced.

EVOLUTIONARY PROCESS

Change as a pervasive reality has marked the human experience since the beginning of time: it was noted by the ancient Greeks and commented on by the writers of the scriptures of virtually all of the world's great religions. Our parents and grandparents and their grandparents before them lamented, "Nothing is the way it used to be." Still, there is a sense that the changes with which we deal seem to be broader and more far-reaching than in years gone by. And the changes appear to be coming at an ever-accelerating pace. Certainly those changes based on technology are vast and rapid. If one focuses only on the environment of the office—the environment in which advancement officers operate—one is struck by the degree to which technology has reconfigured and redefined both the means by which work is done and, at important points, the content of the work itself.

As recently as the seventh decade of the twentieth century, an appropriately equipped advancement office would have contained addressograph machines, a graphotype, mimeograph (or multilith) equipment, typewriters (most, though not all, of which were electric), dictating equipment, telephones, (and, if the operation were of sufficient size, a PBX switchboard), and a copier. Advancement professionals were served by one or more secretaries adept at "taking" and transcribing shorthand.* File folders containing multiple pieces of paper would have been strewn across desks, and banks of file cabinets, packed with records, would have lined the walls. The office was fairly characterized, in those days, as labor intensive and cost inefficient.

That decade saw the first appropriation of computer technology for the purposes of systematizing fund-raising operations, and it quickly gained acceptance and momentum. In some large institutions, the advancement operation was "allowed" to make use of the organization's data processing equipment (which was thought to belong to the Business Office) to store and access contributions records on a limited basis. In most institutions, however, the advancement office, committed to computerizing operations, contracted with an outside service bureau to store, maintain, and deliver, on call, data relevant to fund raising. In all cases, both inputs and outputs were in "batch mode"; that is, they took place in chunks, once a month or once every two months.†

---

*The equipment noted was characteristic of a more or less sophisticated, large advancement office. In smaller offices, the total available technology was apt to be a typewriter, a telephone, and "ditto" equipment; membership or donor records were kept on 3×5 cards in the figurative and sometimes literal "shoebox."

†There was an attitude, then, that although records of past activities and relationships were good, they were not essential to the work of the development officer. It was during this period that the author was named vice president for development of a relatively young, public comprehensive university. The institution had little fund-raising history. A service bureau was contracted to maintain records, provide labels, etc. When I went to examine the university's alumni records prior to sending them to the service bureau, I found, to my horror, that a significant portion (perhaps 30%) of the 50,000 records had been filed by *first* name. The conversion of those records to electronic data processing was a monumental and expensive undertaking.

The situation today in advancement offices is very different. A personal computer sits on the desk of virtually every advancement officer. If the organization is of moderate size or large, the computers are joined in a network allowing for communication among and between staff. Sophisticated software is provided enabling the computer to perform functions as varied as word processing, prospect research, and planned giving. Electronic mail (e-mail) is more common and more efficient than interoffice memos. Data relative to donors and prospective donors is available on demand. Progress toward goals, information about the most recent institutional contact with a particular donor, and friendship circles and business relationships of both donors and prospective donors are routinely requested and accessed from the advancement database.

The technology available to advancement officers and advancement managers is significantly greater than the existence of personal computers and supporting software, exciting though the capacity of computer technology may be. The advancement office and the personnel belonging to that office are in possession of facsimile machines; mobile telephones; high-speed, high-definition copiers; paging devices; telephones with sophisticated features such as call waiting and call forwarding; and multi-color, high-resolution printers. Transportability is assured: much of the current technology is available in equipment designed for use in automobiles or from other remote locations.

Wondrous though the available technology may appear, the capacity of contemporary office technology does not stop here: computers are available in ever smaller packages, and each annual introduction of computer models seems to feature more memory, more speed, more potential, than the last. Donors are enabled to transfer funds to the recipient institution by EFT (electronic funds transfer), without ever writing a check or signing a stock certificate. Voice mail, which takes many forms, makes possible detailed communication among and between persons without concern for immediate availability. The development of digital television, with the potential it holds for splitting signals and simultaneous transmission of multiple signals, has opened new vistas for telling the institutional story; cable television and satellite transmission join with local and long distance telephone carriers to expand services at surprisingly reasonable cost. Interactivity among and between viewers and listeners and the transmitting entity promises to revolutionize selection of personnel, training, conferencing, and countless other parts of advancement operations.

In short, advancement offices hold and promise greater efficiency and productivity than ever before. Advancement officers are able to be reached and engaged wherever they are at any time. Database managers in the advancement office can manipulate their records rapidly and in ways that seem to answer every need. Researchers discover information about prospects and donors that could only have been imagined in former years, and they can array that information according to nearly limitless parameters.

That problems accompany technology with which the advancement manager must deal is clear; some of those problems are addressed later in this chapter. It is a fact, however, that the systems available to the advancement manager and staff promise more information and accuracy, with faster access and contact. Those attributes of the technology of the times are critical elements in assuring advancement office accomplishment.

Brief reflection will lead to the insight that for all the many and varied pieces of equipment to be found in the contemporary advancement office, they are of a piece, that is, they constitute a system. And they must be understood as such: modern telephones, fax machines, and copiers share with computers the fact that they have been made possible by the chip or semiconductor, by means of which great volumes of information or instruction are processed or manipulated. Despite the systemic nature, or wholeness, that characterizes modern office technology, it may prove useful for the manager to understand the equipment available for use in two, admittedly artificial, categories: communications and information.

ACQUIRING COMMUNICATIONS TECHNOLOGY

The office telephone and its related manifestations—the mobile telephone, the facsimile machine, and the pager—make possible virtually instantaneous voice or document interchange. The advancement manager would no more seek to serve the employing institution without these tools than he or she would approach a donor without the case for support clearly in mind.

The particular array of communications technology to which the advancement manager commits is determined after evaluation of the following:

- the flexibility of the particular equipment or system
  1. Is it capable of expansion if and when the need presents?
  2. Does it provide the specific features and capabilities staff members want and need?
  3. Does the equipment or system interface appropriately with that in use throughout the organization?
- the upkeep and maintenance of the equipment provided by the vendor
  1. Are service personnel readily available?
  2. Have appropriate warranties been put in writing?
  3. Are reliability records available?
  4. What has been the experience of other users?
- the ease of equipment/system operation
  1. Is training readily available for staff?
  2. Are manuals of operation written in terms that assure ready and complete comprehension?

- the features of the system and the needs of advancement operations
    1. Do tasks performed by the equipment correspond to the real needs of staff and management?
    2. Are there "bells and whistles" in the system that, though impressive, are not pertinent to actual operations?
- the costs associated with the equipment or the system
    1. Is budget readily available to acquire the equipment?
    2. How does the cost compare to competitors' products?
    3. Does the purchase of the equipment provide savings in other areas (e.g., does it reduce staffing needs or allow for re-allocation of staff)?
    4. Are there hidden costs?
    5. Can unit costs be reduced by expanding the potential purchasing group—internally or externally?*
- the delivery of the equipment or installation of the system
    1. Is it promised in timely fashion?
    2. What has been the vendor's delivery history, as reported by other users?
    3. Is "down-time" anticipated? How much? Is the "down-time" reasonable?
    4. Is the vendor subject to penalties if the equipment or system is not operational by a predetermined date?

A review of the foregoing factors makes it apparent to the advancement manager that, when contemplating the purchase or lease of any of the various communications systems and accompanying equipment, the manager should:

- Develop, in writing, a set of criteria defining the needs which must be met by the new equipment or system.
- Engage staff or relevant volunteers in the development of those criteria.
- Acquaint himself or herself with the manner in which the presenting needs have been met by similar institutions or organizations.
- Identify reputable vendors to review the criteria and bid on the job.

---

*The advancement office in one university was able to reduce costs significantly for its telephone system by convincing other institutions in the same system to purchase their systems from a common vendor. The advancement office in another institution encouraged other offices in the same institution to acquire mobile telephones from the same vendor identified by the advancement office and, as a result, saved nearly 30 percent on the equipment purchase.

136   THE EFFECTIVE ADVANCEMENT PROFESSIONAL

ACQUIRING INFORMATION TECHNOLOGY

Once again, it needs to be recognized that communications technology and information technology are best understood and utilized as an integrated system: we address them separately for convenience of discussion.

Information systems are manifest in two dimensions: hardware and software. The former has to do with the constellation of circuitry and chips contained in processors, displayed on monitors (cathode ray tubes [CRTs]) and manipulated via keyboards; the latter, software, is comprised of the instructions incorporated on discs or other formats that direct the computer circuitry and chips to perform specific functions.

The hardware (or what is commonly called "the computer") may vary as to manufacturer, memory capacity, operating speed, architecture, and operating system.* In general (and there are exceptions), the more recent the date of design and manufacture of the equipment, the more extensive and speedy its operations and the greater the available options.

Software is the product of computer programmers who design and write, in a language capable of being understood by computer hardware, instructions that direct actions of the computer's circuitry and chips. Normally referred to as programs, computer software addresses a vast range of tasks from things as simple as alphabetizing files or holding family recipes to those as complex as calculating human life expectancy.

Over the years, a vast library of programs has been created, much of which is available for purchase from retail stores specializing in information technology. This software comes in the form of discs, which need only be introduced into the computer's disk drive for use by the processor. Other software, more sophisti-

---

*At this writing, two manufacturers' system architects compete for the computer hardware market: IBM and Apple. In many ways, IBM may be seen as dominant, having made licenses available for other manufacturers to build units based on IBM system architecture. Units built on the IBM model by other manufacturers are typically identified as IBM "clones." The IBM term "personal computer" (PC) has become generic and is commonly used to identify hardware that may be built and marketed by one of many component manufacturers and that employ proprietary IBM technology.

Apple computers have depended on a distinct system architecture that, until the mid-1990s, was not licensed to other manufacturers. The result of the differing marketing strategies was that IBM-based equipment secured significantly greater market penetration. Despite the fact that Apple equipment was perceived, by many, to have distinct advantages over IBM and IBM-clone units (more "user friendly," superior graphic capabilities, etc.), Apple and its system proved to be a distant "runner-up" in the computer hardware market.

Despite that fact, Apple won many loyal supporters so that it remains appropriate to speak of nonprofit (and profit-oriented) entities as Apple environments or IBM environments. It remains to be seen if Apple's admittedly late decision to license its brand-specific technology will win for the firm a larger share of the market or even if that decision is taken in time for Apple to survive the competitive pressures.

cated and complex, has been created for purposes required by specific classes of clients—advancement offices, for example—and is purchased from the firms that have designed and written the program in question. Such material usually provides for custom options. A third category of software is comprised of programs created to serve a unique purpose for a given user.

CHOOSING THE BEST SYSTEM

Each advancement office has its own style and way of fulfilling its responsibilities; further, advancement offices exist in all manner of nonprofit organizations. As a consequence, it is impossible to prescribe software required by every well-functioning advancement operation. The need for programs to accomplish the following tasks would seem to be beyond question, however:

- word processing
- e-mail
- spreadsheet
- graphic design and/or desktop publishing
- scheduling
- prospect research
- planned giving
- gift/pledge processing
- database management

The selection of the specific program(s) to accomplish any one of the above tasks must be made by the advancement manager, staff, or the institution itself. *How* such decisions are made, however, is a process to which the manager will want to give thoughtful attention. (It is rarely appropriate, for example, for the manager to stop by the local computer store on the way home and pick up a program based on the color of the box in which it is contained.) Software decisions for each of the tasks to be performed determine how at least part of the work is done in the advancement office over a period of time: these decisions typically impact numbers of people, impose a training obligation on the organization, and imply built-in limits and potentials. The consequence is that such decisions must be taken with care.

When faced with the need to reach decisions regarding information technology (either hardware or software), the manager should:

- Call on the knowledge and experience of the advancement staff member who is responsible for the activities associated with the use of computers in the

office. (In the absence of such a person on the advancement staff, then the person responsible for information technology in the total institution or organization should be brought into the decision process.)
- Involve volunteers in the decision process, ones who are committed to the organization and who have expertise in information technology.
- Consult selected members of the advancement staff to develop detailed knowledge of needs in each of the areas addressed by software applications.
- Consider retaining an independent information technology consultant who will gain an understanding of the organization's actual needs and will be prepared to make recommendations of equipment and programs to meet those needs.

The study of needs and the development of criteria that will inform the decision-making process need not consume the advancement manager at every step along the way; indeed, in a large advancement operation, it is not advisable for the senior-most manager to be caught up in the minutiae of technology decisions. The manager will, however, receive the recommendations of his team, confirm or modify their decisions, and be prepared to back up those decisions.

Probably no decision in the realm of information technology for advancement is more important than the one dealing with database management. The programs addressing the database are ones that determine, among many other items:

- what information may be stored
- how much information may be stored
- how information is filed
- how many files can be handled
- the form(s) in which information is reported
- the manner in which data may be accessed

In short, the database management program deals with the inputs and outputs of that wide range of activities characteristic of advancement operations: members, donors' and prospects' names, addresses, telephone numbers, giving records, solicitation tracking, relevant information about those on the list, progress toward goals, pledges, and so forth.

Programs developed to receive and provide institutions with this broad range of information have been developed over the course of the last several decades, and they have grown more sophisticated with the passage of time. They are available for purchase at prices ranging from a few hundred dollars to several hundreds of thousands of dollars. The distinctions among the programs, from inexpensive to very expensive, have to do with the amount and variety of information that can be stored, the type and characteristics of reports that may be generated, the volume capacity of the program, the speed of operation, the nature of vendor service provided, to name a few. Large organizations claiming constituencies of several hundred thousand persons and raising funds in the scores of millions of dollars tend to be limited to a handful of software vendors for their database management programs; small and moderate-sized organizations have scores of vendors from which to choose.

CONVERSION

There are relatively few advancement operations that do not now make use of one or another form of information technology. The systems in place, however, may have been set in operation many years ago, they may no longer meet the institution's needs, they may have flaws that can no longer be tolerated, or new and improved applications may have come to market. Converting to new hardware or software is an experience with which most advancement managers have had to cope at least once during the course of their careers.

As one of Judie's staff pointed out in the illustration with which this chapter began, conversions can be a pain and they frequently are lengthy processes. In his article entitled "Implementation of a New System,"[1] Michael Ranney reports on a relatively small organization that began discussing a new system five years before it was in place and operational, a fact that probably had more to do with the ethos of the organization than with the process by which decisions were reached regarding the system. That process, as reported by Ranney, was thoughtfully conceived and may be usefully consulted by managers embarking on a conversion. We paraphrase the process here:

- The flow of communication within the organization and the data needs were analyzed.
- Staff readiness for the new system was evaluated.
- An advisory group of persons with computer experience was formed.
- Efforts were undertaken to maximize the effectiveness of the existing system.
- System options were evaluated with counsel sought from staff and advisers.
- Software was selected for use in the new system.
- Hardware supplier was selected based upon such factors as options, costs, and record of support and service.
- Plans were made for and implementation of staff training.

Discussions with colleagues in advancement who have implemented new systems suggest that small and moderate-sized organizations often accomplish a conversion to a new system in 12 months or less, while the implementation, from beginning thoughts to full implementation, of a new information technology system in large organizations (as defined by the size of the database, the level of activity in the advancement office, and the organization's budget) may be expected to require two to four years.

ON-LINE USES OF INFORMATION TECHNOLOGY

The potential for being entertained, amused, informed, counseled, sold, and stimulated that is resident in the Internet (i.e., when the user has a computer equipped with a modem and an access provider)* is staggering. The Internet, an informal, unstructured communications vehicle linking computers, has opened wide the potential for instantaneous exchanges among and between users across geographic boundaries. Since becoming generally available in 1994, the World Wide Web (the Web), an Internet tool with graphics, sound, and animated images, has stirred excitement because of the perceived outreach and marketing potential by which it is defined. The Web is an on-line network on which organizations and persons tell, via the computer, their particular stories to all who show sufficient interest to "sign on." Users of the Web include those who choose to deliver their own messages via so-called "home pages" and those who peruse the information available to them on home pages. The latter may or may not respond via their computer link to the information to which they have been exposed. Many users, perhaps most, fall into both teller and listener categories.

To the degree that on-line capability is available to advancement staff members, they have available—at the click of the mouse—extraordinary sources of information and the distilled experience of others' efforts. That the accuracy of the available information has not been "vetted," that is, that the Web promises neither accuracy nor sober evaluation of the data arrayed, constitutes the Web's greatest limitation and most compelling flaw. It should be noted that the U.S. Supreme Court, in 1997, held that users of the Web are protected under the free speech amendment to the Constitution. One of the consequences of that ruling is that the Web may continue to offer information that is untruthful, inaccurate, scurrilous, or even pornographic.

For those who choose to undertake communications through the World Wide Web, they own the opportunity to present their institutional messages on a home page. A home page may be initiated at small cost, requiring, in the beginning, little

---

*There are a number of paths or access routes to the Internet. Perhaps the most common has been through commercial service providers. With the payment of a modest monthly fee, users are enabled to avail themselves of the specific services offered by their provider and to be readily connected to the Internet; some access providers make charges based on the time the user spends on-line. A few nonprofit Internet providers offer access to organizations serving one or another of several specific segments of the third sector.

more than a graphics display and limited text. With the passage of time, in order to claim the attention of viewers, sound, animation, and text updates will demand growing staff efforts and increased costs.

The Web may also be seen as a vehicle permitting users to query others for information, argue a case, or seek help in addressing problems. It serves, in short, as a means by which users seek to establish relationships with those with like interests, responsibilities, or problems. Very early in the existence of the Web, communications among advancement officers with similar responsibilities were established: engineering development officers, arts fund raisers, directors of development for education schools, and so forth. These mutual help channels for advancement today number in the hundreds if not the thousands, and their use is expanding.

PROBLEMS

The advancement manager will become keenly aware that, for all of the advantages of information technology, there are also problems, some of which are severe. The nature of those problems and the ways in which they manifest themselves vary from time to time and from one independent sector organization to another. The following brief discussion identifies some of the criticisms that have been voiced about information technology.

There is simply too much information available. The sheer volume of information is, factually, more than is needed or can be used. Countless hours may be spent accessing information that, in the end, may be of little value to the advancement officer. All information, from whatever source it is derived, must be prioritized to be useful, and the simple fact of the volume of information available via the computer makes difficult the prioritizing process.* That which is determined to be priority information must be dependable and, if the information was entered by someone within the organization, must be in a manner consistent with strict data entry procedures.

Advancement officers depend on relationships, created and nurtured, to do their jobs; computers add little to the relationship-building, cultivation, or solicitation process. Though it is true that contemporary technology is a means by which advancement staff can learn more about those with whom they work (donors, prospective donors, editors, public officials), knowing about such per-

---

*David Gerlenter, a professor of computer science at Yale, commenting on computer use in schools, says, "We need less surfing in the schools, not more. Couldn't we teach them to use what they've got before favoring them with three orders of magnitude more?"[2 (p.61)] Larry Cuban of Stanford comments, "Schooling is not about information. It's getting kids to think about information. It's about understanding and knowledge and wisdom."[2 (p.61)] Although these citations both have reference to computer use in schools, the advancement manager will recognize their applicability, for he or she wants staff to use information, not simply acquire more for its own sake.

sons does not, by itself, make for a relationship. Advancement officers are called on to deal with the reality of the circumstances in which they find themselves (e.g., prospects, budgets, goals, cases, needs) and not simply with the "virtual reality" of the on-line world. The "remove" that marks on-line activities is, or can be, inimical to the fulfillment of the advancement mission.

Means and ends are differing realities. Information technology serves as a wonderful instrument—a means. It is not, and never will be, the end of advancement operations. The computer has rarely been responsible for placing a story in the media, for arranging an appropriation from the legislature, or for securing a gift or pledge from donors.* The core reality of philanthropy is voluntary action taken by a person who has been claimed by a need or challenged by a favored institution or organization. Whereas an instrument—television, computer, or telephone—may carry the message and even mediate the need or challenge, the fund-raising end-point—check or pledge—is an act apart from technology. So it is with other advancement goals.

Information systems technology, as represented by both hardware and software, is always changing; no matter what the institution acquires today, it is almost immediately obsolete. Clearly, vendors are in the business of presenting ever-new options to organizations that have purchased or are likely to purchase their systems. Some of those options may be seen as improvements on the systems in place. The apparent reality is that whatever hardware and software the organization has purchased, has trained its staff to use, and has depended on to support advancement operations is not good enough. In such cases, commitments for new technology become regular and ongoing projected expenditures year after year. Advancement activities have their own legitimate purposes, separate and distinct from technology acquisitions, and ought not always be defined by the hunt for the latest, the quickest, or the newest. The advancement manager must be in firm possession of an understanding of the needs the technology will answer in order to provide staff with the support required to accomplish their purposes. Then the manager must be prepared to wait for new needs to become apparent before changing and acquiring new technology.

Earl had served for nearly two years as the senior advancement manager for his employer, a national voluntary health agency. He inherited several technology systems with his job. There were problems of which he had become aware concerning both his communications and information technology.

---

*There are efforts currently underway to solicit and secure gifts on-line. At this writing the results of those efforts have been disappointing; as the technology continues to improve and provides for a level of privacy not now possible, successful contributions solicitation, via the computer, may enter the realm of the doable. Success will still depend on the existence of a sound relationship between advancement officer and prospect based on face-to-face encounters.

Although Earl was not a computer technological whiz, neither was he intimidated by the technology: he could turn on the computer, compose letters using word processing software, communicate with staff and peers using e-mail, and define, with some proficiency, the kinds of reports he needed.

The time had come, however, to make some major technology changes. Earl did not feel confident in providing leadership to those changes. Rather than faking his way into the new technology of communication and information that circumstances had thrust on him, Earl queried colleagues in other organizations on the creation of an appropriate technology system for his advancement office. Having spoken with nearly a dozen of his peers, Earl developed something he called a technology checklist.

Somewhat amended from Earl's version, the checklist follows:

- Needs identified by the advancement staff will be directly addressed by the equipment and programs at the time of purchase.
- Staff members, volunteers, board members, and peers within the organization will have been consulted and their concerns or interests satisfied prior to the purchase of major hardware or the conversion to new software.
- The advancement office will employ at least one person who is knowledgable about and adept at using contemporary office technology. (When the advancement office does not employ expert staff, such staff within the larger organization will be regularly available to the advancement office.)
- Contracts for purchase of equipment or software for use in the advancement office will provide for general training of all advancement officers and specific training of staff members with identified assignments.
- Selected vendors will provide assurances of timely maintenance of equipment and prompt answers to software concerns or problems.
- Such issues requiring customized approaches will have been identified prior to purchase, a time frame for customization will have been agreed upon, and actual costs will have been negotiated.
- The communication and information technology vendor will have committed to a specific usable lifetime of their equipment or systems (no less than three years) prior to the signing of purchase agreements.
- Plans will have been set, at the time the systems are acquired, for an evaluation of the system to take place within a year of implementation.

Among the changes that accompany the growing use of technology in the advancement office, none is more important than the fact that the commitment to use of communication and information technologies represents a *strategic* decision on the part of the advancement manager. The kind of equipment or hardware used and the types of software to which the institution commits itself are logistical decisions, they undergird and support the advancement office's overall mission.

Using them is strategic. The appropriation of contemporary technology in the advancement office addresses the singular advancement issue: how the institution in general, and the advancement manager in particular, supports the efforts of the fund raisers, the public relations professionals, the alumni officers, the planned giving specialists, and all the others who are charged with seeking and securing public support.

By providing appropriate technology, the advancement manager demonstrates that he or she understands that the only appropriate role played by management is in support of staff efforts to meet organizational needs and fulfill the organizational mission. The manager provides, via technology, for:

- clear and sure voice communications
- immediate availability of documents from distant locations
- pertinent report generation
- accurate record keeping and list generation
- prospect tracking
- reliable comparison parameters
- flexible scheduling

The skillful advancement manager understands that his or her role is to support and guide staff efforts. Technology is useful precisely to the degree that it serves to undergird the manager's efforts to support and guide.

REFERENCES

1. M.O. Ranney, "Implementation of a New System," in *Improving Fundraising with Technology*, eds. J.D. Miller and D. Strauss (San Francisco, Jossey-Bass, 1996).
2. T. Oppenheimer, "The Computer Delusion," *Atlantic Monthly* (July 1997): 61.

CHAPTER 7

The Manager and Planning

When Patricia was selected as executive director of the agency, it was with the understanding that she would be held responsible for making substantial changes in the operations of her employing organization; however, she was informed that not all members of her board believed there was need for change. The agency had existed for over 40 years and had been operated, for most of those years, by volunteers. It served a significant proportion of the potential client population; the budget was in or near balance most years; and, when there was a deficit, a supporter stepped forward to "pick up" the difference.

The agency in question provided a summer camping experience for young people with a chronic, life-threatening disease, although for almost all campers the disease was controlled. The agency had been founded by two physicians whose specialities served those diagnosed with the disease at issue. Over the years, the agency had been gifted with funds sufficient to acquire land, construct buildings, and provide scholarship assistance to attend camp for needy young people afflicted with the disease. One of the founding physicians, still alive and active, continued to serve as a leader on the agency's board of directors.

The agency's program received extensive and favorable press and other media exposure. Past participants in the summer camp experience, their parents, and their grandparents, were supportive of the program in financial and psychological terms.

Patricia's 40-member board was minimally involved in the agency: they met six times a year with an average attendance of 11; for the most part, the board supported Patricia's efforts in recruitment of summer staff and campers but tended to provide direction (not counsel or advice) about the what, how, and when of the camping program. When camp was in session nine weeks each summer, board members and other volunteers showed up, daily, to tell staff what was to be done. In her first year as executive director of the agency, Patricia found herself taking direction from board members who had never attended a formal board meeting. Moreover, her staff was subject to such direction, even when it was contrary to Patricia's instructions.

On conclusion of the first summer of her term as executive director, Patricia wrote and delivered to the board a detailed report of camp attendance, finances, contributions, and needs. It had been a summer of solid achievement, but also one of frustration. She included, in her report, a series of queries about the responsibilities of board members and her responsibilities to those whose participation in agency activities were limited to their involvement in summer camp operations. Her report was mailed, with the endorsement of the board chairman, to all 40 members of the board.

At the next board meeting a month later, board attendance remained at 11—none of those who had, the year before, inserted themselves into day-to-day camp activities was present. In her frustration, Patricia commented, "We are trying to do something important for these children and families whose lives, today, are impacted by the disease. But board members and parents of past participants in our program feel they can determine, direct, and shape our activities whenever they decide to show up at camp. I would love it if they were here at our board meetings to wrestle with us in the definition of our program. But they aren't."

Then, in words growing out of her frustration, Patricia asked her board, "Are we a serious contemporary social service agency providing needed services, or are we an extension of the kitchens of our inactive board members? Is this a mom and pop operation or a social service delivery system that avails itself of the best insights of our professional and active volunteer leadership?" The members present were taken aback by the anger in the words of their executive director.

Breaking the spell cast by Patricia's words was the founding physician. In measured tones he said, "She's right, you know. Some work all year to create a great experience for our kids, and others do nothing but show up during camp and tell staff what they want done—whether right or wrong. We have grown beyond that kind of operation—or, at least, I thought we had. This issue is of greater importance than a matter of throwing some people off the board; it has to do with who we are as an agency, and where we're going."

Over the next two board meetings, members wrestled with the agency's mission, the relationship of its board to its staff, and future directions for the agency. In the end, four months after Patricia expressed her frustration, the board retained a consulting firm to assist in the creation of a strategic plan—a map to direct the agency's future.

The details may differ, the personalities change, the presenting circumstances vary, but advancement managers will recognize the circumstances: the need to chart a course that is responsive both to the internal realities of the organization and the context in which the organization exists. Such are the challenges of strategic planning, and to such challenges strategic planners address their efforts.

STRATEGIC PLANNING

A strategic plan may be defined as a set of decisions made now that will have an impact on the future activities of the organization. The plan takes into consideration the challenges and capacity of the organization, as well as the environment in which it operates. The strategic plan will have secured the endorsement of the leadership and will reflect the financial, staff, and time commitments of the organization. The strategic plan will, usually, project efforts for two to five years or even longer.

Although the term strategic planning most often has reference to the extended planning efforts of an entire organization in all of its complexity—and is frequently so defined and treated in management literature—divisions or units of organizations, with growing frequency, similarly engage in "strategic" planning.

Three questions arise when an organization sets out to develop a strategic plan:

1. Who are the persons, in the organization, who will participate in the development of the strategic plan?
2. What are the elements to be addressed in the creation of the organization's strategic plan?
3. How will the commitments associated with the plan be addressed in the implementation of the plan?

WHO IS INVOLVED IN CREATING A STRATEGIC PLAN?

A strategic plan "belongs" to the organization. It is not the product of one person's work, nor does it represent the commitments of a selected few. Consequently, the identification of a strategic planning team that is broadly representative of the organization becomes a matter of utmost significance.

In Patricia's case it was determined that the entire membership of the board would be involved in the planning process and that the board would be supplemented by the addition of three parents of youngsters attending the camp. Although 40 (the total membership of the board) was too large a number to serve effectively in the planning efforts, it was reasoned that the changes in agency operations that were likely to result from the process were so important that all board members should be afforded the opportunity to participate. It was also thought that active planning participants would, in all likelihood, not exceed a dozen, a conjecture that subsequently proved accurate.

The common practice is for the senior leadership of the organization to create a strategic planning committee whose members have been selected for both broad and specific knowledge of the organization's operations and for their understanding of the attitudes, skills, and commitments of others within the organization. The strategic planning committee will not be comprised, necessarily or exclusively, of persons with impressive titles, although some from among the organization's senior leadership will be expected to be active participants in the process. Among those to be included in the efforts to develop the plan are persons holding such positions as president, vice-president, headmaster, dean, chief administrator, executive director, and chairman of the board. Additionally, a typical strategic planning team includes consumers of services (students, alumni, or, in the case of a medical center, former patients and/or physicians), donors, advocates for the cause addressed by the organization, junior level staff, and so forth.

The process is best served when the strategic planning committee is representative of the range of activities within the organization. A community college planning team, for example, would almost certainly include members representing the offices of academic affairs, student services, business and finance, and advancement. A typical university committee charged with creating a strategic plan might be comprised of 10 persons: vice-president for academic affairs, a dean, vice-president for advancement, a representative of the finance office, two students (one of whom is active in student government), two well-regarded faculty members, an alumnus/a, and two donors to the university.

The development of a comprehensive strategic plan is time intensive. Members will be alerted to the fact that the committee will meet regularly, at least monthly, and that subcommittees will be formed to address specific issues in the interim between the regular meetings. It is rare for a comprehensive strategic plan to be developed, even with an intensive meeting schedule, in less than six months; 12 months is a more common time frame for the completion of the planning process; and 18 months or even longer is not without precedent.

It is urgent, throughout the planning process, that the CEO, if not a member of the team, be regularly and thoroughly briefed on matters under discussion, on directions taken, and on projections shaped. The advice provided by the CEO will serve as an important ingredient of the team's efforts. In an earlier chapter, there was an extended illustration of a "visioning" process; two elements of that process are informative for strategic planning: (1) a staff member was assigned, full time, to provide leadership to the activity; and (2) that staff member met regularly with the CEO to keep communication flowing about activities undertaken.

A strategic plan may be and frequently is created without full-time leadership. On the other hand, in large, complex organizations, it has become common for the strategic planning process to depend on professional leadership; if not a staff member, then a consultant retained specifically to work with the planning team. Growing numbers of organizations have created the position of director of strategic planning and made the incumbent part of the organization's permanent staff leadership.

It was noted above that some organizations frequently devise divisional or unit strategic plans. When a unit, for example the division of advancement, sets out to develop a plan, it is obvious that the composition of the team will differ from that projected for the comprehensive, organizationwide strategic planning process. The principles, however, remain the same: the team will be representative of the unit, it will meet frequently over a period of time sufficient to accomplish its tasks, and the senior person in the unit will be kept fully informed and provided with opportunity to offer counsel.

Because the plan created during the process "belongs" to the organization and not just to those who worked on it, one of the important activities to be undertaken by the committee is the creation of a process to inform the constituencies of the content of the plan and to secure maximum "buy-in." There are several ways that have proven effective in reaching those ends; they all require the provision of full and complete information to the constituencies and a willingness, by the committee, to listen to comments and concerns and to revise plans as appropriate or necessary. Interim reports to the constituencies—large meetings in which plan details are presented, small meetings for those belonging to the several constituencies, wide distribution of the total written plan, distribution of a detailed precis of the plan—all have proven helpful in assuring the desired "buy-in." The commitment by the members of the strategic planning team to seek and secure the widest possible understanding of the plan and endorsement for the plan—in its totality and in its parts—is key to implementation.

THE ELEMENTS OF THE STRATEGIC PLAN

Strategic plans are not like the Ten Commandments: here is what the content should be and it evermore will be so. In our definition, we identified several characteristics of a strategic plan: it projects the organization into the future; it is concerned with organizational capacity as well as the environment in which the organization functions; it makes financial, staff, and time commitments. There is a sense, then, that so long as a strategic plan is marked by those characteristics, the elements of which the written plan is comprised may address those issues identified by the planning team. However, experience reveals that the process almost always produces a written plan or report in which most, or all, of the following elements are addressed:

- situation analysis
- history
- mission
- macro-environment: demographics and competition
- critical issues
- financial factors
- objectives
- programs
- staffing considerations
- time lines

Sometimes elements will be combined in the document issuing from the planning process, but it is the unusual plan, indeed, that fails to take into account these or similar elements.

Situation Analysis

Frequently requiring much of the time of the planning team, especially in the early stages of the process, the situation analysis is a frank and detailed statement of the status of the organization at the time planning efforts are in process. It is vital, in undertaking the situation analysis, that members of the planning team face honestly the current position of the organization. This is not an occasion calling for the use of rose-colored glasses; rather, the efforts of the organization will be seen with steely-eyed realism. That does not mean, of course, that solid achievements will be ignored or downplayed; they should be reported, of course. It does mean, however, that problems will be honestly faced, failed initiatives identified, unmet needs specified.

Among the data to be gathered to support the stock-taking that is required in this phase of the planing process are:

- persons served (how many?)
- finances (how much? is it enough?)
- organizational trends (are we headed up or down?)
- organizational commitments (what do we say we want to do? are we doing it?)
- staff and leadership (do we have enough? the right kind?)
- facilities (are they adequate?)
- community perception (do they like us? do they even know we exist?)

The situation analysis lays the foundation on which the remainder of the plan rests. It will not be based on feelings or beliefs alone ("I think we're doing fine!"). It requires hard information that will support or refute feelings and beliefs. By themselves, the feelings that committee members bring to the planning process are not bad, not even inappropriate; they are simply not enough. Frequently, professional strategic planners begin with questions designed to elicit those feelings from committee members and they may be among the facts with which the committee will deal.*

---

*It is not uncommon to read sentences in a strategic plan similar to: "Members of the committee are warmly supportive of_____ and share optimism for the organization's future. This is especially important in the face of data revealing a slow but steady decrease in. . . ."

As the data are collected to reveal the circumstances that obtain within the organization, the situation analysis may be drafted by a member of the planning team or members of a subcommittee and distributed to the total committee for discussion and revision as and where appropriate. When the committee is satisfied that the statement of current organizational circumstances is both accurate and relevant, the situation analysis may serve as an agenda of sorts for the future work of the team.

Members of the planning team must reach agreement on the situation in which the organization exists; consequently, time must be allotted to the study and discussion of the draft statement to resolve differences that may exist as to fact and interpretation. Because the projections for organizational action follow from the situation analysis, differences among team members about the organization's current situation will be "papered over" only at the expense of the quality and substance of the remainder of the plan. The situation analysis will be as long or as short as is needed to address, accurately, the status of the organization. It is accurate to say, however, that rarely are one or two paragraphs adequate to the task.

History

Important as it is to understand the position in which the organization finds itself, so is it informative—and vital—to know how the organization got to where it is. Thus, a statement of history is an important element in planning.

An organizational history, for planning purposes, will not, usefully, be taken from public relations materials or the front of the catalog. The history that will prove of value to the planning team will address many of the very issues addressed in the situation analysis, but from the perspective of the longer view:

- persons served (when did we focus on this population? why? have our services made a difference?)
- finances (what have been the long-term trends? have our income sources changed?)
- organizational trends (have we had an up and down history? all up? all down?)
- organizational commitments (have we remained consistent over the years? why not? where have the inconsistencies appeared? why?)
- staff and leadership (can we associate success or failure with certain periods when the staff was marked by particular skills?)
- facilities (when did we acquire our facilities? when have they been especially useful? how has program changed since then?)

- community perception (was there a time when we were better liked by our publics? less well-liked? to what may that be attributed?)

The organizational history, prepared as part of the planning process, assists in putting in perspective the present situation and prepares the organization to make decisions now that will impact the organization's future. It is amazing the degree to which some organizations of the voluntary sector drift away from programs, services, activities, or strategies that once were successful and, thus, important. Reviewing the history of the organization in a detailed and systematic way often reveals promising paths for future action.

Catalogs from the past, old financial statements, annual reports from years gone by, program reviews, or audits done in past years are excellent sources of information to assist in developing the kind of organizational history that belongs in the strategic plan. Personal sources should not be overlooked: former board members, retired staff, past donors, all possess important pieces of the organizational memory, pieces that may be utilized to chart the organization's future course.

Mission

As noted in Chapter 4, the organizational mission is a statement of purpose that tends to be fixed (i.e., it changes slowly or not at all over the course of many years). The mission is the *raison d'etre* for the organization. Despite that reality, and owing to a wide variety of pressures—changing communities, changing societal demands, pressure for funds—organizations of the independent sector, in large numbers, frequently move away from or beyond the purposes for which they were founded.

The time associated with the creation of a strategic plan is an appropriate and important time to revisit the organization's stated mission. Among questions to be asked by the planners, with reference to the mission, are:

- Are we, in fact, doing those things our mission statement says we were created to do?
- Have we expanded on our mission? Are we committed to the provision of related, albeit wider, services and activities than our mission projects? Have our purposes narrowed?
- Does our mission statement capture, in language that is both contemporary and pointed, our reason for being, or are the words and commitments reflective of a different era in American life?

- Is the mission statement direct and understandable, or does it ramble on, appearing to commit the organization to efforts to be all things to all people?*
- Will the mission, as currently expressed, serve the institution into the foreseeable future?

Missions are not to be tampered with lightly. But if the dispassionate review of the mission, here anticipated, reveals that the organizational reality is different from or greater than that which is stated in the mission, a revision is mandated. Once again, a draft of the proposed new or revised mission should be written, distributed, discussed, revised, or adopted by the committee for presentation to the CEO for disposition according to his or her insights and commitments.

The advancement manager has a particular stake in the content of the organization's mission. As previously noted, the mission is the ground on which the case for contributions support rests. It is a cardinal ethic of advancement that funds may be sought and raised only as the recipient institution is competent and able to use them for the purpose for which they were given. Some fund raisers—sadly, a number of whom represented religious or quasi-religious groups—have gone to prison for diverting contributions from the purposes for which they were given.

Macro-Environment

Organizations of the third sector do not exist in a vacuum, even though some act as though they think they do. The institutions of the nonprofit world are set in communities, states, and a nation; they operate alongside other, often competitive, organizations; they are subject to the same, or at least similar, trends as other organizations; they are subject to the laws of the land, the laws of economics, and the laws of nature.

When the planning team addresses the largest context in which the organization operates—the macro-environment—the members are seeking to develop an understanding of how the environment impacts on the organization and the manner in which the organization interacts with it.

---

*Sometime in the not-too-distant past, many colleges and universities fell into the practice of stating the institutional mission in many pages of text. This was often the result of an effort by the senior leadership of the organization to please every faction of the faculty and the community. The resulting complexity did not serve those institutions well; when everything is claimed as the organization's purpose, focus is lost and community perception of the organization tends to become diffuse. Organizational missions need not be stated in one sentence, or even one paragraph; neither should they be encyclopedic or the product of vote-swapping or compromise.

Demographics

As an obstetrician would be unlikely to choose to practice his or her specialty in a retirement community, so the nonprofit organization will want and need to know something of the demographics of the service area in which it functions. That kind of knowledge has broad implications for everything from program to fund raising, from staffing to occupancy.

We know, for example, that persons of Hispanic extraction are susceptible to diabetes at a rate higher than persons of north European origin. If a diabetes-serving agency learns, from a review of available demographic data, that the region in which it operates has experienced a significant growth in the population of persons with Hispanic surnames, the agency can conclude that such a population switch will carry with it major program imperatives. Similarly, because the African American population suffers a greater number of strokes per capita than other groups, an area with a heavy concentration of African Americans can be expected to require services from agencies addressing the needs of stroke victims and from medical centers providing both acute and rehabilitative care of stroke patients.

The acquisition of demographic data and an understanding of the implications of such data are imperative for members of the strategic planning team. Organizations of the voluntary sector exist to serve people; it is imperative, for sound decision making, that those organizations know who those people are and what characteristics they exhibit. Obviously, the Bureau of the Census is one source of the information sought. The local Chamber of Commerce is another. The relevant state Department of Health and federal Department of Health and Human Services are prepared to provide morbidity and mortality statistics and data about incidence rates for specific diseases and accidents.

Sometimes, the relevant data is close at hand: in a college or university, the database management office is able to supply significant amounts of detailed information about graduates or former students; in a hospital, the discharge office can make available to the planning team a wealth of information about former patients and their families.

The need for demographic data and the use to which that data may be put by the organization are not always immediately apparent. As relevant demographics begin to accumulate, however, it is remarkable how disparate bits of information begin to take shape and form and to suggest purposes to which the data may be put to benefit the organization.

Competition

Another component of the macro-environment with which the members of the planning team will want to familiarize themselves is the competitive environment.

The basic questions to be asked, here, are: Who else is out there doing something similar to what we are doing? How successful are they? What are their sources of students, or patients, or clients? When do they get their funding? How much of it do they get? What are their trends?

At first glance, it may seem that collecting information about the competition in such quantity and with such specificity will be difficult. I have found that not to be the case, however. After acquiring a list of those organizations who are, in some sense, "the competition," I have called the executive director, the administrator, or the president and asked for an appointment. Then, in a manner not dissimilar to conducting a feasibility study, I have asked the questions to which I seek answers. To an altogether remarkable degree, the information has been made readily available. Where that has not been the case, I have made an effort to pick up an annual report of the competitor organization. Surveying the competition is an activity that lends itself to the use of the services of the members of the planning team. When they inform "the competitor" that they are participating in a planning study, a high percentage of the leadership of other organizations is willing—sometimes eager—to help.

Failing a cooperative interview subject, your planning team may always request copies of the Form 990 filed with the Internal Revenue Service by the competing organization. Those forms, and the data they contain, are matters of public record and available on request. The form will not provide all the information sought; it will, however, give relevant financial data for the organization in question.

It remains for the planning team, armed with demographic data and information about the competition, to select, from all of the material at hand, that which is most useful and informative for inclusion in the written plan that is evolving. This is an occasion when member teams can be appointed to sift through information, look for trends, identify items of particular relevance, find the implications for their own organization (one team with the demographic material, the other with the competition information). Drafting conclusions, complete with charts and graphs as necessary, can be circulated to colleague team members, discussed, revised, and adopted.

Critical Issues

It is helpful to think of the "critical issues" element in the strategic plan as a distillation of the materials, uncovered in the foregoing analyses, that are of major importance for the life of the organization. To the degree that the situation analysis, the organizational history, the mission, and the review of the macro-environment have been accomplished with the precision and objectivity anticipated, the critical issues for the organization's life and future will have become readily apparent.

Critical issues may be positive or negative; they may suggest continuation of some efforts and elimination of others. The enumeration of critical issues—often a simple list of items of overreaching importance with, perhaps, a paragraph or two of explanation or supporting documentation for each issue identified—takes on the character of the platform from which organizational action will be launched.

The critical issues list, prepared during the strategic planning process of an independent, non-residential secondary school started with the following six items (explanatory, accompanying paragraphs have been excluded):

1. Enrollment has shown growth in all but two of the last 20 years.
2. Although income has also grown, it has not kept pace with student growth; tuition income has lagged behind the increase in expenses.
3. The school has ceased being sure of the population it serves: a major percentage of the students have been enrolled after experiencing difficulty in public schools; others come expecting a traditional college preparatory experience. The headmaster, the teachers, and the parents aren't altogether sure to whom the school appeals.
4. Contributions income, though valued, has never been one of the school's priorities. As a consequence, the names and locations of affluent parents of former students have been lost. There is, for all practical purposes, no list. Contributions are now needed to address major facility needs.
5. The building currently occupied by the school is inappropriate to institutional needs: it is too large and too expensive.
6. The board of the school is weak and ineffective. All of the members have been selected because of their personal relationships with the headmaster.

The critical issues list for the school in question goes on through 23 items. Each of the identified issues surfaced as members of the planning team worked their way through the previously identified elements in the strategic planning process. Although, on the surface, it appears that this institution is successful (enrollment growth, slower but real income growth), the data gathering reveals significant problems (critical issues) in the school's operations that must be addressed if the institution is to survive. Decisions must be taken, now, that will provide for a future marked by clarity of purpose and focused activities designed to ensure organizational health.

One of the sensitive matters that may arise as critical issues are defined is the identification of a problem area that some constituencies do not want to or are afraid to address. Not infrequently such sensitive matters have to do with the performance of specific staff members or the leadership of the organization. In the independent school illustration above, the planning team became painfully aware of the problems posed for the school by the headmaster. He was a warm, caring man who had been with the school for all of its life. He was deeply loved by much of the faculty, many students and alumni, and significant numbers of the parents. But he was a person time had passed by, at least in his present role, and almost everyone knew it except the headmaster. He was persistent in the belief that nothing was wrong with his institution that couldn't be "fixed" with more money.

What can be done when the identification of one or more of the critical issues and the proposed actions to address those issues is profoundly threatening? Neither of the potential answers is easy or comfortable. One option is for the members of the planning team to face the matter squarely and directly. This means stating the problem with clarity within the context of the strategic plan. Because critical issues are ones that lead, directly, to action plans, the planning team selecting this option will be required to state what is to be done about the issue: dismiss the offending party? destroy an icon? retire the headmaster?

The other option is for the team to agree that the issue at hand is so sensitive, so threatening, that it must remain unstated and, thus, ignored. Of the two courses available to the planning team, the first is clearly the one to be favored from the perspective of organizational health and well-being; the second calls for a degree of dissembling and temporizing that will result in the presentation of an incomplete and inadequate plan.

It may be argued that one way to escape from the horns of the dilemma is to find or construct a third horn—another option. Offer a compromise that will, presumably, provide advantages both to the institution and to the ideas or persons who pose the dilemma. Rarely does such a strategem serve either the institution or the problem area. In any event, whichever option is chosen, the planning team will be required to face the issues with a spirit that transcends personal advantage.

Financial Factors

The elements addressed to this point in the strategic planning process have focused, largely, on the present and the past—the "where have we come from?" and "where are we now?" materials. With the identification of the issues of critical importance to the life of the organization, the members of the planning team are prepared to turn their faces to the future—the "what do we need to do now?" concerns.

Earlier efforts have produced materials in the plan that have been largely, if not exclusively, presented in narrative form. The financial factors section will, in all likelihood, be heavily statistical. It will be comprised of numbers set in specific future time frames. (It is not uncommon, in many commercial enterprises and some organizations in the voluntary sector, for the strategic plan to consist, in large measure, of statistical material. A significant disadvantage of expressing the plan in numbers alone is the difficulty such a presentation makes for obtaining the desired organizational "buy-in." An organization's publics are more likely to proceed forward in harmony with the planning team when they are able to read and understand why certain decisions have been made and how. Numbers alone may stifle the impulse to understand.)

Projecting financial needs and targets into the future is difficult. The financial factors section of an effective strategic plan will not be an exercise in "wishing." It will, rather, grow out of sober reflection and analysis of the following elements:

- financial history of the organization
- nature of the constituencies
- demonstrated or articulated support for the organization among the constituencies
- financial needs of the organization
- resources available for allocation to strategies for income growth
- state of the area's economy as responsibly projected into the near-term future
- activities that are projected to grow out of implementation of the strategic plan

As with the institutional budget, the financial analysis presented in the strategic plan will include both expense and income sections. All factors related to the organization's financial life will be taken into consideration. Many strategic planning teams, recognizing that neither expenses nor income in voluntary sector organizations are evenly distributed over the months of the year, choose to do their financial projections by quarters. The financial projections of a small but active operating foundation for a two-year period are represented in Table 7–1. Although this example comes from a simple (i.e., not complex) organization, some factors, applicable to much larger third-sector organizations, become clear in studying these short-term financial projects: (1) funds are not expended evenly, one month to the next; (2) there are cycles that apply to fund-raising activities (some periods of the year produce significantly more income than others); (3) growth in both expenses and income tends to be relatively slow (if at all) and steady (windfalls are rare and cannot usually be anticipated); and (4) the costs associated with fund raising have a direct impact on dollars raised.*

---

*It should be noted that the organization cited in the illustration follows a conservative fiscal policy: funds raised in the current year are not expended until the following fiscal cycle. This organization does not budget "on the come."

Table 7–1 Financial projections for a small foundation

Expenses	Year 1 Q1	Q2	Q3	Q4	Year 2 Q1	Q2	Q3	Q4
Exec. Dir.—part-time	$5,000	$5,000	$5,000	$5,000	$6,000	$6,000	$6,000	$6,000
Admin. expenses:								
Postage	400	600	800	800	400	625	850	850
Telephone	250	250	375	500	275	250	375	500
Supplies	175	250	300	400	1,450	150	150	175
Fund-raising expenses	600	1,600	500	2,800	600	2,000	1,500	3,900
Promotion & recognition	700	350	400	900	500	500	850	1,500
Scholarships	13,000	—	14,000	—	16,000	—	18,000	—
Grants	—	18,000	—	18,000	—	2,000	—	2,500
Board meeting	2,000	—	2,000	—	2,500	—	2,000	—
Quarterly totals	22,125	26,050	23,375	28,400	27,725	11,525	29,725	15,425

Income	Year 1 Q1	Q2	Q3	Q4	Year 2 Q1	Q2	Q3	Q4
Endowment	$5,000	$5,000	$5,000	$5,000	$5,300	$5,300	$5,500	$6,000
Interest	1,250	1,250	1,250	1,250	850	850	850	850
Special events	1,000	—	20,000	1,500	1,500	1,000	2,500	2,000
Named scholarships	500	—	1,000	—	1,500	1,000	1,500	1,000
Direct mail	10,000	16,000	13,000	21,000	11,000	17,000	14,500	24,000
Quarterly totals	17,750	22,250	40,250	28,750	20,150	25,150	24,850	33,850

The financial factors section of the strategic plan for large complex organizations will be, of course, considerably more lengthy and detailed; grants funds, both governmental and foundation, will be included; United Way or other federated giving income will be projected; service fees (or tuition) will be reflected; fees realized from the provision of ancillary services will play a part. On the expense side, financial projections will take into account the number and type of professional staff employed, the expenses associated with personnel (benefits, equipment, expenses, training), the number and classification of support personnel, rent, maintenance, future needs, and so forth.

In projecting funds available to expend, one of the factors of importance to the advancement manager is the degree to which he or she may anticipate and plan on growth in the support for advancement operations from the employing organization. Regrettably, many large voluntary sector organizations do not make funding commitments to divisions within the organization for more than one year at a time. Because the success of advancement operations is heavily influenced by the financial resources committed to advancement, the one-year-at-a-time budgeting methodology has a serious, and negative, impact on planning for advancement growth. It is, therefore, a matter of the greatest importance that the CEO be kept well informed, during the planning process, of the understandings of fiscal support for advancement on which the projections are based. The CEO may feel unable to commit resources beyond a single year; full disclosure will, however, alert the leadership to the formal funding requests that are to flow from the implementation of the strategic plan.

Objectives

The planning team has reached the point at which decisions must be made relative to those actions to be undertaken to address the identified issues. These decisions will be expressed in the form of objectives to be reached. In a previous chapter (see Chapter 4), it was noted that objectives are both measurable and time specific. To say that is also to say that the objectives contained in the strategic plan will go well beyond citing a critical issue and observing, "We'll fix that!"

The questions to be answered by the objectives linked to the critical issues are: How are you going to fix it? When are you going to do it?

To return to our illustration drawn from the planning of the independent secondary school, one of the critical issues identified was a weak and ineffective board whose members were selected on the basis of friendship with the headmaster. The objective as written by the planning team read:

> "The Board of Directors of _____ School will be augmented by the addition of three new members. These members will be identified and recruited by the Chairman of the Department of Social Studies of the school and will be representative of the business and/or commercial interests of the county. The members of the current Board of Directors will be provided opportunity to meet and query the candidates prior to voting on their membership. The above activities will have been accomplished by _____." (The completion date was fixed six months following the presentation of the strategic plan.)

The objectives proposed for years two and three addressed by the plan contained similar, though not identical, objectives producing, by the end of year three, the cumulative effect of setting in place and making operational a majority new board for the school.

Working their way, systematically, through each of the critical issues, the members of the planning team should ask and seek to answer for each one, "What needs to be done?" "When can it be done reasonably assuming responsible efforts?" If the plan on which the team is working is a three-year plan, each issue will be faced toward the end of delineating the desired accomplishments in year one, year two, and year three. If theirs is a five-year plan, objectives will be set for each of the years of the plan.

Although the strategic planning team was selected for each member's knowledge of the organization, it cannot be expected that they will be expert in every matter that comes before them. It is totally consistent with the purposes and processes of strategic planning that members will be free to seek the insights and advice of persons outside the planning team membership whose areas of expertise touch on issues under consideration. Not only will the team (and the organization) be advantaged by the wisdom gained from others, the participants in the process, as they have involved others, will have commenced building bridges to the plan's larger constituency, thus, laying the groundwork for the desired "buy-in."

Brief reflection on identifying objectives to address each of the critical issues facing the organization leads inescapably to the conclusion that this is a large undertaking with vast implications for the organization. There are no shortcuts if critical issues are to be addressed toward the end of organization improvement. One by one the planning team must face them, reach agreement on the course of action desired, come to a conclusion about when it is desirable and possible for the proposed action to be completed, and reduce those agreements and conclusions to written form.

What is at stake is nothing less than the reformation of the organization. The responsibility resting on the members of the planning team is heavy. But the members of the team are enabled to bear their burden secure in the knowledge that they have gathered their information with seriousness of purpose, that the information is both accurate and accurately understood, that they have analyzed the data carefully, and that the actions proposed are appropriate.

Programs

As objectives spell out, to the organization, the what and the when of actions to be taken, programs are meant to define the how. It is apparent that not all critical issues necessarily result in programs (see, for example, the objective addressing the need for board renewal, above); many, however, do. The scope of strategic planning is such that all aspects of the organization are examined, and actions are identified that are necessary for organizational strength and viability. Thus, one can imagine the planning efforts of a health care organization dealing with such varied and vital issues as service mix, location, equipment, staffing, outreach, facilities, third-party payers, and service contracts. To consider each within the context of the organization's opportunities to provide service is to move inexorably in the direction of program development.

Programs may be seen as means by which services are delivered, objectives met, and institutional life strengthened. They consist of structured efforts that are supported by staff or volunteers. Programs are meant to serve a purpose, and they usually exist within a "mix" of related but differing programs. In large, complex organizations, the members of the planning team usually will not be proficient at or involved in delivering all of the services provided by the organization. As the strategic planners begin to map out the programs needed to meet stated objectives, they will depend on the knowledge and skills of those who are involved in the delivery of programs.

"We want to make certain that those who live in the new community east of the hospital have available the same quality of health care as those who live close to us." With those words, a member of the strategic planning committee expressed one of her team's major programmatic concerns. She was speaking with the hospital's director of social services. She went on, "We're not certain what we should do, but we're convinced we have an obligation we're not meeting." The director responded, "Well, you know they are almost 11 miles distant. It hasn't been easy for us to serve that community. We do have a small outreach office out there that we staff about 10 hours a week. We have done some simple, basic things through that office: blood pressure screening, a quarterly "well-baby" clinic, some health education classes. Not much. And not enough. What we really want to do is get a larger facility; staff it with a nurse practitioner or physician's assistant, add a part-time counselor or social worker, and expand health education offerings."

The doors were opened to identifying and mounting programs that would address one of the critical issues identified by the planning team and meet the objective of serving the new community in a responsible way. The planning team member had an opportunity to tell her contact something about the process in which she was so deeply involved. The social service director was glad to be heard, for she had given careful thought to the needs of the community in question, and she was pleased that her employing institution was taking a hard look at all of its operations and commitments.

Programs, as they are articulated in comprehensive (i.e., institutionwide) strategic plans are characterized by more tentativeness than other elements in the plan. Team members, as noted above, may not have program expertise and are required to seek input from those who do; programs, themselves, have a way of evolving, of starting to be one thing and metamorphosing into something a bit different. Still, the projection of programs has an important place in the plan, making clear that concrete activities will emerge to meet identified issues and objectives.

Divisional or unit plans, on the other hand, may be extremely specific about the programs that are projected because many of the members of the planning team are, themselves, staff within the unit. As a consequence, the program component of unit strategic plans may be extensive, innovative, and detailed. It tends to be realistic and less subject to change than are the programs projected in institution-wide plans.

Staffing Considerations

The various and varied organizations of the voluntary sector share an important trait: their budgets are skewed toward the personnel side. It is not uncommon for nonprofit institutions to have staffing costs consuming 70 percent to 80 percent of the organization's operating budget. The delivery of services, whether education, health care, or child protection, requires people: teachers, physicians and nurses, social workers, and the like. The advancement manager, especially, understands that the resources acquired to support the organization bear a direct relationship to the number of quality personnel that can be hired, trained, assigned, and supported.

The Rev. Richard E. Moore, a retired Synod Executive of the Presbyterian Church U.S.A. and a gifted manager, observes, "The best source of new money for your organization is money you already have." What he points to, of course, is the need to evaluate each activity to which organizational funds are committed, to ascertain that the activity is needed, that the funds expended on the activity are expended appropriately, and that assigned staff are effectively distributed across the spectrum of organizational programs. Moore's insight is valuable for those charged with the design of the strategic plan.

As the members of the planning team arrive at the staffing implications of their study and projections, they will ask pointed questions.

- What are the staffing levels for each of the activities in which the organization is engaged? Are they appropriate and necessary?
- What are the staffing levels required of each of the plan's initiatives?
- When must staff be assigned to these initiatives, given the time frames projected in the plan's objectives?
- Among the skills and abilities possessed by current staff, are there glaring gaps? Are current staff properly placed and assigned?
- What are the skills and ability levels required of proposed new staff for projected initiatives?
- Are the salaries currently paid by the organization competitive?
- What salary levels will be required by those retained to staff the proposed initiatives?
- Does the organization currently employ and assign staff who are being underutilized?

- Are currently staffed activities within the organization appropriate to the fulfillment of the mission?
- Does the organization persist in supporting activities that are no longer effective or needed?

The sensitivity of issues involving personnel is apparent; dealing with those issues, however, is unavoidable if the planning effort is to bear fruit. (No one ever said that planning was easy or that the lives of those involved in planning would be lived out on a bed of roses.) Some strategic planning teams choose to address only those personnel issues that have to do with staffing levels and the desired mix. That approach serves to minimize or eliminate the sensitivity that may be associated with the consideration of staffing. Unfortunately, it also reduces the potential for utilizing the strategic plan as an occasion for the consideration of the quality and effectiveness issues that cluster about staffing considerations. Careful evaluation of staffing concerns, as part of the strategic planning process, may result in decisions that will enable the organization to redirect effort—and therefore funds—so as to embark on new initiatives at an earlier date.

Dwight was an experienced and successful development officer who was assigned to one of the constituent schools of the university for which he worked. The school to which he had been assigned had been without a development director for some years. Dwight faithfully undertook his assignment with enthusiasm. Soon, however, it became apparent that his dean didn't value the disciplined services of this careful development director; regularly, the dean interfered with Dwight's efforts, sending him this way and that, pursuing the immediate big gift. The result, of course, was that neither large nor smaller gifts were being secured: prospective donors were not being identified, cultivated, or solicited in a disciplined fashion.

In the planning process, the team had identified an immediate need for a senior level person to give leadership to the office of prospect research and management. The financial projections, however, made it apparent that funds would not be available to hire a leader for that office for two years. During consideration of the staffing implications of the strategic plan, it became evident that Dwight's considerable talents were being underutilized. The team recommended, in their plan, that the advancement manager meet the prospect research need by reassigning a staff member whose talents were not being fully used. The manager immediately agreed and arranged to move Dwight to the leadership position in the office of prospect research and management. An important need was met by utilizing more appropriately the services of an existing staff member.

Note that the planning team did not tell the advancement manager what to do with his staff; they presented the results of their studies and recommended action to address one of the institution's immediate challenges.

Another staffing consideration to which the strategic planning process should give attention is the identification of persons responsible for addressing the actions proposed in the plan. This cannot be effectively accomplished if the planning team reaches this point in the process and insists on working in secret. They will consult with the persons thought to be in the best position to provide the required leadership, with that person's supervisor, with the CEO. Although it is true that plans, when presented, often undergo change and modification, the factor that provides for implementation of strategic plan objectives and programs is the specificity with which the plan is marked. Consistent with the common criticism of studies, reports, and plans, many do end up "on the shelf" gathering dust. A thoughtful review of such well-intentioned but ineffectual documents is that they have been cast in general (i.e., non-specific) terms. Identification of those responsible for meeting objectives and initiating actions takes the plan out of the category of an exercise in futility; its preciseness provides the strategic plan with the very elements of seriousness and intentionality that make for committed implementation.

To the degree that the objectives and programmatic thrusts proposed by the plan require new or additional staff, the fiscal details related to those needs will need to be reflected in the section of the plan dealing with finances. The team will remember that new staff do not show up only on the expense portion of the plan; new staff may, depending on the assigned responsibility, produce greater income.

Time Line

A fully realized strategic plan will, on presentation, make clear when the actions envisioned will be undertaken. The immediately preceding plan elements—objectives, program, financial matters, staffing consideration—have all been time specific. That portion of the planning team's organization that studies the plan in detail and in its entirety will have seen and identified when particular actions are to be taken. Some in the organization will not review the entire plan with the thoroughness for which the members of the planning team might hope. For both groups, however—those who devour the plan and those who skim it—the time line will serve to bring the recommendations and actions into bold relief. The discipline of preparing the time line assures the planning team that the elements of the report mesh one with another, that proposed actions intended to follow (or precede) other actions do, in fact, follow (or precede).

In the execution of their time lines, most strategic planning committees utilize categories such as year one, year two, year three. Some, however, divide their time lines into quarterly segments for the greater precision such fine tuning provides.

PLAN IMPLEMENTATION

In his masterful retelling of the Lewis and Clark expedition, *Undaunted Courage,* historian Stephen Ambrose writes

> It was a favorite saying of one of President Jefferson's twentieth-century successors, Dwight Eisenhower, that, in war, before the battle is joined, plans are everything, but once the shooting begins, plans are worthless. The same aphorism can be said about exploration. In battle, what cannot be predicted is the enemy's reaction; in exploration, what cannot be predicted is what is around the next bend in the river or on the other side of the hill.[1 (p.81)]

In the life of the advancement manager in the contemporary nonprofit organization, the factors that defy prediction are legion: the state of the economy, the health of a major donor, the public's steadfastness (or fickleness), the initiatives of a competitor, the tone of a media response. As the general at war does not withdraw from the field of battle when his foe responds in an unexpected way, and the explorer presses on even when an apparently impenetrable obstacle is set in his path, so the manager is called on to continue on course when desired ends fail to result from planned effort. This is certain: plans do not—in all their details—work as anticipated. The manager is required daily to assess, improvise, try something new, or to double and redouble efforts to reach the results the plan was created to assure.

If that is true, why plan? Why attempt to make those decisions today that are intended to affect future outcomes? The answers are clear, even simple. If our organization does not examine itself, does not respond to issues and needs, or does not set objectives and budget to reach them, then our organization will never be more than it is today. Planning is preparing to meet the challenges the organization was founded to address. Planning is bringing together all of the available information and our most disciplined thinking toward the accomplishment of the organization's mission.

A study of successful organization—in business, in government, and in the independent sector—will reveal that all, without exception, are committed to planning. They are not content to let the future shape them; they insist that they have it within their power to shape their own futures. They study to understand themselves, the people they serve, the needs they seek to meet, and the nature of the world that is coming. And they put all of that information together to take the decisions today that will enable them to prevail in the future.

For all the imprecision with which planning is marked, for all of the unexpected that is waiting around the next bend, growing numbers of successful organizations have determined that strategic planning is a continuing process. They have created staffs whose job it is to acquire information, overlay that information on the organization and its work, and project the actions the organization must undertake to prevail in the future. For such organizations, strategic planning is not an activity in which to engage every five years or so, but a continuous cycle involving input, analysis, plan, output, and evaluation. The organization that is committed to planning does not say, "These are the things we must do at some time in the future." Rather, it says, "Given what we know about our organization and its challenges, these are the actions we must take now, and at defined points along the way, in order to claim our future."

The details may change as the organization and circumstances evolve, but the decisions taken in the planning process prepare the organization to meet the unexpected. The planning-focused institution, and the manager committed to the efficacy of planning, return to the plan repeatedly to "tweak" it: to rethink, to evaluate, to incorporate new information, and to engage in fresh analysis. The strategic plan is a beginning, not an end; an itinerary, not a destination.

REFERENCE

1. S. Ambrose, *Undaunted Courage* (New York: Simon & Shuster, 1966).

CHAPTER 8

The Manager and Motivation

There is scarcely a manager anywhere who does not ponder the question, "How do I get those with whom I work to fulfill their obligations to the organization?" The manager, characteristically, sorts through the complex of organizational challenges and needs, relates them to the staff, and comes to terms with two realities: (1) "These are the things I must accomplish," and (2) "These are the people whose efforts I must utilize in their accomplishment." The advancement manager concludes either "If my organization is to reach its dollar goals and fulfill its programmatic objectives, those purposes must be accomplished with the staff I currently have available to me" or "I must acquire different or additional staff to reach the goals and objectives to which my efforts have been directed."

STAFF COMPOSITION

With rare exceptions, managers work with staffs that were created (i.e., hired, trained, and assigned) by others. The manager may help to shape that staff with new hires, extended training, revised assignments, or organizational/structural changes, but most often it falls to the manager to address needs, meet challenges, and reach goals through the efforts of available staff, many of whom owe their employment to someone else, usually the person who held the manager's job previously.

Reaching organizational objectives by harnessing the human resources available constitutes the great challenge faced by the advancement manager. How does one take a disparate staff, comprised of persons with varied talents and commitments, and attain the results required by the organization? Of a certainty, the advancement manager can't accomplish the necessary results alone. By virtue of staff retained and assigned, the organization recognizes that fact. Simple logic leads to the conclusion that results—good or bad—are the product of staff skills and effort. Harnessing the two—skills and effort—is a major test of the advancement manager's ability. The advancement manager depends, as do other managers, on motivating available staff to accomplish the purposes for which he or she is responsible.

Motivation has to do with the internal drive to achieve and accomplish recognized and accepted goals. Motivation is behavior's engine: it builds on the "is" to create the "what can be." Although motivation is internal, it can be affected and shaped by external forces and acts. One of the gratifying characteristics of a career in advancement is that one's colleagues in the field share, to a remarkable degree, the drive for attainment and success. Rarely are advancement staff members satisfied with their efforts except as those efforts lead to growth, goal achievement, and focused and results-oriented efforts.

Managers have adopted, in collaborative efforts with their organizations, a variety of strategies that are perceived to be motivational, that is, activities designed to result in the commitment of maximum effort by employees utilizing the full range of their knowledge and skills. Among efforts in which organizations in the independent sector engage to motivate employees are: the promise of job security; the provision of financial incentives; the potential for career growth and advancement; assignments which, on their successful conclusion, afford the staff member with a sense of achievement; and recognition.

JOB SECURITY

Advancement staff members, by virtue of the field in which they work, are sensitive to the reality that employment is characterized by a high degree of transiency. Indeed, almost every advancement staffer has learned from articles in the professional press or from conversations with colleagues that job tenure is often brief for those whose task it is to seek and encourage public support. Recognition of the tenuousness of employment may produce a shallow commitment to the organization and to the field of advancement; and a shallow commitment, not infrequently, has as its product effort withheld.

It is hypothesized that employees who have confidence that the hard-working (i.e., the achieving) staff member will be rewarded with a secure employment situation tend to remain in place for longer periods of time and exert greater effort toward the achievement of desired institutional behaviors. However, it is only minimally effective for the manager to say to staff, "Give me your best, and you will keep your job!" Such a message is, at root, negative: "Malinger, and you are out of here" is the corollary. Few contemporary advancement managers are prepared to position their efforts among staff within the framework of threat, even implied threat; employees often move on when threat is the context in which they are required to work. Fear can be enervating. Rather than producing greater effort, it often results in lassitude and unfocused (pointless) activity. Fear can produce hostility, backbiting, "politicking," and self-serving behavior. Moreover, because the advancement job market, at century's turn, abounds in opportunities for movement and relocation, even those whose past employment record raises competence questions are able to find another job. Fear, the product of threat, is ineffective as a motivator.

The reality is that the advancement manager is best served in efforts with employees, and these efforts are most motivational when the manager can provide evidence of job security for staff members whose efforts are both effective and consistent. Personnel complements that include several staff members who have been with the organization for several years suggest, with a power greater than words alone, that skills plus effort equals job security (S + E = JSec).

The emphasis on employment security is not meant to suggest that every employee will possess all of the traits, knowledge, or personal characteristics that are ingredients of high advancement achievement. The advancement manager often feels it necessary and appropriate to suggest and provide for employee training to augment and sharpen skills. Focused opportunities to upgrade skills often serve as powerful staff motivators.

Employee job security is not a benefit for the employee alone; the values, derived by the organization as a consequence of a stable workforce, are manifold:

- sustained and continuing leadership in advancement operations
- reduced costs associated with recruitment, interviewing, and hiring
- enduring relationships with donors, the media, and organizational colleagues
- reduced time required for orientation and training

A few advancement managers are wary of providing for job security. They purport to believe that secure employees will become complacent, that brief tenure among staff members controls salary expenditures, and that newly hired employees bring higher levels of energy to operations. Experience suggests that such beliefs are ill-founded.

- Security in employment tends to produce confidence, a trait that has been found to be of value for the advancement manager and significantly different from complacency.
- Costs incurred in recruiting, hiring, and training new staff members are almost always greater than those associated with salary enhancements for existing staff.
- The efforts of longer-term employees are usually more focused and less diffuse than those of new hires.

The realization that the employment situation is secure serves to drive staff members to consistent effort; the provision of secure employment serves the organization by creating circumstances in which relationships can build, personnel costs can be controlled, and objectives can be met.

FINANCIAL INCENTIVES

Persons working in advancement are, on average, paid at higher levels than at any time in the history of the craft. Nevertheless, many in the field have been brought in at and held to compensation levels that are lower than those long-term employees working in clerical support or custodial positions.

The advancement manager, always constrained by budget realities, understands that many staff are motivated by financial rewards. To be sure, persons vary widely in their need for and response to compensation: for many, it appears that the pay raise represents the single most important motivator applicable to work behavior; for others, the organization's mission is of greater significance than the pay level; a high proportion of staff are arrayed at other spots along the "important/not so important" continuum as that scale applies to salary. Given those distinctions in response to salary-as-motivator, how is the organization (and the advancement manager) to deal equitably with those funds that are or may become available for salary enhancements?

Many organizations in America's third sector have determined that equity in salary administration means that everyone employed by the organization, that is to say everyone on staff, should share equally in the salary increase pool: "Effective June 1, all employees will receive a 4 percent increase in salary." It is commendable that organizations have stepped up to the responsibility to reward employees through increases in their compensation levels. Such a practice (i.e., identical salary enhancements for everyone) may prove ineffective, however, in motivating staff to higher levels of performance. The high-effort, high-achieving employee logically inquires "If everyone gets the same raise, why am I working 60 hours a week and Mary Lou won't even put in her 40 hours?" Some organizations have recognized the appropriateness of this query and have developed a salary administration policy in which the pool of money available for financial enhancements is divided into two segments: one portion goes to fund across-the-board increases while the other portion is set aside to fund merit increases. Thus, "Effective June 1, all employees will receive a 2 percent increase in salary; some employees are eligible for a merit increase based on job performance. Supervisors will inform staff members who will receive a merit increase."

Such an announcement may well cause a stir among employees—"Did Steve get a merit increase? Why didn't I?"—but advancement managers in organizations utilizing a salary administration policy that splits available resources into the two categories can use the circumstances created by the inevitable questions to discuss the reasons for salary differentials as well as the activities in which employees must engage and the results they must achieve to be eligible for a merit raise.

Some nonprofit organizations have committed to a pay-for-performance approach to salary enhancements. These organizations go to great lengths, at the onset of each fiscal year, to set specific performance objectives for each employee. When the year comes to an end, the manager is enabled to measure achievement against expectation. Funds available for raises are then distributed based on results. Within organizations utilizing the pay-for-performance approach, money (as reflected in salary) is seen and utilized by the manager as a primary motivator of work behavior. Exhibit 8–1 identifies some of the advantages and disadvantages of each of the approaches to salary enhancement and the use of each as a motivating factor.

Among the issues related to compensation for advancement staff members, few have occasioned more discussion than commissions or bonuses. It has long been the position of the major professional organizations related to advancement that compensation based on funds sought or raised (commissions) are to play *no part* in the compensation packages of their members. The professional codes of ethics and standards of conduct relating to advancement have consistently incorporated a proscription on commissions. The reason commissions are excluded as legitimate compensations are compelling and go to the potential for abuse in commission arrangements.* (See the discussion in Chapter 10, The Manager and Ethics.)

Those who enter into contracts that provide for compensation based on a percentage of the revenue sought or raised pursue their professional efforts outside the bounds of advancement legitimacy. (There are few who work in advancement who have not been offered, at some point, a commission package: "If you get me $50,000, I'll give you $20,000," the agency director said recently.) It is to the credit of those who work in philanthropy that most routinely and immediately reject such offers.

Although bonus arrangements for advancement personnel have usually been treated by professional organizations in a manner similar to commissions, there is growing (albeit not a majority) acceptance among advancement practitioners (and some professional organizations) that incentive arrangements, providing for income opportunities beyond salary, may play a legitimate role for those working in advancement operations. It was rumored for years that incentive compensation packages were made available by some independent sector organizations and

---

*There is ample and continuing evidence that commission arrangements lead to activities that produce high fund-raising expenses with only minimal funds available for programs consistent with organizational mission. Donors have made it clear that they don't want and will not approve of a percentage of their gifts being "drained off" to benefit a commissioned fund raiser.

Exhibit 8–1 Approaches to salary enhancements

Everyone gets the same raise

Advantages

1. Complaints among employees are minimized.
2. Team relationships—"we're all treated the same"—can be built.
3. Salary enhancements are easily administered.

Disadvantages

1. The efforts of high achievers go unrecognized.
2. Marginal performers are rewarded at levels equal to others.
3. The desire for upward mobility in salary is frustrated; everyone moves upward in lock-step.

The enhancement pool provides for both across-the-board and merit increases

Advantages

1. All employees have their efforts rewarded, albeit at differing levels.
2. High-achieving employees are rewarded to a higher degree.
3. "Average" and marginal employees learn that extra effort results in higher pay.

Disadvantages

1. The amount set aside to provide merit increases is diminished by the amount committed to the general pay raise.
2. Employees performing at an "average" level may develop negative feelings from having been left out of the merit group.
3. Managers must commit time to explaining why specific salary decisions have been made.

Pay-for-performance

Advantages

1. Salary enhancements are available for high achievers.
2. Available funds are focused on achievement and, thus, serve to motivate effort.
3. Limited resources for compensation are committed to the most deserving.

Disadvantages

1. Loyal employees who may be "average" in performance go unrewarded.
2. Performance, when measured solely in quantifiable terms, can be a limited factor in compensating valuable employees.
3. Events or circumstances beyond employee control can negatively impact results and, thus, compensation.

institutions and that some fund raisers were being advantaged by incentives based on the realization of performance goals. The fact that those arrangements have been rumored rather than confirmed suggests that neither the organizations nor the advancement officers involved felt entirely comfortable with incentive packages. Recently, some organizations within the philanthropic community have set out to define and implement employee incentive programs based on a complex of factors (not simply dollars raised).* The issue of bonuses and incentive programs sparked a lively debate within the National Society of Fund Raising Executives in the early 1990s. The debate resulted in reworking the language in a clause in the organization's Code of Ethics and Standards of Professional Practice.†

It would seem likely that incentive packages for advancement officers that are above and beyond base salaries will become increasingly common in the next decade. That there are potential dangers associated with such a possibility is clear. ("It's a very small step from bonuses to commissions," a thoughtful advancement manager observes.) The pressures for ever-growing amounts in philanthropic support are so intense as to make it seem inevitable that extraordinary financial arrangements will be offered to exceptional advancement performers in the years ahead. The fact that incentive packages stir strong feelings and that there is continuing debate about bonuses underscores the belief that the compensation level is a powerful motivator and, for some, the single most powerful motivator.

Funds in support of salary enhancements are not available to the advancement manager every year, and they are rarely available in the amounts for which one might hope. More frequently than the advancement manager might desire, the organization releases information, the implications of which require that all salaries be held at current (i.e., no increase) levels, and sometimes such information even mandates reduced salaries. Taking the behavior seriously that is driving such outcomes for employees, the advancement manager is faced with the task of informing staff that, no matter the scope and success of staff efforts, available funds will not support expanded rewards. No one, least of all the advancement

---

*Among factors written into one such incentive program and determinative of prospective bonuses are goals reached and surpassed (not only dollar goals), new donors secured, new staff recommended, and former donors re-acquired.

†When NSFRE adopted the Standards of Professional Practice, the organization was responding to issues raised in the debate over ethical behavior. The controlling standard with reference to bonuses (Standard No. 5) was promulgated by NSFRE in 1992 and provides "Members may accept performance-based compensation, such as bonuses, provided that such bonuses are in accord with prevailing practice within the members' own organizations and are not based on a percentage of philanthropic funds raised." The reader should be alert to the fact that some NSFRE chapters retain vigorous opposition to performance-based bonuses.

manager, likes to be placed in the position of making the announcement that raises are unavailable. How can the manager, constrained by budget and restrained by policy, produce results within a situation in which it is recognized that the "fiscal cupboards are bare?" To state the problem in different terms, what happens when budget constraints require that staff must go without increased rewards that recognize exemplary achievement? What happens when the promise of salary growth seems sure to be delayed?

In such admittedly difficult circumstances, nothing substitutes for frank talk and honest perspective as the following scenario illustrates.

"The state's economy is in an awful mess," the vice-chancellor reported. "You know that, but before it becomes common knowledge, I want you to be aware that income available for operations next year will be significantly reduced. We are attempting, to the best of our ability, to ensure the continuation of advancement operations at our current level. We are not sure we can succeed, but we're trying. Please believe in the honesty of our efforts. The immediate and predictable result of our situation is that there will be no funds available for salary increases in the coming year. I know that some of you are counting on raises, and I know that many of you, by virtue of your successes, have earned increased compensation. Our efforts to maintain operations at current levels are real. The best I can offer for the future is my commitment to 'catch up' with your needs and your results as the economy improves and institutional funds become available to support, more adequately, our efforts."

Note the characteristics of the vice-chancellor's message:

- It is provided early—before everyone knows.
- It is honest—there is no equivocating, no false hope.
- It acknowledges the legitimacy and the needs and wishes of the entire staff.
- It addresses a better future.

No member of the vice-chancellor's staff will be happy with the content of the message, least of all the vice-chancellor who delivers it. However, when the manager has taken staff into his confidence, has reported circumstances in candor, has identified priorities (keeping the staff intact), has acknowledged both the needs of some and the rights of others to increased compensation, and has promised, when possible, to "catch up," staff is inclined to take seriously the message to delay gratification. Communication with staff will not erase disappointment, but it will serve as a useful, albeit temporary, substitute for financial reward. That frank explanation of the situation may serve for one year, perhaps two, and—in the extreme—three years to satisfy or mollify staff with respect to anticipated rewards. Raises or financial growth may not, in a dynamic economy, be postponed indefinitely when high-achieving advancement personnel and their expectations are at stake.

CAREER GROWTH AND ADVANCEMENT

Few things have greater negative consequences for the advancement staff member than the fact that the route upward is unsure or, most of the time, dimly visible. Highly motivated though they may be, advancement staff see their upward mobility and their career paths only with the greatest of difficulty. The thoughtful advancement manager understands, however, that few factors have greater impact on staff behavior than the promise of job or position advancement.

With few exceptions, advancement managers provide hope for career advancement and chart courses for staff poorly and reluctantly. "Come to work for us. Do our bidding. We'll pay you as well as we can. Stifle your ambitions." So we communicate, certainly not with our words, but by our behaviors. Again and again, advancement staff members lament, "The only way up for me is out." By their words and their actions they express the belief that career growth depends on seeking and finding employment outside their current organizations. Contributing as it does to short-term employment tenure, the "up means out" attitude deprives third-sector organizations of their best, most experienced, and highly committed employees.

In recent years, the self-defeating nature of practices that do not provide for career mobility has captured the attention of thoughtful advancement practitioners throughout the nation. CASE has included "career-path" discussions in conference agendae; institutions of the third sector have commenced taking seriously the idea that promotion from within has the potential to serve a variety of organizational needs; employers within the nonprofit community have committed to the process of "growing our own" senior staff and have allowed for concomitant growth in responsibilities. In short, career advancement opportunities for staff members have begun to claim the attention and commitment of some managers and organizations within the nonprofit world. With that attention and commitment, recognition has grown concerning values to be derived from provision of career growth opportunities. The unvarnished fact is that few efforts are more effective in the motivation of employees than those that give promise of career advancement—more responsibility, larger salary, greater challenges.

Shirley had offered her candidacy for a new advancement position in the university. The position was one that would put her on a new and promising career track. The vice-president, having been made aware of her application, caught her attention in the hall one day. "I see you have applied for the opening in the school of physical sciences," he offered. "Yes," she responded, "I'm really excited. With my experience and my background, I know I can be a success. I hope I can survive the selection process." The vice-president thought for a moment before he asked, "Where do want your career to take you? How do you see yourself 10 years from now?" Shirley was quick to respond, "That's easy! I want your job!"

Few advancement managers can say, with honesty, that they have never had a staff member who expressed himself or herself thusly. Several factors go into voicing such an aspiration: The staff member may be revealing that the manager is a role model; he or she may believe that the manager's job is an easy one; or it may be that the junior-level advancement professional wants to test skills with the big donors or the national media. Whatever the reasons, the manager is called on to recognize that the very traits for which he or she has searched in selecting staff are the ones that contribute to professional ambition.

It is impossible to provide promotional opportunities to everyone working in the advancement function, especially in organizations that have a pyramid-like structure. Among the mechanisms the advancement manager may employ in addressing the desire for upward mobility (and, simultaneously, providing motivation) are the following:

- provision of training opportunities designed to prepare staff for career growth
- institution of a cross-training program to provide an ever-broadening professional horizon even in circumstances in which promotional opportunities are limited
- initiation of a job classification system that is characterized by the potential for steady, if small, steps upward
- commitment to the use of strategies (task forces, teams, work groups) that place reliance on employee self-direction
- exploration of an organizational structure that is not strictly hierarchied or pyramidal (hub, spokes, wheel style)
- initiation of a mentoring program involving the pairing of junior staff members with selected senior staff members

Committing to activities associated with one or more of these approaches to address employees' desires for upward mobility acknowledges employees' impulse to seek growth. More, the organization and the advancement function will be advantaged by enhancing the range of employee skills and knowledge. Such efforts must be understood by the manager as more than efforts to manipulate employees into believing that they are "moving up" when, in fact, their careers are in a steady state or are stagnating. The manager who seeks to utilize professional growth among motivational strategies will not be content with providing only the image of opportunity. As in all the manager's dealings with staff, the reality and the substance of what is offered is the basis for quality relationships and the ground on which institutional loyalty stands.

ACHIEVEMENT

Among the factors motivating superior job performance, perhaps none is more important than providing the employee with challenging assignments, the achievement of which results in personal satisfaction. Such assignments must be capable of accomplishment and accompanied by the manager's expressed confidence in the ability of the staff member to whom the assignment is made.

For years it has been known in manufacturing industries that the least desirable jobs, in the eyes of employees, are those on mass-production assembly lines. The functions performed are highly repetitive, they make no room for individual creativity, and the tempo of activities is outside the control of individual employees. Jobs that, to the uninitiated, might appear more demeaning, dangerous, or stressful are held by employees in manufacturing industries to be more desirable than jobs on the assembly line, because they allow for some measure (even if it is minimal) of individual expression. Work on the assembly line, well-paying though it may be, denies the worker the understanding of self-worth that comes from meeting and overcoming challenges, from a sense of achievement.

Contrast that kind of job assignment with the one given Keith by the vice-president for advancement at the independent school for which Keith worked.

"We have an alumnus who has, in recent years, become extraordinarily successful. The problem is, he doesn't like us. When he was a student here, he had—according to the information I have gathered—a very difficult time of it. He left, unhappy, before he graduated. He's never made a gift to us. "Since he made his fortune as an entrepreneur in the arts, specifically record producing, he can be considered a prospect for a gift to our new theatre. He has the money to make a $2,000,000 gift, easily. I know this doesn't seem very promising, but I'd like you to take a shot at him. If any of us can do it, you can."

Fourteen months later, Keith delivered to his vice-president a pledge from the previously disaffected alumnus for $1,000,000 for the theatre. The details of how the pledge was secured (there were two "turn-downs" in the process) are of less importance here than the pride of accomplishment that Keith felt when he handed the pledge to his boss. He later reported, "I was ready to leave advancement altogether until I was given this challenge. When Valerie expressed confidence in my ability to meet it, I decided to give this assignment my best shot, to see if she knew what she was talking about. I promise you, nothing ever gave me a greater thrill than receiving that pledge. At the beginning, it was difficult even to see my prospect. It was almost impossible to engage in anything vaguely resembling donor cultivation. And, along the way, it was devastating to be turned down. But

I kept hearing my boss's voice expressing confidence and, finally, I found the key to our prospect's lock. I don't ever want to do anything else; seeking and securing the gift is my calling."

Keith may seem overly enthusiastic, but his words and the energy that empower those words demonstrate the motivation to perform, which is resident in challenge and achievement. Not all of the tasks assigned to advancement staff members are so difficult of achievement or so laden with opportunity as that which was given to Keith. And not all results are so positive; sometimes the response to challenge is not success.

One of the ways in which advancement employees deal with routine, ordinary assignments is to establish goals and standards of achievement for themselves.

"I have a bunch of marginal prospects," Carol said. "I'm going to set a goal of four face-to-face meetings a week with those marginal prospects. I know I'm pushing the percentages, but I want to average two gifts or pledges a week. There may be better ways to do this, but I'm going to keep doing this for the next six months—26 weeks—and then I'll evaluate the effectiveness of my efforts.

"Every one of my prospects can afford to make a significant gift to the college. No, my boss hasn't given me this assignment or the plan. It is simply what I must do to meet the expectations I have of myself. We're pretty new here at the business of private fund raising, but in a few weeks we're going to establish the fact that people will give when asked—or they won't. I prefer to base my efforts for the positive expectation. I'm grateful I was hired to do this job, and I'm even more grateful that my boss believes I can do it."

Her need for achievement—indeed, her compulsion—is driving Carol. However it was that she was challenged by her supervisor, she has fed this challenge into the stream of her own need and charted a personal quest for accomplishment. The advancement manager can't count on such drive and commitment from all staff. Neither can he or she ignore the reality that some need only be alerted to possibility to commit to the effort to shape achievement. Gifted with such staff (or individual staff members), the manager is called on to provide the necessary time and opportunity to hear and understand staff, to share beliefs in individual staff member's abilities, and then to stay out of the way—with this proviso: the manager will inquire about progress with frequency sufficient to communicate involvement and support.

The implications of achievement as a motivator have some very practical dimensions. The manager will:

- Assure that challenging, high-potential assignments are not saved for the one or two staff members in whom the manager has greatest confidence.

- Rotate the mundane, routine, or housekeeping chores of advancement among several staff members in the interest of maintaining high energy and interest among all staff.
- Be continually aware that employee motivation has to do with the internal drive of staff and that the most important role the manager can play is in shaping external circumstances so that the employee can achieve.

Distributing challenging assignments among the entire complement of advancement employees carries with it the threat that some will not rise to the challenge or will not achieve as hoped. "I assigned one of our best prospects to Sarah, and she failed to get the gift. And this prospect was primed to make a gift to us," complained the vice-chancellor. "Sarah temporized, she spent too much time preparing for the solicitation. She put off making the ask. In the end, the prospect, who apparently had some tax issues with which he was dealing, made a major gift to the hospital in town. If I had assigned that prospect to one or another of our best people, that gift would have come to us."

Few advancement managers in multiple staff operations have not had a like experience. In the case cited in the illustration, however, Sarah learned a difficult and vital lesson about the way to do the work of advancement. When she had worked through the disappointment and embarrassment of her failure, Sarah took stock of her job commitments. She re-evaluated her priorities. She vowed that never again would she allow herself to take casually an assignment to a prime prospect.

Sarah was as good as her promises to herself. The care she gave to major donor prospects became a standard to which her professional peers held themselves. Her "failure" became a goal to achievement. Did that, somehow, compensate for the missed opportunity? Not immediately, of course. But over the next several years, Sarah's job performance was such that she "made up" for her lost gift many times over. Hear her vice-chancellor three years later: "I was really angry when we lost that gift because of what I saw as dereliction of duty on Sarah's part. Her job was in jeopardy. I could have terminated her. As it turned out, however, nothing I might have said or done to improve Sarah's job performance could have been of as much value, to her or to the university, as assigning her that prospect and having her fail in her efforts. She has made herself—in large measure because of that event—one of our most reliable and successful advancement officers."

RECOGNITION

Despite routine disclaimers ("Oh, I was just doing my job!"), most employees want, value, and thrive on recognition of their efforts. Owing to the relationship-intensive nature of advancement operations, advancement staff are especially sensitive to, and desirous of, recognition from the boss, the boss's boss, and peers. Efforts and results that are recognized and appreciated are efforts and results that are likely to be repeated.

Recognition may take many forms; all effective recognition scenarios have several elements in common:

- The staff member is singled out individually.
- There is an expression of appreciation or involvement.
- Both the work and the end results are identified. ("I was so pleased with that $10,000 gift from the Smiths. I know how hard and long you worked on it. Thanks.")
- Recognition is not matter-of-fact as though the employee were a cog in the institutional machine.

  Weak: "The hospital is pleased to express gratitude for your efforts."

  Better: "Jim and I really appreciate what you are doing for us, Mary. That $10,000 gift from the Smiths was unexpected. You outdid yourself this time. What's your secret?"

Midway in my own advancement career, I took note of—and marveled at—how much better I felt about my work when I saw, and could talk with the president at least every other week. I really thought I was beyond the need for that kind of validation; obviously I wasn't. Just two weeks ago, prior to writing these words, I had an experience that reminded me of that need. I was on an elevator in the administration building of one of our client organizations, a large, well-known university. The chancellor stepped onto the elevator and warmly, engagingly, greeted me and inquired about progress on the project on which I was working for the university. I didn't know that she would even remember me, let alone have—at hand—some of the details of our firm's work. Once again, I had thought to be beyond the need for the validation such recognition afforded me, but I wasn't. My brief elevator encounter with the chancellor made me feel good, and, yes, even important. So it is with advancement staff members; they appreciate appreciation and they are encouraged by recognition of effort and accomplishment.

In addition to the private words spoken by supervisors to individual staff members in contemporary third-sector organizations, recognition is also provided by:

- articles in organization newsletter(s)
- press notices
- awards lunches or dinners

- public expressions of gratitude in staff and other meetings
- extra time off
- tokens and trinkets

The latter two items deserve brief attention. The manager may recognize extraordinary effort or accomplishment on the part of an advancement staff member by granting an additional day or even more as a paid holiday. The manager, seeking to provide such recognition, may call the staff member into the office and say, simply, "You have done some remarkable things for us of late, and I'd like to let you know that I realize it. Why don't you take a couple of days off? You'll be paid, of course, and the days won't be charged against your regular vacation." Under those circumstances, the employee understands that his or her efforts are valued and those efforts are being endorsed.

By way of guidelines for granting extra time away from work, these three points should be considered: (1) it should be employed sparingly so that it will be understood as "special"; (2) it should be related directly to a specific activity in which the employee has engaged and will not be expressed in general terms (e.g., "You're a good guy"); and (3) it should be utilized, by the recipient employee, in a relatively limited time frame—three weeks or a month.

Tokens and trinkets are used, in some nonprofit organizations, to provide recognition; many give service awards—5 years, 10 years, and so forth; others identify a deserving staff members as "employee of the month" (or year); some grant a convenient and visible parking place as a reward for unusual effort or achievement; still others distribute pins (in a fashion similar to medals in the military) for service "above and beyond."

Organizations create and perpetuate their own cultures. If a third-sector organization or institution is comfortable with and committed to the token and trinket approach to recognition, and if management believes that such an approach succeeds in motivating employees to significant effort in the performance of job responsibilities, then it should, by all means, be continued. If an organization wants to initiate a more or less tangible approach to recognition and motivation (pins, parking places, etc.), it should do so. The question to be answered—and it is of overwhelming importance—is do our efforts at recognition, whatever they may be, produce employees who are motivated to perform at the levels expected and required by the employing organization? Or do staff members see them as trivial and unworthy of the efforts expended or expected?

Motivation of employees constitutes a significant responsibility within the constellation of activities required of the advancement manager. The internal drive to achieve, which is characteristic of motivated employees, may be encouraged by external forces available to the manager: job security, salary enhancement, the potential for career mobility, challenging assignments producing a sense of accomplishment among staff, and recognition. The beliefs managers hold about the behavior of employees and the expectations managers have of staff members shape the behaviors of both.

MANAGEMENT THEORIES ABOUT MOTIVATION

Few issues in management have been subject to more study than the issue of employee motivation. The study has led to analysis, analysis has led to theories, and theories have taken form in lectures and publications. The "alphabet theories"—X, Y, and Z—have exerted considerable influence on management thinking for more than a generation. They seek to provide the manager with a conceptual framework to assist in understanding human and thus employee behavior. The advancement manager's view of human behavior serves to inform the ways in which he or she utilizes the services of staff in the accomplishment of the organization's mission, the attainment of its objectives, and the prosecution of its programs.

Douglas McGregor, in his work *Human Side of Enterprise*,[1] identified two contradictory views of human behavior that could be found among managers. One view, which McGregor identified as Theory X, was based on an understanding of humans in fundamentally negative terms: they were thought to be basically lazy, to dislike work, to require control and close direction, and to place the highest value on stable employment.

Theory Y (and its adherents) was characterized by a significantly more optimistic view of human nature: work was identified as a human activity as natural as play or rest. According to adherents of Theory Y, work provides for significant satisfaction; humans are capable of exercising self-direction and are able to embrace organizational objectives; they understand achievement as a determinant of rewards.

If the manager is convinced that employees don't *want* to work and do so only by virtue of the coercion implicit in the need to eat and have shelter (if the manager is an adherent of Theory X), then the manager will insist on exercising tight, authoritarian control over staff, will distrust employee initiative and creativity, and will emphasize job security ("You've got a job, haven't you?") as the fundamental motivator. There should be no mistaking the fact that the Theory X manager is hard on staff and is thought, by them, to be difficult to work for. Perhaps of greater importance, the Theory X manager creates significant difficulties for himself with the potential for massive stress: every issue and project must be micro-managed, every idea depends on manager initiation, every employee undertaking is to be distrusted, and isolation must be accepted as the natural condition of those in management positions.

The Theory Y manager is positioned to take greater advantage of employee talents and skills: this manager understands that staff are capable of focusing their efforts on the important and significant where organizational mission and objectives are concerned. He or she believes that employees can be challenged to achieve, will not respond only to threat, and are capable of innovation and creativity. The Theory Y manager generally lives out his or her professional life in a milieu characterized by greater warmth, cooperative endeavor, and tolerable levels of stress.

Management "guru" Peter Drucker examined the understanding of employee behavior as explicated in theories X and Y and taught those who were prepared to learn that "knowledge workers" have long since replaced blue-collar workers as the majority employee group in the United States (and, indeed, in much of Europe and parts of Asia); he also taught that knowledge workers require management of a very different order than was predominant in earlier decades. In short, Drucker held that the beliefs associated with Theory X are inoperative in a society in which the large majority of workers operate in a knowledge context. The contemporary manager is called on "to engage the minds, rather than simply control the hands of their employees."

Although Drucker was not, by any means, the first to propound the concept, his insight that treating employees well—in all dimensions of that concept—was as important to the long-term success of the organization (business or institution) as it was to the employees. He added the insight that an organization is a human, a social, indeed a moral phenomenon.

William Ouchi[2] is credited with the insight that employees involved in an organization's objectives are critical to the delivery of product—whether goods or services—in the required quantity and marked by the necessary quality. He held that organizational objectives are best served by meeting the needs and objectives of the employees. Ouchi, clearly seeking to have his work represent a culmination of McGregor's earlier theorizing, used the designation Theory Z for his emphasis on employee/organization involvement. (*Note*: Ouchi's parallelism to McGregor's work is not exact: the former is based on perceptions of human behavior and the implications of those perceptions for managing workers. The latter is organization focused even as it emphasizes involvement between employee and organization.)

Among attributes ascribed by Ouchi to Theory Z organizations are long-term job security, education and training focused on organization-specific skills, participative decision making, diminished emphasis on superior-subordinate roles, decision criteria that hold in balance the needs for productivity (dollar goals in the case of advancement), and consistency with organization purposes. The central issue is that the attitudes and assumptions of managers, as those attitudes and assumptions touch on the nature of employees and their approach to work, are determinative of the ways in which managers motivate their employees. And, at some level, they are determinative of the success the manager will have in his or her efforts to utilize the efforts and the skills of staff.

Among the extensive research into factors that serve to motivate employees, Frederick Herzberg's classic studies[3,4] have special relevance for the advancement manager. His original research was undertaken 40 years ago[3] and was later updated and set in a more contemporaneous context.[4] Herzberg's original research focused on engineers and accountants and sought to identify what made these professionals feel good about their jobs. He sought to understand how employees' feelings affected performance as well as personal lives and what actions or factors returned their feelings to normal. Analyzing the data he gathered, Herzberg posited a two-factor theory of employee satisfaction: to one set of motivators, Herzberg and his colleagues assigned the designation *motivators* (or satisfiers), for he found that these factors, when present for any given employee, produced job satisfaction; to the other set he applied the term *hygiene* factors (or dissatisfiers), sometimes called maintenance factors (see Exhibit 8–2).

Even a casual reading of Herzberg's hygiene or dissatisfier list will reveal that many of these factors are widely understood as employee motivators, and, indeed, we have treated two of them (salary and security) as such in this chapter. How is it, then, that Herzberg includes them in his list of dissatisfiers? What he and his colleagues found, in their study, was that the factors on the motivational list produce job satisfaction when they are *present* in the job to the degree that the employee believes or feels them to be adequate. The factors on the hygiene or maintenance list cause dissatisfaction when they are absent or *deficient*: thus, the two-factor theory.

The implications for the advancement manager are clear, and they are challenging: the manager can provide for career growth, recognize noteworthy efforts, and make challenging assignments, but until and unless factors expected by the

---

Exhibit 8–2 Satisfiers and dissatisfiers

Motivational Factors or Satisfiers	*Hygiene Factors or Dissatisfiers*
1. Achievement	1. Organizational policy or administration
2. Recognition	2. Technical supervision
3. Advancement	3. Interpersonal relations with supervisor
4. The nature of the work	4. Interpersonal relations with peers
5. The possibility of growth	5. Interpersonal relations with subordinates
6. Responsibility	6. Salary
	7. Job security
	8. Personal life
	9. Work conditions
	10. Status

employee (quality relationships, appropriate compensation, job security, etc.) are present, advancement staff will feel, and in fact be, inadequately motivated to perform their assigned tasks at a level that is consistent with potential. Shaping Herzberg's argument in the negative: Activate all of the motivational forces at your command, but if you are deficient in providing your staff with appropriate levels of the factors on the hygiene list, they will not perform to their maximum.

Employees vary widely in their responses to their assignments, to their peers, to the potential for career growth, to the power of salary enhancements, to virtually every issue addressed in this chapter. It remains to note that the listening/communicating/involving advancement manager will learn the interests and drives of individual staff. Based on that knowledge, he or she will, with subtlety, sensitivity, and trust, engage them in the accomplishment of the organization's mission, the accomplishment of their specific tasks, and the satisfaction of their own personal and career aspirations.

REFERENCES

1. D.T. McGregor, *Human Side of Enterprise* (New York: McGraw-Hill, 1960).
2. W.G. Ouchi, *Theory Z: How American Business Can Meet the Japanese Challenge* (Reading, MA: Addison-Wesley, 1981).
3. F. Herzberg, et al., *The Motivation to Work*, 2nd ed. (New York: Wiley, 1967).
4. F. Herzberg, "One More Time: How Do You Motivate Employees?" *Harvard Business Reveiw* 87 (September-October 1987): 109–117.

CHAPTER 9

The Manager and Change

In the last 50 years, the production and sales of books and articles about change, and the accelerating pace of change, has become a cottage industry. There can be no doubting the fact that the last half of the twentieth century has seen vast and far-reaching changes on many fronts: scientific, technical, political, and economic. It is important to realize, however, that ours and our fathers' eras are not the only times in which change has been a dominant and continuing element in the human experience. The first half of the nineteenth century, for example, saw the opening of the American West, the invention of the telegraph, the harnessing of steam power to serve commerce and transportation, the reshaping of national boundaries in Europe, the demise of some of that continent's historic dynasties, and the rush to independence of the people of Central and South America. In brief, the changes that swept across the globe 150 to 200 years ago were as comprehensive, bold, and, in their own way, as challenging as those that twentieth century Americans have experienced in their lifetimes. Chronicles of change could be written about most periods in human history.

Change is one of the conditions of human existence; it is pervasive, and it is continuing. Change takes place within persons—as they take on new responsibilities or cast off old ones, as they re-order priorities, as they enter into or fall out of relationships. Organizational change takes place as the organization engages its environment, seeks to serve better its identified constituencies, hires and assigns staff, and creates programs to assure the accomplishment of institutional purposes.

The advancement manager faces the reality of change on a daily basis: within himself or herself, among staff, in the employing institution, on the national and world scenes. The way in which the manager deals with change and helps others to meet change serves either as an ingredient in the creation of professional attainment and success or leads to frustration and failure. Whatever the advancement manager's level of comfort in accommodating personal change, he or she is called on to lead in addressing the fact of and need for change within the employing organization. This response to organizational change will, inevitably, shape staff and constituency response and will impact results.

Harmon knew what had to be done to bring his university to new levels of fundraising effectiveness: he had to add staff and restructure advancement operations on a decentralized model. It was "tough sledding": people didn't understand the need for all of the new fund raisers. ("They are already thick on the ground," complained one faculty leader in a particularly infelicitous phrase.) But Harmon persevered, and in a little over two years had his people in place in each of the schools of the university and in several other units.

To his dismay, Harmon had to face the fact that his staff was raising little more in the way of contributions than they were prior to launching the new and expanded structure. Media coverage was unimproved, perhaps worse. And, Harmon found that neither advancement staff nor deans were happy with the arrangement so painstakingly set in place: the staff complained that the central advancement office provided them with instructions while their respective deans gave them different instructions and set different priorities; the deans were unconvinced that contributions could grow, even with great effort, and they unhesitatingly assigned "their" advancement staff to other, unrelated responsibilities.

Two years after his system had become operational, Harmon determined that he had to back away from it for the good of the institution and to accomplish his purpose of raising more money. To his great surprise, when he announced that the institution would return to a centralized advancement operation, almost everyone was "up in arms."

What's going on, here?

First, Harmon did not prepare the way for the initial change, the implementation of a decentralized model. He was so certain decentralization would work ("After all, institutions all over the country have had success utilizing this model") that he felt the benefits would be obvious to all. They weren't. Neither his own staff nor the deans of the academic units were drawn into conversation about the reasons for the change, the parameters of decision-making authority, or the benefits anticipated from the implementation of the decentralized model. Communication was nil.

Second, the decision to decentralize was imposed: Harmon had a vision of what he wanted, he was the vice-president for advancement so he had the power, and he thrust his system on those who did not understand it or ask for it, but who were required to make it work. Resentment and distrust were the nearly inevitable products.

Third, the goal of his plan—to raise the level of contributed income—was not one everyone accepted as necessary or doable. Harmon's approach to his goal was perceived as a deficient strategy or, at best, a partial strategy. "Shouldn't we hire a really good prospect researcher if we are going to see our fund-raising goals double and triple? Assigning me to the School of Business is fine, but that in itself won't raise more money," one of Harmon's advancement staff members observed.

Last, when Harmon scrapped his decentralized structure, he repeated his errors: he didn't consult, he didn't communicate, he made and acted on his decision in isolation, and, as a consequence, his decision was perceived as inappropriate and ineffective.

Clearly, there were behaviors available to Harmon that might have resulted in better outcomes. Before identifying the courses of action that, when employed, improve the chances that change will be accepted, let us examine tactics to which staff members may resort when faced with change.

REACTIONARY TACTICS

Resist

This is the immediate response of some when change—in fact or in prospect—is on the horizon. It is fair to say that most healthy people prefer comfort to discomfort. Because change often results in learning and doing new things, and unlearning old and practiced ways, change often produces discomfort. The discomfort may be great or small, but because change, by definition, replaces the old and familiar with the new and unknown, it has a disquieting effect on most persons.

Forms of resistance vary widely depending on the nature and scope of the change itself, the perceived threat, and the personal traits of those who are affected. For some, resistance may be nothing more than unusually quiet behavior accompanied by a transient, albeit observable, emotional distance from others. Some will express their distress openly and directly. Some will institute a pattern of behind-the-scenes complaining, backbiting, and finger-pointing aimed at frustrating and overturning the changes. A few will frankly challenge the organization's leadership in an effort to return to a secure status quo.

Accommodate

When faced with the reality that circumstances require new and different behaviors within the organization, many will respond by giving the appearance—even unenthusiastic—of acceptance. "If that is the way it's got to be, I'll go along, of course, even though I don't believe it's the right thing to do." That is not only the attitude of the accommodator, but in many cases those are the actual words used. There is a sense of grudging acquiescence when accommodation is the tactic employed by a staff member facing the necessity of change. The job, the level of compensation, the local employment market, status, mortgage, kids, all may play parts in motivating the "I'll go along" response. Some who work in the field of organizational development argue that accommodation is the tactic of preference for most staff members. It is, however, dangerous for the advancement manager to place faith in the fact that a given change has been accepted and that staff stands squarely behind him or her as "the new" is implemented, when staff members have made clear that they are merely accommodating to the new reality. In some instances, a staff that has "given in" to change will metamorph, in a short time, into active resisters.

Although it may not be feasible to secure 100 percent enthusiastic response to every innovation, the advancement manager should freely acknowledge that he or she covets both unanimity and enthusiasm and will work toward that end.

Negotiate

Some employees, faced with changes, will seek to use the circumstance to negotiate an advantage for themselves. "Well, George, moving me over to the capital campaign staff doesn't improve on my job security one bit," Ira complained. "All the campaigners I've ever known vanish when the campaign is concluded, as a matter of fact, a lot of them move on a year or so before the campaign reaches its goal. I had planned to stay here, working in advancement for this hospital, for the rest of my career. I want to help you out, of course, but it seems to me, if I agree to this move, you ought to be prepared to make some adjustments. I'd like a significant raise—say 15 percent—and I want the hospital to lease a new car for me. You can handle these requests, can't you?"

What is necessary for a successful negotiation to take place, in this circumstance and others, is that strength and weakness are juxtaposed one to another and both are present in the circumstances of both parties. George's strengths are that he is the superior and has the acknowledged right to make job assignments; he is, by virtue of his position, in control of budget. His weaknesses are that he presumably needs an experienced and knowledgeable person to staff the campaign, and he has specifically assigned Ira to work on the campaign. Ira's strengths are that he knows the hospital, he has earned at least a measure of George's confidence, and he is clear that he wants to leverage this proposed change in his life to his advantage. His weaknesses are that George has the power to assign him where he will, and Ira is lacking in the power to enforce his will on George.

Facing negotiation as a consequence of actual or proposed change, the advancement manager will:

- Begin an evaluation of potential responses by determining what is best for the organization.
- Evaluate the capacity to pay what is asked (not always money) without harming the ongoing operations of advancement.
- Determine the impact that granting the request will have on other staff.
- Weigh the quantity and quality of the contributions of "the negotiator" to the organization.
- Make the decision.

Somehow, regrettably, negotiation and compromise recently have come to be seen as disreputable, disgusting, and disagreeable processes to be avoided. They are not, at root, bad things: we negotiate and compromise on a regular and continuing basis: "You wash and I'll dry," "I'll pick up Cathy at school if you can take Doug to his Scout meeting," "I'll be pleased to accept your job offer if you'll meet my salary needs," "I'm happy to pay a premium for my dry cleaning if you will have it ready for me by three o'clock this afternoon." Negotiation becomes distasteful, and worthy of condemnation, only when it takes on the character of threat and intimidation (e.g., a negotiation over the lives of hostages). In some measure, social intercourse requires bargaining: here is what I will do for you, here is what I need—or want—from you.*

The advancement manager is free to accept the terms offered in negotiation, to agree to new and presumably more reasonable terms, to reject either the idea of negotiation or the specifics of a particular request, or both. The outcome flowing from outright rejection is rarely predictable: some staff members will treat it as though their ace had been trumped and accept the changed circumstances more or less meekly; some will accept the rejection but become, as a result, problem employees; and some will resign and move on.

Embrace

Despite the fact that change carries within it the potential for and reality of personal and organizational discomfort, some staff members willingly embrace

---

*Indeed, the solicitation of a donor may be seen in terms of negotiation: "Your contribution of $3,000,000 will enable us to name this new clinical facility for your mother." Gary W. Phillips reflects, "There are very few truly anonymous donors." That sage, and accurate, observation moves much of the work of advancement into the arena of negotiation.

new realities. They are ones who may be feeling some degree of dissatisfaction with the status quo and are eager to reach for the potential they hope exists in the change with which they are presented. They could be persons undergoing personal growth and evolution who are caught up in the opportunity and dynamic that they sense exists within change. They are often the "company" men or women who have great commitment to and belief in the organization and its leaders and who not only adapt to the new circumstances but speak in support of the proposed changes.

Staff embrace change when they become convinced that some advantage is available to them, to someone, or to something as a consequence of the change. The advantage may be vague and unfocused: "I'm for doing anything to support this organization, and it is in the long-term interests of every one of us to help make this the best prep school in the western United States." Or the perceived advantage may be specific and immediate: "As a result of these changes, every one of us is going to get a 5 percent mid-year raise. I can't wait to see how our new staffing arrangement contributes to our success."

Some staff court change as they might court a lover. They believe that opportunity is always around the next bend, they enjoy the upheavals that may accompany change, they feel alive and excited when things are new and different, or they are easily bored and are energized by the new and the different. For the advancement manager, one concomitant of the varying motives of those who welcome change is that he or she will keep the nature of the changes in perspective: "We're committed to a revision of our institutional mission, which, in turn, will have an impact on almost everything we do—student recruitment, the way we raise funds, the size and nature of our donor prospect pool, the stories we make available to the media. The point is this: we're making these changes so that we will be a better, more respected school in touch with contemporaneous realities and so that those who come to us to learn will be served as well as any school in the United States." Another concomitant is that the advancement manager is responsible for helping staff and others recognize that the changes have not been proposed and set in motion in the belief that they will solve all problems, improve all relationships, or cure all ills. The manager strives to shape expectations of staff in terms that, though challenging, are realistic.

Especially among those who eagerly accept change and embrace it, the manager will be challenged to set it within a context of tentativeness. "We will revisit these modifications of past practices in six months. I need your frank reactions to them—are they making things better? worse? do we need to add some new elements? Don't wait for six months to give me your reactions; as soon as you begin to get a clearer idea of how these changes are impacting your work, please come in and let me know. One of the things I like most about working here, with you, is that we are always evolving, always getting better. These modified practices are aimed at continuing our evolution. Keep me informed of all your thoughts on this matter; believe me, we're prepared to tinker with it—or give it a complete overhaul—until we get it right."

Note how this advancement manager accomplished the following:

- asked for staff involvement in the change process
- supported the changes
- kept expectations realistic
- projected future modifications
- provided endorsement for staff in terms related directly to the changes they were experiencing

Retreat

The fifth tactic utilized by those who are presented with change is to turn and run from it. The form such an ultimate rejection of change usually takes is the letter of resignation or occasionally an "I quit" blurted out in frustration or anger. A variety of changes may occasion retreat.

The appointment of a new CEO frequently results in significant changes in personnel, especially at the upper levels of the organization. The CEO may bring a managerial style that is unfamiliar and unwelcome. He or she will, doubtless, identify priority interests and set action agendas that are different from those previously in place. (Most CEOs want to be known as a leader who has "made a difference" so they mount efforts designed to set them apart, not unlike most advancement managers.) The new CEO may have been given specific instructions by the appointing authority to trim budget, "bring in some new blood," redesign the structure of the organization, or shift organizational emphasis. When the CEO sets forth on fulfilling commitments made on accepting the position, it is not uncommon for the actions proposed and taken to unleash anger, resentment, and frustration.

Resignations that are occasioned by new senior leadership appear to come in clusters: a few soon after the CEO has been named; significantly more, about one year out; and a third group around the time the CEO celebrates the two-year anniversary. Reasons given for resignations due to the appointment of a new CEO vary from the simple ("I just don't like the s.o.b.") to the complex ("I reached a point where I could no longer support her agenda in the community, so it was time for me to leave").

A change in the leadership of the advancement function frequently results in the resignation of some of the advancement team. The reasons may be similar to those ascribed to departures occasioned by a new CEO: different style, different agenda, or initiating policies or practices seen as destructive or dismissive of past efforts. Another factor plays into departures brought on by the naming of a new advancement manager: advancement success depends on creating and nurturing relationships, not only with donors and media representatives but also with colleagues. When the relationship with the advancement manager who may be a mentor to many staff, is sundered (the old one leaves, a new one arrives), the meaning and purpose of advancement efforts may be put in question leading to the decision by some to retreat from the field and to resign.

Many other changes may be deemed sufficiently unacceptable as to lead to resignation and departure. They include

- the appointment of someone as a middle manager
- the imposition of new, stringent fiscal policies
- job reassignment to another area within advancement
- difficult relationships with supervisor or colleagues
- a personal failure or mistake followed by disciplinary action considered excessive or unfair
- decisions to provide for salary enhancements in new and different ways

Faced with a staff resignation the advancement manager presses forward to the accomplishment of the tasks over which he or she has been given authority. At the risk of sounding trite, it is important to remember that no one is unexpendable. Advancement staff members, sometimes the ones on whom the manager has lavished the most attention and on whom he or she depends the most, resign, move on, or move up. What remains for the manager to recall is the claim on his or her talent and commitment that the employing organization has made. When organizational changes have caused some of the advancement staff to leave, the manager returns to the process he knows well and has used in the past: recruit, interview, select, train, assign, motivate.

POSITIVE TACTICS

Organizational changes need not result in profound disruption in advancement operations. Thoughtful prosecution of actions that are sensitive to the threat posed for employees by change will result in an increase in those staff who embrace change and a consequent decrease in those who exhibit the negative responses to change—resist, accommodate, retreat. The process incorporates five actions: preparing, planning, implementing, evaluating, and looping.

Preparing

Change is likely to produce maximum resistance when it happens unexpectedly. Staff members, unaware of the prospect of change, tend to act on the belief that things are okay. When change is thrust suddenly on the unsuspecting, even if it is intended to have positive impact on staff, the result is characteristically one of disequilibrium: "I had no idea!" "Why weren't we told earlier?" "Where did this come from?" "Who is behind this?"

The advancement manager, intent on making changes in operations, structure, budgeting, or assignments and seeking the willing cooperation of staff is called on to prepare the way for the proposed change. Conversations with staff are steered to discussions of current reality, and staff is asked to respond to the apparent needs for modifications of that reality.

David met with the members of his staff, one on one, every other week. The practice required lots of time but was well worth it, in David's mind, because of the communications that took place and because of the relationships built. Following is a partial transcript of a dialogue between David and Margaret, one of the senior development directors reporting to David.

> David: That reminds me; I've been concerned that we don't use our senior directors as well—mm, as we could—no, should.
> Margaret: I don't know. You've asked each of us to serve as a mentor to one of our newer, uh . . . junior people, I guess they are. I'm working with Amy right now.
> David: Yeah, I know, and I feel good about that. Our younger people speak highly of the mentoring program—and of the people assigned to mentor them. But, you know, I don't think we're taking full advantage of you—your talent and insights, I mean.
> Margaret: Mm—I guess I don't know what you have in mind. I don't have any more hours to give to this place.
> David: I know (long pause). I'm not sure I have anything specific in mind right now. Just a hunch that you and the other two senior directors have more to give than I'm letting you give. I just wanted to—you know—surface the subject. I'm going to talk to Phil and Marty. Maybe together we'll come up with something.
> Margaret: Well, uh, thanks for the "heads-up," I guess.

David's conversation with Margaret was not as casual as he wanted it to appear. For some time he had been thinking, in general terms, about giving his three senior directors some specific supervisory responsibilities, a major change for them and for the staff. His preparation for this change commenced with his words to Margaret. He had similar conversations with Phil and Marty during the same week he spoke with Margaret. At the next prospect management meeting, he made a point of speaking of the abilities of his three senior directors, of what they had to give. All of these events transpired in April; during the subsequent three months he continued to prepare staff for the forthcoming change. By early June, he had developed a specific plan that he shared with Margaret, Phil, and Marty. When the formal announcement was made on August 1 of the supervisory responsibilities to be assumed by the senior directors, staff was well prepared for the change. There were some expected questions and concerns voiced by staff members, requiring answers, but the transition to the new approach was smooth and only minimally disruptive.

What this advancement manager had done to prepare his staff for a significant change was to commence early to communicate with and involve staff in the shape and nature of the change. By mid-June, it had become pretty obvious to the entire staff that new reporting relationships would soon be announced. In their regular meetings with David, staff were given opportunity to discuss their anxieties ("If we do change our reporting relationships, Dave, does it mean I won't have occasion to meet with you, in our private sessions, anymore?") and to make suggestions to make the new system more effective.

The extended illustration above focuses on a change that, in the end, was widely understood and accepted; in fact, during the preparation stage, support for the modified reporting relationships coalesced rather quickly. What happens, during the preparation stage, when the manager discovers significant opposition? There are four options:

1. The anticipated change can be dropped or postponed.
2. The advancement manager can determine he or she must persevere and uses involvement techniques to gather support.
3. Revisions of the anticipated change, based on staff inputs, can be incorporated.
4. As a last resort, the change can be implemented against staff wishes.

It needs to be added that when significant changes in advancement operations are anticipated, others in the organization will be informed and involved. It is not only the staff of advancement with whom preparation is made: the CEO, other departments, selected persons who comprise the constituencies, and key donors should be included. Alerting them to the perceived needs driving the proposed changes, defining the outcomes expected as a result of the change(s), encouraging questions, and seeking input will smooth the transition from the old to the new.

Also to be addressed during the preparation stage of the change process is the question of what others are doing (i.e., others whose work is in the same or similar arena). The advancement manager will seek out two or three counterparts in other organizations, identify concerns that are driving the changes under consideration, and gather information on how those organizations are answering the identified needs. (The advancement manager can be certain that someone in the course of the change process will ask, "What is XYZ doing about it?" "How does ABC approach this issue?") Not only will external consultation prepare the manager to answer those questions knowledgeably, he or she will have gathered ideas and learned of approaches that may help to shape the changes to be initiated.

Planning

Sometime during the preparation phase, the manager will commence efforts to give form to the change under consideration. He or she has listened to many persons within and outside the organization, has gathered a body of information and data that informs the proposed change, has weighed the impact of the change, and has committed intentions to writing. In creating the plan for change, the advancement manager should consider:

- The responses of those with whom he or she has worked during the period of time devoted to the preparation for change
- The perceived need(s) to be addressed by the anticipated change
- Results or outcomes anticipated as a consequence of the new approach
- Timing appropriate for the initiation of the change
- Problems that may result from the implementation of the change(s)
- Fiscal implications of the proposed change, both expense and income

Reducing the plan to writing, rather than carrying it about in one's head, requires the disciplined and ordered thought to which the advancement manager is committed as the changes move toward implementation. Questions or disagreements that may arise in response to the proposed change may be addressed with greater confidence and accuracy as a result of having reduced the plan to written form. Many experienced, successful managers are prepared to show their plan for change to others, in draft form, believing that such openness serves to advance the preparations to garner the needed and desired support. They report that by having easy access to early versions of the plan, staff are prepared to suggest changes and modifications to address such concerns as they may harbor. An advancement manager from the southern United States reports, "Sharing an early draft of planned changes just gets everybody involved in creating change. By the time we're done and ready to announce how things are going to be in the future, nearly everybody's got their fingerprints on it. They believe, and at some level they're right, that the changes are their work."

Advancement managers seek to hire the best, most intelligent, creative people they can find. They work with those people on a daily basis to inspire them to commit the full range of their abilities to securing support for the organization. Under most circumstances, it is counterproductive to exclude those gifted staff members from the decision process as that process relates to advancement operations. Secrecy in planning leads to surprise, and surprise leads to resistance.

The written plan, in its early versions, will be open to amendment of both its overall content and the specific changes proposed. There is, almost always, more wisdom in the group than in the individual. Involving many in planning for change will, with rare exceptions, produce a better plan and a cohort prepared to endorse the proposed changes. Those managers who believe that, by virtue of office, they have and should exercise power to order their staffs and operations, frequently are the ones who run afoul on issues of change.

Implementing

Changes, once determined to be necessary or desirable, must be set in motion. That usually requires that a specific date be set on which the new replaces the old. "Commencing August 1, the following will be standard policy." Rarely is it desirable for change to be effected on a staggered basis, starting here in August, there in October, and someplace else in December. If every place that will be impacted by the change is not ready on a given date, the implementation should be delayed. Confusion reigns when the several components of advancement operations are functioning in differing ways, according to differing policies and procedures. The exception to the rule of instituting change on an identified date is if a proposed change is to be tested in one or two places before it is incorporated in all of the relevant operations.

Because change may be required and is initiated in so many areas of advancement life, it is impossible to identify rules that apply, across the board, to the implementation of change. There are, however, some questions the advancement manager must ask and answer as changes are instituted.

- When are we going to do it?
- Who are the persons responsible for overseeing this activity?
- Has staff been appropriately trained so that each person knows what is expected as a consequence of this change?
- If new forms are required by the nature of this change, is a supply on hand?
- Are necessary funds available now or will they be available on the starting date?
- To the degree changes will impact others, within and outside the organization, have all of them been notified?
- Has a date been set for a meeting with staff to give input on the way in which the implemented changes are working? When is it?

- Are the record-keeping tools in hand to allow the institution to track the results achieved as a result of the changes?
- Do we know the results anticipated at the end of three months, six months, one year? What are they?
- Do these changes lend themselves to media coverage? When? Has the story been assigned?

The ability to answer each of these questions with precision and clarity will aid in assuring that the changes implemented will have been set in a context that provides maximum opportunity for success.

Evaluating

As a matter of course, everything attempted in the name of advancement should be evaluated on a periodic and ongoing basis. Evaluation is especially important as it relates to changes that have been implemented. The evaluation process asks the sharp question, "What was achieved?"

Evaluation will, most usefully, focus on the gathering of hard data and the comparison of current data with that gathered in past months or years. For too long, nonprofit organizations would proffer excuses for less-than-stellar performances by saying something like, "We didn't do what we said we wanted to do, but so many good things happened along the way!" or "Our agency didn't reach its goal, but we identified some wealthy new prospects so our future looks bright!"

Evaluation that is useful is hard and uncompromising. If the changes implemented were designed to create a 15 percent growth in income after one year, the evaluation process will measure actual performance against ambition, and the report will state the facts with clarity, eschewing obfuscation.

Evaluations may be undertaken internally by a staff member assigned to the task. They may utilize the services of an outside consultant retained for the purpose (in which case they may be called "development audits"), or someone from within the institution but outside the advancement function may be requested to serve as an evaluator.

Formal evaluations are undertaken at predetermined intervals, intervals that are usually spaced relatively far apart. It is common for evaluations to be conducted annually or biennially, rarely more frequently. Information uncovered in the evaluative process should be made available to staff, to the CEO, to selected representatives of the institution's several constituencies, and to others related to or impacted by advancement operations (chief of the medical staff, deans, vice-president for finance). The temptation to bury the evaluation report, if it is perceived to be "bad," is scrupulously to be avoided. Even less-than-flattering evaluations of effort and performance are utilized by thoughtful managers to stimulate staff efforts to prepare the ground for new (and presumably more successful) initiatives and to serve to motivate innovation. Yet another temptation to avoid is "killing the messenger." There are, unfortunately, instances when evaluators, on presentation of an honest but partially unfavorable evaluation, have been ordered by the manager to alter the content of the report on threat of dismissal. Effective managers, however, understand that evaluations may be and often are effective teaching and learning devices. Such managers possess sufficient self-esteem to give them confidence in using "bad" or "so-so" evaluations to benefit staff, advancement, and the employing organization. "We did some dumb things," a foundation president said. "This evaluation tells me we need to undo those things and get back on course. This study is going to help us get turned around."

Although formal evaluations of advancement performance take place occasionally, there is another evaluation process best understood as an ongoing responsibility. Informal, largely unstructured, ongoing evaluation serves to keep the advancement manager informed of trends, performance, problems, and attitudes. In the role as informal evaluator, the manager utilizes questions (the Socratic method, if you will) to gather data on which opinions can be based and strategy and tactics developed. While seeking to avoid creating the feel of "grilling" staff, the manager, in conversation, will become specific in posing questions that provide information pertinent to evaluation. The information gathering may start with an unthreatening "How's it going?" and move on to:

- Have you gotten an appointment with Mr. So and So yet? When is it?
- Tell me about the quality of the information you received from the prospect research officer. Do you have good prospects? What can we improve?
- Have the changes we instituted last year helped or hindered you?
- Should we be revising other parts of our operation? What? How?
- Is this office giving you all the support you need or want? That's why we exist, you know—to serve you.

Such a string of questions, put in rapid fire order, one after the other, are certain to intimidate. When asked in the context of an extended conversation however, interspersed with expressions of support for and confidence in the staff member, the questioning can take on a collegial quality. The skilled advancement manager will understand that his or her purpose is not to put a valued staff member on the spot but to elicit sufficient information to assure currency about effort and results and to learn if additional changes in operations must be made. Asking questions of the right persons with sufficient frequency can identify problems early enough to plan effective solutions, rather than waiting to discover problems when they have grown to catastrophic proportions resistant of solution.

The very size and complexity of large advancement staffs often serves to inhibit the kind of information gathering proposed; the manager simply lacks the time to meet one on one with everyone whose information might be valuable. One accomplished senior-level advancement manager, with a total staff over 100, meets the challenge of informal evaluation by engaging his 30-member fundraising staff in quarterly report meetings. In those meetings, the manager painstakingly goes around the room asking the kinds of questions suggested above and uncovering, in the process, the information he needs to form opinions, structure new programs and initiatives, and assist in shaping operational changes. (Yes, it's a long meeting, but it happens only four times a year. The public nature of the gathering imposes obvious limitations, but staff quickly grow accustomed to the exercise and learn to be remarkably forthcoming.)

Looping

As used here, looping refers to the process of returning the change process to the beginning. Following on formal and informal evaluations, looping is the more or less structured effort to look at the instituted changes in a fresh and unbiased way.

"A year ago, we made some major changes in the way we do things here. The results of our changes have been pretty good, though not startling in some areas. I want us to go back and think through where we were then, what we changed that produced positive results, what we decided that has not been so effective. And, of course, I want to identify what we need to fix." So began the meeting called by the senior advancement manager of a national health agency—a looping meeting, though she did not give it that designation.

It is clear that a single meeting was not going to accomplish all that Lillian wanted, so when the meeting concluded, she appointed a task force to address the scope of her concerns with instructions to report back to the entire group in 45 days. Carefully, the task force considered each change that had been set in place some 12 or 13 months earlier. The members reviewed the evaluation of results. They spoke with the senior advancement manager, probing her sense of the strengths and weaknesses resulting from the changes instituted. They interviewed several staff members.

When the task force had concluded their fact finding, the members undertook an analysis of the data they had gathered. On reporting their findings to staff colleagues and the senior advancement manager, they identified the several changes of a year previous that had produced significant positive results, a few that had proven inappropriate or unworkable, and some others that needed "tweaking."

The senior advancement manager understood, and the members of the task force discovered, that changes in operating activities, policies, or structures never provide final or ultimate answers. The entire range of activities associated with the advancement function must admit to ongoing review. It requires organizational commitment to ask and ask again "What are we trying to accomplish?" and "Have we identified the best ways to assure the desired accomplishments?" Looping is a structured approach to posing those questions and seeking their answers.

The tendency in undertaking the looping proposed here is to see the exercise in global or cosmic terms, to look at every piece of organization and advancement operations. The intent, however, when looping is seen as part of the change process, is to focus the effort on the specific changes instituted, the results expected and obtained as a result of those changes, and the modifications required to maximize the effect intended by the changes.

So far, we have discussed change initiated by and within the organization—internal change. It is important to recognize that not all change of internal origin starts with or is initiated by the senior advancement manager. Change in today's independent-sector environment often begins among staff members who surface areas demanding modification or who offer innovative ideas leading to new operational or organizational approaches. When the impulse and the nature of change have a "bottom-up," as opposed to a "top-down," origin, staff responses are often impacted in positive ways. The advancement manager who seeks to engage staff fully will encourage and welcome changes initiated by staff.

EXTERNAL CHANGE

Some changes with which organizations must deal are a result of external actions, influences, or forces. Among external influences that have had profound impact on advancement operations in recent years are those that are technological in nature. The rapid application of electronic data processing, commencing in the 1970s for most independent-sector institutions and continuing to this day, has produced widespread change in the ways in which advancement officers and staff have accomplished their several tasks—record-keeping, research, information exchange, communication, and funds transfer, to name but a few—and has revolutionized efforts to seek and secure public support. Similarly, telephone technology continues to shape new ways of doing the work of fund raising and public affairs: multiple line telephones, voice mail, pagers, and cellular and digital phones allow for instantaneous and near-universal contact. Cable television and interactive television offer avenues to the public that, at this writing, are largely uncharted but appear to hold vast promise for philanthropy.

Other external forces demanding and creating change for advancement operations are those having to do with the standards required for reporting gifts and pledges and the means by which funds are counted: Financial Accounting Standards Board (FASB) and Government Accounting Standards Board (GASB).

Federal, state, and even county governments legislate and regulate the endeavors of philanthropic organizations and force changes on the organizations of the third sector. Tax laws, standards for fund raising and administrative costs, and guidelines for assistance programs are but three of the many examples of areas in which government impacts third sector organizations.

Demographic shifts, economic swings (both up and down), political trends, even changes in the make-up of the boards of the institutions can and do serve to force or influence changes in advancement operations within the organization. In some cases, changes brought on by external influences result in staff responses similar to those triggered by changes of internal origin: resist, accommodate, negotiate, embrace, retreat. There is this difference, however; changes required or influenced from outside the organization almost always prove to be less responsive to staff attitudes than those that have their origin within the organization.

When external forces are demanding organizational response in the advancement arena, it falls to the advancement manager to accomplish several tasks:

- to evaluate the nature and potency of the external influences
- to determine the required organizational response (change)
- to identify the time and sequence in which the required changes will be effectuated

The new members of the Board of Trustees of a moderate-sized liberal arts college, with stars in their eyes caused by the large sums being raised by a nearby college, instructed the president of the institution to focus all future fund-raising efforts on "large gifts," which they defined as gifts in excess of $10,000. The president passed along this instruction to his vice-president for advancement and asked that steps be implemented to set in motion this large gift emphasis.

Questioning the directive, the vice-president pointed out that direct mail and the annual telefund were raising, together, more than $500,000 a year for the college with individual gifts averaging about $125. He was told that he was to cease such efforts and direct all of his staff's energy into "large" gift solicitation. Recognizing the strategic and tactical dangers implicit in the decision pressed on him, but unsuccessful in modifying the instruction, the vice-president restructured his staff assignments and developed plans to seek only gifts of the magnitude identified in his charge. He provided for a four-month transition period that allowed his staff to complete the spring telefund.

In the succeeding two years, so-called large gifts to the college showed modest increases in both numbers and dollars raised, but the annual fund, of which direct mail and the telefund had been parts, dwindled to near nothing—less than $50,000—all unbidden, by the end of the second year. There had been an overall net reduction in income when the board finally rescinded its action 24 months after it had been taken.

The vice-president (1) had assessed the environment and found an unbending board, (2) had determined the changes that had to be made in response to the environment and had restructured staff assignments, and (3) had determined the optimal time to effectuate the changes and had, thus, "bought" four months to complete the spring telefund.

The external influence (the action of the board) had been determinative of the changes required of the advancement manager. Even though he knew, with near certainty, that the decisions would do damage to his institution's efforts to acquire public support, based on his understanding of the donor and prospect profiles, he responded in the manner required by the environment external to advancement.*

So it is with many changes brought on by the play of external forces on the organization: much of the time the advancement manager is called on to act, to create and implement changes with which he or she is uncomfortable or feels are inimical to the organization. Under those trying circumstances, the advancement manager can only resist the impulse to complain, berate, sabotage, or resort to subterfuge. The manager may explain concerns, may advocate vigorously for his or her position, or may seek reconsideration from those in power. In the end, however, the manager is called on to respond in good faith to the changes brought on by external forces and to rally staff and others to the new circumstances.

READINESS FOR CHANGE

We have seen that change is a constant in life, that it causes discomfort and serves to threaten the individuals and organizations involved, that responses to change vary widely among and between persons and organizations, and that thoughtful approaches are available to the advancement manager to incorporate change into organizational life in ways that are supportive of the organizational ethos. We have noted that the response of the manager in initiating and gaining acceptance of change is crucial.

---

*It may seem unusual for the board of the college, in this example, to have been identified as exercising *external* force. The board was, however, external to advancement operations in the sense that the majority of its members were new, they acted without a detailed understanding of the importance of the income strategies pursued by the advancement office, and they did not seek counsel from the president.

It remains to ask if there is a theoretical basis that will inform and guide the manager through the flux that characterizes the contemporary independent-sector institution. There are many, of course, for concomitant to the pressures to create useful, fresh responses to contemporary realities is the structured effort to understand and win acceptance of change. For the advancement manager, Thomas Harvey's preconditions for unfreezing the organization are perceptive and accessible. In *A Checklist for Change*, Harvey writes that organizational readiness to address change requires strain, valence, and potency.[1]

By *strain*, he means that an organization must be in a situation of stress and that the people within the organization understand and recognize the reality of the stress. Strain has many faces for the advancement manager: increased competition, growing financial need within the organization, diminished results or results that are less than those required, media disapproval or media indifference, lack of leadership endorsement of advancement. To the degree that strain exists and is recognized within the organization, change becomes a reasonable, an expected, and a hopeful course for the future.

Valence refers to the understanding that existing conditions within the organization are configured in such manner as to lead those involved to commit to the belief that change has the potential to improve prevailing conditions. Valence connotes, therefore, the reality that change proposed depends, for its effectiveness, on change endorsed. Valence, in Harvey's construct, deals with the issue of "buy-in," of acceptance.

Potency, as a precondition for change, goes to the issue of effectiveness. The actors in the organizational drama must commit to the belief that the organization can make meaningful change and that such change will address the identified strain in a manner and with a force that may produce desired, or at least improved, results.

When the large and prestigious research university 10 miles distant hired a nationally prominent and highly regarded advancement executive to lead efforts to secure public support and made greatly expanded financial resources available to the new executive, the vice-president of the comprehensive university recognized that the success of advancement operations for his employer was placed at risk (strain). With a thoroughness that defied the limits of the time available, the vice-president devised a plan that charted a new course for the comprehensive university, one that called for minimal additions to advancement staff and supporting resources. Existing staff and the president of the university agreed that the changes proposed had the potential to sustain the modest advantage the comprehensive university had achieved over the research university in garnering public support (valence).

As the vice-president worked his way through the labyrinth that was the financial allocation process operative within his institution, he was met with the belief that though his plan was timely and pertinent, it was unlikely to enable the institution to maintain a competitive edge on the research university. The resources requested and the changes proposed were rejected on the grounds that they could not succeed. The race had been lost before it had been run. There was no belief in the potency resident in the vice-president's proposal.

Were the financial managers of the comprehensive university right in their judgment? Wrong? There is no definitive answer to those questions. What is certain is that the research university went on, in subsequent years, to secure growing public support in both contributions and media attention far outstripping the continuing modest efforts of the neighboring comprehensive university, whose vice-president has long since moved on to make his knowledge and skills available in a more responsive environment.

Change is not a legitimate response when its end is its own existence. We do not seek, propose, or implement change for its own sake. But when there is strain, valence, and potency, change is the appropriate—perhaps the only reasonable—response of the advancement manager committed to growing public support for his organization.

REFERENCE

1. T. Harvey, *A Checklist for Change* (Boston: Allyn and Bacon, 1990).

Chapter 10

The Manager and Ethics

A senior advancement manager was about to retire from the position at a university that he had held for nearly 15 years. His replacement had the opportunity to consult with him just prior to the retirement party. The manager-elect asked the retiring manager if he could pass on some words of wisdom and advice on how to be successful over the long term in this position. The executive thought for a while and responded that the secret to being a good advancement manager was contained in two words: "right decisions." Although this advice was helpful, the new manager wanted to know what the key was to making correct decisions. The incumbent pondered again and then stated that the essence of making right decisions came down to one word: "experience." The manager-elect once again quizzed the senior executive, wanting to know how to get that kind of experience. The astute expert went on to conclude that in the final analysis, experience was gained and achieved through a process summarized in two words: "wrong decisions."*

Ethics, in its simplest terms, is about how to make choices between right and wrong decisions. In another sense, ethics is the base of norms or standards that we use to make choices in situations that have an inherent right-wrong or proper-improper tension. Critics of the ethics phenomenon complain that ethics are based on a rigid set of constraints in conflict with the individual's right to independent thinking. Others contend that ethical issues are more like a personal religion (i.e., subjective) and therefore outside the realm of consensus resolution.

The attempt to apply ethical principles to the business setting is, as one author notes, much like trying to nail jello to a wall.[1] In some of the toughest ethical

---

*Adapted from A. Sikula, *Moral Management: Business Ethics* (Dubuque, IA: Kendall/Hunt Publishing, 1989).

situations in the nonprofit world, ideals of fairness in human behavior—even when the right choice may be clear—can be inconsistent with the reality of competition and organizational pressures.

Jan Williams struggles with pressures to be a team player and "fudges" to improve results on a status report to senior executives by including a large contribution that is nearly, but not completely, assured. Despite the real pressure from above, she is aware that she's partially responsible for the misleading report.

Robert Stein knows that it is time to fire an employee but delays doing so because the employee is a single mother with a young child. Robert has tracked this employee's performance over the past six months and recognizes strengths in some areas, but with stringent financial goals for his small group, he can't afford mediocre performance on the part of even one employee.

Jim O'Day has been told that a suspect project has suddenly become the senior executive's priority for the advancement office, raising new questions for him about the real nature of fund raising at his institution.

Sarah Benton is responsible for managing the press during a crisis in which her institution is clearly at fault, but she has been instructed by the CEO to deny any allegations of impropriety.

Some ethics violations are so apparent that their violation is immediately rejected by everyone concerned. Imagine the indignation of the fans if a referee allowed the home team an additional free throw in a close basketball game after the final buzzer had sounded, just because he felt bad about the team's losing streak. Unfortunately, most of our ethical dilemmas are less clear and their resolution more challenging. Harvard Business School lecturer Joseph L. Badaracco Jr. put it well when he described ethical challenges as not so much issues of right versus wrong but conflicts of right versus right.[2]

Although standards of conduct are required of any organization and its members, if the organization is to exist for long, the ambiguous nature of many such standards makes their application problematic. Managers face tough issues; solutions are not always obvious. The challenge for the manager is twofold: to develop a sense of ethics that can be of guidance in situations of moral conflict and to discern how to incorporate these standards when ethics and business issues are in contention.

The really creative part of business ethics is discovering ways to do what is morally right and socially responsible without ruining your career and company.

—Joanne B. Ciulla[3]

ETHICS DEFINED

The word "ethics" derives from the Greek "ethos," connoting a deep sense of values that direct a person to recognize the inherent goodness or badness of individuals or organizations of which they are a part. "Moral" from the Latin root "mores" is similar in that it refers to the customs and accepted rules of a group or society.[4] Although "ethics" and "morality" are sometimes distinguished, they are basically synonymous in suggesting a comparison of an act to a standard of what is right and good. Exhibit 10–1 indicates the definitional differences between "moral" and "ethics."

THE DEVELOPMENT OF ETHICS: VIEWS FROM RELIGION AND PHILOSOPHY

Ethics has played a part in business since the early days. As far back as the time of the Greeks and Romans, most business transactions were viewed as ethically immoral because they were so often associated with fraud and required engaging with ruthless barbarian merchants who did not share the moral standards with the countries' leadership.[5] Later, Christianity, with its hesitation to endorse worldly success and money-making, applied a strict prohibition on usury.

> The sin called usury is committed when a loan of money is made and on the sole ground of the loan, the lender demands back from the borrower more than he has lent. In the nature of the case, a man's duty is to give back only what he borrowed. (Pope Benedict XIV)[6 (p.5)]

Early Christian ideals tended to put an ethical stigma on business, which served to thwart its development. As history would have it, Calvinist protestantism came to justify interest-taking as a legitimate participation by the lender in the profits accruing from the money he had lent.[7] Therefore, protestantism understood business success as the fruit of a rational way of life, indeed, as a mark of God's favor. Such an understanding opened the way for careers in business, particularly for devout and ethical people, contributing, though unintentionally, to the development of rational western capitalism. The early Christian suspicion of business was not shared by most Jews, who tended to regard wealth as a gift from God. The leaders of Judaism, Buddhism, Zoroastrianism, and the Chinese religions viewed success in business as a blessing. Mohammed is reported to have said that "he who makes money pleases God."[8 (p.5)] The Talmud could be viewed as another critical stage-setter for the development of western capitalism, with its compilation of

Exhibit 10–1 Selected definitions of moral and ethics

Moral

1. Of or concerned with the judgment of the *goodness* or *badness* of human action and character; pertaining to the discernment of *good* and *evil.*
2. Arising from conscience or a *sense* of right and wrong.
3. Being or acting in accordance with standards and precepts of goodness.
4. Having psychological rather than physical or tangible effects, for instance, the effect on one's character.
5. Based on strong likelihood or firm conviction rather than on actual evidence or demonstration.
6. A concisely expressed precept or general truth, a maxim.
7. Instructive of what is good or evil.

The key is *judgment* made according to some perceived standard of *good* or *evil.*

Ethic; Ethics

1. The *discipline* dealing with what is *right* or *wrong* or with moral duty and obligation.
2. A group of moral principles or set of values.
    a. A particular theory or system of moral values.
    b. The principles of conduct governing an individual or a profession; standards of behavior.
3. The character or the ideals of character manifested by a group of people.

Ethical

Self-position, one's own condition or place, custom. Being in accord with approved standards of behavior or a socially or professionally accepted code.

The key is *conformity* to some *code* or *standard* of *conduct.*

Source: Copyright © 1996 by Houghton Mifflin Company. Adapted and reprinted by permission from *The American Heritage Dictionary of the English Language, Third Edition.*

---

with its compilation of beliefs and ethics that addresses issues of social justice and provides ethical principles for dealing with property, profits, prices, weights, measures, and quality.

From the field of philosophy, we find commentary on a broad range of ethics topics from their practical interpretation to the potential for teaching ethical standards. One ethics historian noted that Aristotle devised the concept "virtue" to provide a workable notion of ethics. After all, as a man of moderation, Aristotle didn't view ethics as putting radical demands on behavior. In *Ethics and Excellence,* Robert Solomon suggests that Aristotle used the word "moral" simply to mean "practical." Ethical toughness then implied a "willingness to do what was necessary" and "insistence on doing it as humanely as possible."[9] (p.46)

Can managers learn to be ethical judges in ambiguous situations? Immanuel Kant made the distinction that judgment is a faculty that is inherent in the person and can only be developed, but an understanding of the rules—a needed precursor to judgment—can be taught.[10] Text learning may work well for basic knowledge, but when faced with actual situations, the manager benefits most from real-life examples of ethical choice and discernment.

But whose standards of right and wrong should be used to teach others? John Dewey and James Tufts highlight the dilemma faced by the person when:

> . . . he goes from a protected home life into the stress of competitive business, and finds that moral standards which apply in one do not hold in the other . . . If he tries to face (the conflict) in thought, he will search for a reasonable principle by which to decide where the right really lies. In doing so, he enters into the domain of moral theory.[11] (p.169)

To understand and resolve ethical conflicts in business, managers can benefit from an examination of reasons, the ground on which they stand (the "moral theory"), when making moral determinations. According to some theorists, there is only one universal moral standard for everyone (moral absolutism), or there is no such standard (moral relativism). Some moralists believe that certain actions are wrong in themselves and no rationale justifies performing them (e.g., murder, suicide, lying). Others hold that circumstances and social conditions play a determining role in whether a given action should be judged as wrong.[12] Proponents of cultural moral relativism argue that moral obligation lies solely in the customs, mores, or laws of a culture or society. To be moral, all you have to do is obey society's accepted practices.

In a rather dramatic deviation, utilitarian theory focuses on overall consequences as the sole criterion for deciding whether an action is justified. In case this approach has too much appeal for the advancement manager's pragmatic spirit, consider the caveat that beneficial consequences in one situation might infringe on the rights of individuals or the ethics of justice. Peter Drucker reminds us that not all actions can be rationalized by good intentions:

> There is the temptation to say: We are serving in a good cause. We are doing the Lord's work. Or we are doing something to make life a little better for people, and that's a result in itself . . . (but) that is not enough.[13] (p.30)

The end does not always justify the means. Getting the contribution has never justified lying about how the money will be used.

Another approach to actions and consequences was taken by Thomas Aquinas, who proposed a natural law theory in which actions that promote the individual's intellectual, physical, and psychological well-being are right; ones that detract from it are morally wrong. Consequences are useful in determining the morality of a particular action, but they are not viewed by Aquinas as the ultimate criterion for that judgment. The corollary of this theory points to an underlying dilemma in this approach: certain actions are intrinsically wrong (murder, suicide, lying), even if they would result in generally good consequences. This difficulty is partially balanced by what's known as the "double-effect" principle under which a person may directly produce a good effect even though an evil effect occurs as well, as long as the person doesn't intend the evil effect or use it as the means to achieve the good outcome.[14]

The bottom line for moral theory is that different belief systems can generate different judgments of whether an action is ethically right or wrong. Managers who are aware and comfortable with their own principles of morality are better able to make judgments about applying them in specific, and conflicted, circumstances.

CODES OF ETHICS

> *"Tut, tut, child" said the Duchess. "Everything's got a moral if only you can find it."*
> —Lewis Carroll
> *The Adventures of Alice in Wonderland* (1865)

The nonprofit world is not new to ethical issues. Some of the most hotly debated national issues—abortion, euthanasia, genetic engineering—fall within the purview of nonprofit organizations to address as ethical dilemmas. Some nonprofit organizations have existed long enough and are sufficiently organized to have their own code of ethics. Social workers, Girl Scouts, and college presidents come to mind. It is relatively recently, however, that those who work for nonprofit organizations in the field of advancement have been seen as part of a distinctive sector, in need of their own identity and ethical standards. Practitioners in advancement, much like practitioners in advocacy, educational, or religious organizations, assume a public trust that can be guided by ethical standards.

Increased media attention to ethical violations by a few organizations has also served to reinforce the need for ethical standards. "Whenever any nonprofit is found to have abused its trusted position, the reputation of trustworthy nonprofits also suffers; the value of nonprofit status as a signal that an organization deserves contributions of money or time is debased."[15 (p.26)] Within the moral and idealistic culture of fund raising, high ethical standards are congruent with the nature of the work that we perform.

Earlier, the distinction was made between "moral" defined as a judgment based on a standard of good and evil and "ethics" as conformity to some code or standard of conduct. The written standards or codes of ethics represent an established group's efforts to guide employees in their judgments of acceptable behavior within that organization.

Exhibits 10–2 and 10–3 are examples of codes of ethics developed by organizations for the advancement professional, with additional samples included in Appendix A. The detail and apparent careful wording of each of these documents speaks to the hours of toil that went into their development. CASE even includes a note about the "year's deliberation" by their leadership and countless volunteer members who participated in writing what is necessarily a consensus document, which was completed in 1982. NSFRE developed its Statement of Ethical Principles in 1991, added Standards of Professional Practice in 1992, and amended these documents in the subsequent two years.

CASE and NSFRE begin their codes of ethics with broad introductory statements about the mission of their respective organizations, followed by a respectful acknowledgment of their members' service, experience, high-level skills, and lofty motivations. After this preamble, organizations may include Standards of Membership before addressing Standards of Professional Conduct (Appendix A). The number of items included in the list of standards varies from 10 to 20, with some items more specific than others.

Each organization's statement usually consists of a mixture of higher ethics in business dealings and specific antifraud practices, quite likely promulgated in reaction to publicized abuses or regulatory directives. The American Association of Fund Raising Counsel (AAFRC; a trade group of fund-raising consulting firms), however, directs all of its standards to very specific guidelines for practice, reflecting its members' role as counsel to not-for-profit organizations. The CASE statement reads "Their [institutional advancement professionals'] words and actions embody respect for truth, fairness, free inquiry, and the opinions of others," while AAFRC states "Contracts providing for a contingent fee, commission, or percentage of funds raised are prohibited. Such contracts are harmful to the relationship between the donor and the institution and detrimental to the financial health of the client organization." Fairly consistently mentioned in most codes of ethics for advancement professionals are statements about privacy and confidentiality of information, not accepting favors for personal gain, and avoiding even the appearance of a conflict of interest.

Organizational codes of ethics apply to all advancement professionals, often explicitly including members of the board of directors of the organizations they

Exhibit 10–2 CASE Code of Ethics

Statement of Ethics

Institutional advancement professionals, by virtue of their responsibilities within the academic community, represent their colleges, universities, and schools to the larger society. They have, therefore, a special duty to exemplify the best qualities of their institutions, and to observe the highest standards of personal and professional conduct.

In so doing, they promote the merits of their institutions, and of education generally, without disparaging other colleges, and schools;

Their words and actions embody respect for truth, fairness, free inquiry, and the opinions of others;

They respect all individuals without regard to race, color, marital status, sex, sexual orientation, creed, ethnic or national identity, handicap, or age;

They uphold the professional reputation of other advancement officers, and give credit for ideas, words, or images originated by others;

They safeguard privacy rights and confidential information;

They do not grant or accept favors for personal gain, nor do they solicit or accept favors for their institutions where a higher public interest would be violated;

They avoid actual or apparent conflicts of interest and if in doubt, seek guidance from appropriate authorities;

They follow the letter and spirit of laws and regulations affecting institutional advancement;

They observe these standards and others that apply to their professions, and actively encourage colleagues to join them in supporting the highest standards of conduct.

The CASE Board of Trustees adopted this Statement of Ethics to guide and reinforce our professional conduct in all areas of institutional advancement. The statement is also intended to stimulate awareness and discussion of ethical issues that may arise in our professional activities. The Board adopted the final text in Toronto on July 11, 1982, after a year's deliberation by national and district leaders and by countless volunteers throughout the membership.

Courtesy of Council for the Advancement and Support of Education, Washington, DC.

serve. Some development offices also apply their code to fund-raising consultants. Unlike a company code of ethics, organizations for the advancement professional do not include provisions for the code's administration or consequences for noncompliance.

Exhibit 10–3 NSFRE Code of Ethics

NSFRE Code of Ethical Principles and Standards of Professional Practice

Statements of Ethical Principles

Adopted November 1991

The National Society of Fund Raising Executives exists to foster the development and growth of fund-raising professionals and the profession, to preserve and enhance philanthropy and volunteerism, and to promote high ethical standards in the fund-raising profession.

To these ends, this code declares the ethical values and standards of professional practice which NSFRE members embrace and which they strive to uphold in their responsibilities for generating philanthropic support.

Members of the National Society of Fund Raising Executives are motivated by an inner drive to improve the quality of life through the causes they serve. They seek to inspire others through their own sense of dedication and high purpose. They are committed to the improvement of their professional knowledge and skills in order that their performance will better serve others. They recognize their stewardship responsibility to ensure that needed resources are vigorously and ethically sought and that the intent of the donor is honestly fulfilled. Such individuals practice their profession with integrity, honesty, truthfulness and adherence to the absolute obligation to safeguard the public trust.

Furthermore, NSFRE members

- serve the ideal of philanthropy, are committed to the preservation and enhancement of volunteerism, and hold stewardship of those concepts as the overriding principle of professional life;
- put charitable mission above personal gain, accepting compensation by salary or set fee only;
- foster cultural diversity and pluralistic values and treat all people with dignity and respect;
- affirm, through personal giving, a commitment to philanthropy and its role in society;
- adhere in the spirit as well as the letter of all applicable laws and regulations;
- bring credit to the fund-raising profession by their public demeanor;
- recognize their individual boundaries of competence and are forthcoming about their professional qualifications and credentials;
- value the privacy, freedom of choice, and interests of all those affected by their actions;
- disclose all relationships which might constitute, or appear to constitute, conflicts of interest;
- actively encourage all their colleagues to embrace and practice these ethical principles;

continues

Exhibit 10–3 continued

- adhere to the following standards of professional practice in their responsibilities for generating philanthropic support.

Standards of Professional Practice

Adopted and incorporated into the NSFRE Code of Ethical Principles November 1992

1. Members shall act according to the highest standards and visions of their institution, profession, and conscience.
2. Members shall avoid even the appearance of any criminal offense or professional misconduct.
3. Members shall be responsible for advocating, within their own organizations, adherence to all applicable laws and regulations.
4. Members shall work for a salary or fee, not percentage-based compensation or a commission.
5. Members may accept performance-based compensation such as bonuses provided that such bonuses are in accord with prevailing practices within the members' own organizations and are not based on a percentage of philanthropic funds raised.
6. Members shall neither seek nor accept finder's fees and shall, to the best of their ability, discourage their organization from paying such fees.
7. Members shall effectively disclose all conflicts of interest; such disclosure does not preclude or imply ethical impropriety.
8. Members shall accurately state their professional experience, qualifications, and expertise.
9. Members shall adhere to the principle that all donor and prospect information created by, or on behalf of, an institution is the property of that institution and shall not be transferred or utilized except on behalf of that institution.
10. Members shall, on a scheduled basis, give donors the opportunity to have their names removed from lists which are sold to, rented to, or exchanged with other organizations.
11. Members shall not disclose privileged information to unauthorized parties.
12. Members shall keep constituent information confidential.
13. Members shall take care to ensure that all solicitation materials are accurate and correctly reflect the organization's mission and use of solicited funds.
14. Members shall, to the best of their ability, ensure that contributions are used in accordance with donors' intentions.
15. Members shall ensure, to the best of their ability, proper stewardship of charitable contributions, including timely reporting on the use and management of funds and explicit consent by the donor before altering the conditions of a gift.
16. Members shall ensure, to the best of their ability, that donors receive informed and ethical advice about the value and tax implications of potential gifts.

continues

Exhibit 10-3 continued

> 17. Members' actions shall reflect concern for the interests and well-being of individuals affected by those actions. Members shall not exploit any relationship with a donor, prospect, volunteer, or employee to the benefit of the member or the member's organization.
> 18. In stating fund-raising results, members shall use accurate and consistent accounting methods that conform to the appropriate guidelines adopted by the American Institute of Certified Public Accountants (AICPA)* for the type of institution involved. (*In countries outside of the United States, comparable authority should be utilized.)
> 19. All of the above notwithstanding, members shall comply with all applicable local, state, provincial, and federal civil and criminal law.
>
> *Amended: March, 1993; October, 1994*
>
> Courtesy of the National Society of Fund Raising Executives, Alexandria, Virginia.

Conflicts with Advancement Codes of Ethics

Codes of ethics are never meant to include comprehensive treatment for the totality of situations confronting the advancement manager. Even with extensive procedural detail, the codes can't give direction to the professional in all circumstances. That leaves the responsibility for seeking counsel and interpretation, and for reporting any noncompliance, with the staff member. As such, it is a managerial responsibility to ensure that all employees receive an orientation and updating on the behavioral and ethical standards of their respective institutions and departments.

It is rare for a code of ethics to include direct reference to the protective measures for those who report noncompliance or to the shared responsibility for the manager who has condoned or even approved the alleged violations. Failure to report an employee's ethics violation can be just as significant a problem for the manager as the original infraction.

In case of doubt, it is mandatory to disclose any actual or potential conflict-of-interest occurrence. Conflicts of interest for advancement managers can include a variety of situations that arise out of the very nature of their work.

- Advancement professionals are in the business of asking for gifts; however, it is an ethical violation to do so for personal gain.
- In the course of conducting research on a potential donor, considerable information about that person or group's financial status is uncovered. Laws of privacy and confidentiality must prevail.
- Although performance-based bonuses may be acceptable, percentage compensation for funds raised is not acceptable.

- After securing funds, advancement managers must, to the best of their ability, ensure that contributions are used in accordance with donors' intentions and as stated in the ask.

DONORS' EXPECTATIONS OF ADVANCEMENT STAFF

In the voluntary business that is philanthropy, donors support specific causes or institutions with their contributions. The level of trust that these endeavors require is extensive—trust primarily by the donor in the organization requesting funds. To foster that essential trust, four advancement organizations have joined together to develop a Donor Bill of Rights. AAFRC, CASE, NSFRE, and the Association for Healthcare Philanthropy (AHP) published this document to instill confidence in the not-for-profit organizations that donors are asked to support (see Exhibit 10–4). Areas covered in this statement include the right to: specific information related to the organization's mission, use of funds and gifts, governing body, personnel, and financial statements; and assurances of recognition, privacy, confidentiality, professionalism, and honesty.

Yet another document useful for managers in search of thoughtful guidance for ethical behavior is the Model Standards of Practice for the Charitable Gift Planner developed by The National Committee on Planned Giving and the Committee on Gift Annuities (see Exhibit 10–5). Unlike the Donor Bill of Rights document, these model standards address a broader range of individuals and disciplines involved in the complex process of solicitation, planning, and administration of a charitable gift: charitable institutions and their planned giving officers, independent fund-raising consultants, attorneys, accountants, financial planners, and life insurance agents.

This statement of planned giving standards consists of principles that, in part, echo the fund raisers' code of ethics and the donor's bill of rights in calling for:

- professionalism, fairness, honesty, and integrity
- compliance with federal and state laws and regulations
- compensation that is not based on personal gain from the gift
- fully informed donors

Creation of a code of ethics is a noble endeavor, consistent with professional ideals and public trust. As a "document on the shelf," however, it also has the potential to be a substitute for honorable actions. Robert Payton[16] reflected on the role of guidelines when he commented that making ethical decisions involves the process and the result. We are uncertain about so many facts and consequences but may attempt to deal with our uneasiness by forcing situations into set categories.

Exhibit 10–4 A Donor Bill of Rights

Philanthropy is based on voluntary action for the common good. It is a tradition of giving and sharing that is primary to the quality of life. To assure that philanthropy merits the respect and trust of the general public, and that donors and prospective donors can have full confidence in the not-for-profit organizations and causes they are asked to support, we declare that all donors have these rights.

I.

To be informed of the organization's mission, of the way the organization intends to use donated resources, and of its capacity to use donations effectively for their intended purposes.

II.

To be informed of the identity of those serving on the organization's governing board, and to expect the board to exercise prudent judgment in its stewardship responsibilities.

III.

To have access to the organization's most recent financial statements.

IV.

To be assured their gifts will be used for the purposes for which they were given.

V.

To receive appropriate acknowledgment and recognition.

VI.

To be assured that information about their donations is handled with respect and with confidentiality to the extent provided by law.

VII.

To expect that all relationships with individuals representing organizations of interest to the donor will be professional in nature.

VIII.

To be informed whether those seeking donations are volunteers, employees of the organizations or hired solicitors.

IX.

To have the opportunity for their names to be deleted from mailing lists that an organization may intend to share.

X.

To feel free to ask questions when making a donation and to receive prompt, truthful and forthright answers.

Developed by
  American Association of Fund Raising Counsel (AAFRC)
  Association for Healthcare Philanthropy (AHP)

continues

Exhibit 10–4 continued

> Council for Advancement and Support of Education (CASE)
> National Society of Fund Raising Executives (NSFRE)
>
> Endorsed by (in formation)
> Independent Sector
> National Catholic Development Conference (NCDC)
> National Committee on Planned Giving (NCPG)
> National Council for Resource Development (NCRD)
> United Way of America
>
> Courtesy of the National Society of Fund Raising Executives, Alexandria, Virginia.

We can hide behind guidelines, making them so precise and inflexible that they make the decisions for us.

Effective codes of ethics can serve the advancement manager, providing a standard to which the manager's and employee's behavior can be compared. Ethical standards can be incorporated into individual objectives, becoming a part of performance reviews. When resources are allocated, a reference may be made to the code of ethics to ensure compliance. Reputation, recognition, and appreciation are the currency of the advancement professional. The advancement manager's code of ethics can help ensure a morally rich future.

ADVANCEMENT MANAGER'S FIDUCIARY RESPONSIBILITY

In David Mason's six-part series on ethics for the nonprofit sector, he notes that before leaders can effectively address ethics, they have to get serious about identifying their value systems. Among the core values that he identifies is "stewardship," defined as the "recognition that a person or an organization is obligated as a caretaker to manage its property and operations in a prudent and responsible manner with proper regard to the rights of the society, the community, and those who developed the organization in the past and who will inherit it in the future."[17 (p.25)]

Nowhere is stewardship more obvious than when the fiduciary responsibility of the manager is examined. Stewardship is an essential value in relation to contributors (and in addition to management's use of resources), for managers are ultimately accountable for their organization's ethical and fiduciary status.

At the most basic level, managers have an obligation to allocate resources and account for their use. A traditional accounting budget can determine whether the manager has stayed within the limits of the annual budget. The ethical challenges faced by managers in relation to their fiduciary responsibilities, however, are decidedly more complex than their job descriptions would imply.

Exhibit 10–5 Model Standards of Practice for the Charitable Gift Planner

Preamble

The purpose of this statement is to encourage responsible charitable gift planning by urging the adoption of the following Standards of Practice by all who work in the charitable gift planning process, including charitable institutions and their gift planning officers, independent fund-raising consultants, attorneys, accountants, financial planners, and life insurance agents, collectively referred to hereafter as "Gift Planners."

This statement recognizes that the solicitation, planning and administration of a charitable gift is a complex process involving philanthropic, personal, financial, and tax considerations, and as such often involves professionals from various disciplines whose goals should include working together to structure a gift that achieves a fair and proper balance between the interests of the donor and the purposes of the charitable institution.

I. Primacy of Philanthropic Motivation

The principal basis for making a charitable gift should be a desire on the part of the donor to support the work of charitable institutions.

II. Explanation of Tax Implications

Congress has provided tax incentives for charitable giving, and the emphasis in this statement on philanthropic motivation in no way minimizes the necessity and appropriateness of a full and accurate explanation by the Gift Planner of those incentives and their implications.

III. Full Disclosure

It is essential to the gift planning process that the role and relationships of all parties involved, including how and by whom each is compensated, be fully disclosed to the donor. A Gift Planner shall not act or purport to act as a representative of any charity without the express knowledge and approval of the charity, and shall not, while employed by the charity, act or purport to act as a representative of the donor, without the express consent of both the charity and the donor.

IV. Compensation

Compensation paid to Gift Planners shall be reasonable and proportionate to the services provided. Payments of finders fees, commissions or other fees by a donee organization to an independent Gift Planner as a condition for the delivery of a gift are never appropriate. Such payments lead to abusive practices and may violate certain state and federal regulations. Likewise, commission-based compensation for Gift Planners who are employed by a charitable institution is never appropriate.

V. Competence and Professionalism

The Gift Planner should strive to achieve and maintain a high degree of competence in his or her chosen area, and shall advise donors only in areas in which he or she is professionally qualified. It is a hallmark of professionalism for Gift Planners that

continues

> **Exhibit 10–5** continued
>
> they realize when they have reached the limits of their knowledge and expertise, and as a result, should include other professionals in the process. Such relationships should be characterized by courtesy, tact and mutual respect.
>
> **VI. Consultation with Independent Advisers**
> A Gift Planner acting on behalf of a charity shall in all cases strongly encourage the donor to discuss the proposed gift with competent independent legal and tax advisers of the donor's choice.
>
> **VII. Consultation with Charities**
> Although Gift Planners frequently and properly counsel donors concerning specific charitable gifts without the prior knowledge or approval of the donee organization, the Gift Planners, in order to insure that the gift will accomplish the donor's objectives, should encourage the donor, early in the gift planning process, to discuss the proposed gift the charity to whom the gift is to be made. In cases where the donor desires anonymity, the Gift Planners shall endeavor, on behalf of the undisclosed donor, to obtain the charity's input in the gift planning process.
>
> **VIII. Explanation of Gift**
> The Gift Planner shall make every effort, insofar as possible, to insure that the donor receives a full and accurate explanation of all aspects of the proposed charitable gift.
>
> **IX. Full Compliance**
> A Gift Planner shall fully comply with and shall encourage other parties in the gift planning process to fully comply with both the letter and spirit of all applicable federal and state laws and regulations.
>
> **X. Public Trust**
> Gift Planners shall, in all dealings with donors, institutions, and other professionals, act with fairness, honesty, integrity, and openness. Except for compensation received for services, the terms of which have been disclosed to the donor, they shall have no vested interest that could result in personal gain.
>
> *Adopted and subscribed to by the National Committee on Planned Giving and the Committee on Gift Annuities, May 7, 1991.*
>
> Courtesy of the National Committee on Planned Giving and The Committee on Gift Annuities.

Tom Henderson, advancement manager for Nonprofit X, is offered a lucrative book and lecture deal based on work his organization did to establish and support a multidisciplinary health care development team in Vietnam. Should the manager personally benefit from organizational expenditures? After all, the project's money was solicited legitimately.

Henry Robertson is up for consideration as the next vice-president due to his track record of high performance as an advancement manager for the president's office. But the competition is stiff, especially from external candidates. Could he allocate resources in such a way that the president's new cultural center at the university meets its funding goal, even though it means that funds for updating his staff's antiquated MIS system would have to be postponed for his replacement to handle?

Tammy Sue holds the advancement manager's position at an organization dedicated to cancer research. The organization's executives receive excessive salaries compared to their counterparts in similar nonprofits. However, the executives defend their salary levels as necessary to their duty to be recognized and socialize with wealthy potential donors.

One measure of success for the advancement manager has always been reaching the fund-raising goal. The way in which goals are established, however, can diminish or reinforce the success of matching the goal. In many institutions, all sources of income are added and the results compared to the wished-for expenditure list; the difference is the fund-raising goal. The result of that kind of goal-setting process—even if the goal is met—is unsatisfied fund raisers, high anxiety, and unfunded programs. One seasoned advancement manager was once told to raise $300,000 for postage. He sought and found other employment after his remonstrating with his superior brought no results.

The fiduciary responsibility of advancement managers is integrated with the organization's ethical standards. Good stewardship requires a sound goal-setting process and reliable accounting systems and processes in place to resolve conflicts in the allocation of resources. In the end, advancement managers are not hired as fund raisers to add numbers together; they are hired to help make things different and better for those served by the organization. Money is raised for important and necessary things, not to set records.

LAW AND ETHICS

Enlightened self-interest; corporate social responsibility; from a historical perspective, the development of professional ethics can be viewed as a process of catching a new wave of interest and embodying it in voluntary standards, without waiting for legal compulsion in order to head off the law.[18] Ethics paid, this view went, because even short-term incurred costs were offset by the market's favorable response to the company in the long run.

Today's business ethics, as embodied in employer-employee relations, must reach beyond the legal avoidance mentality to embrace new realities that impinge on internal organizational contracts and ethical behavior. No longer do we have the "psychological" contract characteristic of stable, predictable, and growing companies: hard work and loyalty are recognized with jobs providing financial rewards. Today's downsizing and right-sizing plus mergers and acquisitions challenge the very basis of the prior contract's tenets of fairness, equity, and justice.[19]

When an employee senses that the old rules of the loyalty "game" no longer apply, unethical behavior may take root. Sims[20] suggests four situations in which enlightened management can take steps to create and maintain ethical working relationships with employees, and therefore foster ethical practices among employees, from the first moment of interview to termination of employment.

Job Interviews

Just as fund raisers have a responsibility to represent accurately the purpose(s) to which a contribution will be put, managers have an obligation to be realistic and truthful about what a potential employee can expect upon accepting a specific position. Favorable and unfavorable aspects of the job must be presented. With realistic information, the applicant can either decline or commit to the job with a more realistic psychological contract in place.

Training

Improvements in the employee-employer contract can be made during employment by additional training and development to assist employees in adapting to changing needs in the workplace. From increasing computer skills to diversity training, human resource development should begin with clear mutual expectations of training and the evaluation of effectiveness.

Understanding Ethical Expectations

Employers and employees are similar to a family constellation. When ethical expectations are clarified and discussed, the chances are increased that ethical behavior will follow. Managers can give life to the company's attitudes and aspirations. The more ethics are discussed, the better the potential for ethical behavior to become second nature or fully integrated within the institution.

Dismissing or Firing Employees

There are few situations for managers that equal the ethical challenge of dismissing an employee. And there are few processes that undermine employees' views of themselves and the company than going through this event. This ultimate violation of the employment contract can still be handled fairly and equitably if certain conditions are met. The terms of dismissal must be clear and not arbitrary; they must be administered equally to all employees in the same or similar situations.

When managers pay attention to each stage of the employer-employee contract and deal with each step ethically, they can reasonably expect ethical behavior in return from their employees.

ETHICS AND CHARACTER

Since the time of Watergate, now more than two decades ago, we have witnessed a pitiful series of government scandals. Iran-Contra stands out, as does the hemorrhage of federal officials who, upon leaving office, sold their contacts and influence to the highest bidders. Whitewater and the political contributions' scandals raise a variety of ethical, if not legal questions. The public has had to read about and listen to stories about the head of a major and historic rights organization paying hush money with organization funds in order to avoid sexual harassment charges. In a violation of public trust that particularly affected advancement efforts, the leader of the United Way of America misappropriated charitable funds to finance a lavish lifestyle and was sentenced to prison.

Each time there is a scandal of major proportions, inside government or out, a legislator or bureaucrat sits down and writes another set of rules by which conduct should be judged. It is as if the act of defining what to do, what not to do, what must be done, and what cannot be done will make our population ethical. To a remarkable degree in the popular mind, ethics have been reduced to rules and codes.

Such a rules-oriented approach to ethics leaves latitude for those inclined to self-serving behavior. No set of rules or detailed code can cover every eventuality; so the gaps between what the rules say and what they were meant to imply provide the opportunity for the sleazy to take advantage. The fact remains that ethics cannot be reduced to a set of rules any more than morality equates to commandments—ten or otherwise. Ethics has to do with character; it has to do with core values by which lives are lived and behavior is shaped.

Although ethical issues are part of the routine practices of management, they are less frequently focused on legal issues than with concerns about relationships and responsibilities. Ethics are the values at work in our relationships in society. This "social ethic" determines the manner in which we exist in relationship to the people and the structures of society around us. How do we function alongside our peers, our bosses, our staff? How do we relate to the demands of the job? How do we serve the needs of our donors? How do we see and help the less fortunate, the sick, the immigrant? How do we respond to the questions of our age, the laws of the land, the policies of government? These are ethical questions, questions that point to the social dimensions of behavior.

Although societal ethics may seem far removed from the work of the advancement manager, they are, in fact, germane to the issue of character: the individual and his or her relationship to society; the advancement manager and his relationship to colleagues, donors, or the employing organization. The Josephson Institute of Ethics has identified "Six Pillars of Character," which have applicability to the work of the advancement manager.

Pillars of Character

Trustworthiness

As men and women of good character, people can unqualifiedly count on us. What we say is truthful. What we promise to do is done. What we offer, we can and do deliver. Trustworthiness is a root virtue for advancement managers. We ask donors for their personal wealth, the fruit of their labor. Donors have the right to expect that they have heard the full, accurate story from us when we make our "ask" and that we will make good on our promise to assure that the donors' wishes are fully and completely honored.

Trustworthiness means that our colleagues know that we won't steal the march on them with a prospect, that we won't shade the truth with the boss to make ourselves look better than they, or that we will make our calls and attend our meetings as expected.

A sign outside a Broxville, New York, church announced one week that the sermon for the next Sunday was "On Being the Kind of Person I'd Like to Go Tiger-hunting With." The sermon was about trustworthiness. A trustworthy person is the kind of person with whom you'd be willing to hunt tigers—or dollars.

Respect

The advancement professional shaped by respect judges people on their merits, accepts individual differences, and allows others to make decisions about their own lives. In essence, respect implies honor and regard given to those with whom the manager deals: donor, colleague, mate, family member, neighbor, or boss.

One of the ironies in the advancement profession is that its successful members are often characterized as articulate, even glib, with opinions expressed well and at length. This asset becomes a liability when verbal skills are used to overpower someone, to refuse to listen to them, to insist that we know what they should do better than they do, or when we don't honor their opinions or hold their being in high regard.

T.S. Eliot once observed that the greatest sin is doing the right things for the wrong reasons. In like manner, if the advancement professional bullies a donor—or a colleague—he or she may manage to get his or her way, but long-term relationships will be damaged because of the failure to regard, honor, and respect that person.

Responsibility

This concept has two essential meanings: one is a posture or attitude that implies, "If I did it, I'll own up to it"; the other is a commitment to meeting responsibilities by figuring out which tasks are ours and doing them without hesitation.

William Bennett writes in the *Book of Virtues*, "Responsible persons are mature people who have taken charge of themselves and their conduct, who own their actions and own up to them—who answer for them."[21 (p.186)]

Advancement management is a high-stress occupation. There isn't a single professional in this field who doesn't make an occasional mistake. A lot of the manager's errors get overlooked. When they are noted and called to the manager's attention, he or she has a choice: offer excuses, blame someone else, or take responsibility. Strong, vital character implies that the manager admit the error and move on.

Debbi Adams missed a meeting—not just any meeting, but an important one during which significant decisions were to be made. She simply forgot the meeting. That was not responsible behavior, but it happened. Immediately after discovering it, Debbi called her manager and admitted, "I messed up. I don't know how or why, but I forgot." That was responsible behavior, and the manager was more proud of that colleague than disappointed. Later, when the missed meeting led to some criticism by those who attended, the manager was able to say, "The development officer admitted the mistake and is truly sorry. She has taken full responsibility for her error. It won't happen again." Their concerns died down. Taking responsibility is a mark of strong character and a wise course of action.

The other dimension of responsibility—figuring out which tasks are ours and then setting out to accomplish them—is the very definition of daily challenges. Managers don't have someone assigned to them to determine, minute by minute, what is to be done. Except over a period of time, no one is assessing that we continue to do what our work entails. It is in being responsible, in systematic tenacity, that the work of the advancement manager takes shape, that goals are met, and visions transformed into reality.

Character is shaped in the daily routines. Heroes are not only those who lay down their lives for a cause; they are also the ones who quietly and uncomplainingly consistently go about the mundane business of doing what must be done. Fundraising colleagues who are most admired for their professionalism are those who are responsible. They are the heroes, the persons of character.

Caring

The projects for which the advancement manager raises funds are not simply excuses to increase institutional wealth. These projects can make a difference in the lives of the sick, the destitute, the hungry, and the student. They make a difference to faculty members, scientists, and physicians; they alter how the organization is perceived and affect the entire voluntary sector.

Caring means engaging in acts of kindness, compassion, and empathy. Likable or not, board members, volunteers, staff members, doctors, and faculty matter and need to be within the advancement manager's sphere of caring. This spirit of caring cannot be simply mechanistic or pragmatic. It reaches beyond pragmatic caring because of the potential for money to be raised. Development professionals have the privilege of putting energy and talent to work to achieve beneficial outcomes; that's something to care about. The real bottom line for the fund raiser is not just the dollar amount; it's what the dollar amount will do for people.

Justice and Fairness

Although advancement professionals are not involved in the business of adjudicating great questions such as those addressed by the Supreme Court, they are involved in the business of working within a complex world that is devoted to serving people. Occasionally, circumstances arise that do not represent fair play, perhaps situations in which someone has been ignored, abused, or hurt. The advancement officer who is to be respected is the one who stands in solidarity with victims of injustice, whether it is a faculty member who has been inappropriately denied tenure or a member of an unpopular minority who has been discriminated against.

Life is not made easier, nor is more money raised by a commitment to justice. However, the manager with this allegiance will be viewed as reliable and fair; that fact alone justifies this commitment.

Civic Virtue and Citizenship

As consuming as work can be, it is not all of life. We live in a community and are citizens of a nation. With talent and ability, the educated man or woman has high energy and can be a high achiever. The world needs what the advancement professional has to give. Good character suggests that part of our commitment is to give of ourselves to the world of which we are a part. Whether it is service on the board of a small nonprofit organization; leadership in a church, synagogue, or mosque; or coaching third base for a Little League team, it is important to be a contributing member of the society of which we are a part. The most admired fund raisers carve out time from their crushing schedules to contribute. Our world is better for their efforts and so are they.

The elements of character—trustworthiness, respect, responsibility, caring, justice and fairness, civic virtue and citizenship—are challenged daily in our society and in our work. In recent years, fund raisers across the United States have been accused of engaging in numerous practices that defy the essence of character.

- Some institutions have vastly inflated the value of gifted properties in order to accommodate specific and favored donors.
- Some institutions have encouraged donors to make large "gifts" to them and, when the gifts have been matched by the donors' employers, have returned the original "gifts" to the donors.
- Some organizations have raised significant amounts of money for well-publicized purposes, only to convert the money involved to other purposes once the gifts were in hand.
- Institutions have touted their ability to accomplish certain things, often based on potential research, that the institution was not prepared to do and knew that fact when solicitations were made.

There are two reasons that give advancement managers the right to ask people to give money to the organization they represent: (1)The organization is doing something of worth; and (2) donors can be assured that the funds they contribute will be strictly applied to the purposes for which they are given.

If advancement managers are at peace with these propositions, they can serve the public good as fund raisers; if not, they should move directly and without delay into other work. Both of these reasons for asking are at the core of the issue of ethics. Advancement professionals define themselves by their ethical commitments, not merely by their solicitation skills.

REFERENCES

1. A. Stark, "What's the Matter with Business Ethics?" *Harvard Business Review* 71 (May-June 1993): 38–48.
2. A. Stark, "What's the Matter with Business Ethics?"

3. J. Ciulla, "Business Ethics as Moral Imagination," in *Business Ethics: The State of the Art*, ed. E.R. Freeman (New York: Oxford University Press, 1991) 215.
4. M. Rion, *The Responsible Manager* (San Francisco: Harper & Row, 1989).
5. F. McHugh, *Business Ethics* (New York: Nichols Publishing, 1988).
6. F. McHugh, *Business Ethics*, 5.
7. F. McHugh, *Business Ethics*.
8. F. McHugh, *Business Ethics*, 5.
9. A. Stark, "What's the Matter with Business Ethics?" 46.
10. C. Powers and D. Vogel, *Ethics in the Education of Business Managers* (Hastings-on-Hudson, NY: The Hastings Center, 1980).
11. G. Williams, *Ethics in Modern Management* (New York: Quorum Books, 1992).
12. G. Williams, *Ethics in Modern Management*.
13. D. Mason, "Ethics and the Nonprofit Leader" *Nonprofit World* 10, no. 4 (1992):30–32.
14. G. Williams, *Ethics in Modern Management*.
15. D. Mason, "Keepers of the Springs: Why Ethics Make Good Sense for Nonprofits," *Nonprofit World* 10, no. 2 (1992):25–27.
16. D. Mason, "Put the Power of Ethics to Work in Your Organization" *Nonprofit World* 11, no. 1(1993):30–33.
17. D. Mason, "Values for Ethical Choices: Rate Yourself," *Nonprofit World* 10, no. 3 (1992).
18. A. Stark, "What's the Matter with Business Ethics?"
19. R. Sims, *Ethics and Organizational Decision Making* (Westport, CT: Quorum Books, 1977).
20. R. Sims, *Ethics and Organizational Decision Making*.
21. W. Bennett, *Book of Virtues* (New York: Simon and Shuster, 1993).

Appendix A
Standards of Membership and Professional Conduct

PREAMBLE

Member firms of the AAFRC are primarily organized to provide fund-raising counsel and direction to not-for-profit organizations throughout North America. Our members share a deep commitment to philanthropy and respect for the men and women who voluntarily commit their time and resources in the service of philanthropic organizations operating today throughout society.

This statement of standards of membership and professional conduct reflects decades of service and experience by member firms, and has been carefully formulated to address the best interests of our not-for-profit client organizations and their extraordinary generous donor constituencies.

The philanthropic community recognizes the high ideals, competence, and integrity of the individuals who comprise the member firms. Through years of experience, these professionals have honed their skills and achieved acknowledged leadership in strengthening and expanding the philanthropic potential of their clients.

STANDARDS OF MEMBERSHIP

AAFRC member firms are organizations whose consulting and program services benefit a wide array of national, regional, and local not-for-profit institutions. Client relationships often include Trustee Boards, not-for-profit executives, and senior fund-raising professionals. AAFRC member firms have significant records of achievement across every sector of American philanthropic activity. Membership standards in the Association are rigorous and include the following:

- A formal application and review process which examines current and recent client engagements; the minimum credentials, experience and longevity of senior staff; and the organization, management and financial stability of the firm itself.
- Fees should be mutually agreed upon in advance of services;
- A flat, fixed fee is charged based on the level and extent of professional services provided. Fees are not based on the amount of charitable income raised or expected to be raised;

- Contracts providing for a contingent fee, commission, or percentage of funds raised, are prohibited. Such contracts are harmful to the relationship between the donor and the institution and detrimental to the financial health of the client organization;
- Fund-raising expenditures are within the authority and control of the not-for-profit organization.

FURTHER:

- It is the best interest of clients that solicitation of gifts is undertaken by board members, staff, and other volunteers;
- Member firms do not engage in methods that mislead the public or harm the client, such as exaggerating past achievements, guaranteeing results, or promising unrealistic goals;
- Subsequent to analysis or study, a member firm should engage a client only when the probability for fund-raising success exists;
- Member firms should not profit directly or indirectly from materials provided by others, but billed to the member firm, without disclosure to the client;
- Any potential conflict of interest should be disclosed by the firm to clients and prospective clients.

AND:

- Member firms will not acquire or maintain custody of funds and/or gifts directed to the client organization.
- Evidence that the firm has achieved and sustained high standards of performance, and that the work of its senior professionals is well regarded by current and former clients.
- Demonstrated integrity and ethical conduct in all of its client practices, and ongoing adherence to the standards set forth in this document.
- Ongoing participation in the work of the Association through quarterly dues, reflecting a significant financial commitment to the profession.

Services Provided

Member firms provide consultation to gift-supported organizations whose purposed and practices are deemed in the public interest. These include a wide range of religious, educational, health care, human services, arts, cultural, humanitarian, environmental, international, and other organizations benefitting society.

Member firms offer a wide range of services, all designed to increase giving to client organizations. Services include: feasibility and planning studies, market surveys and research, professional staff and volunteer training, program evaluation, public relations counsel and communication services, campaign counsel full-time campaign management, and other related services and counsel.

STANDARDS OF PROFESSIONAL CONDUCT

Payment of Services

Member firms believe it is in the best interest of the client that:

- Initial meetings with prospective clients should not be construed as services for which payment is expected. No payments or special consideration should be made to an officer, director, trustee, employee, or advisor of a not-for-profit organization as compensation for influencing the selection of fund-raising counsel;
- Fees should be mutually agreed upon in advance of services;
- A flat, fixed fee is charged based on the level and extent of professional services provided. Fees are not based on the amount of charitable income raised or expected to be raised;
- Contracts providing for a contingent fee, commission, or percentage of funds raised are prohibited. Such contracts are harmful to the relationship between the donor and the institution and detrimental to the financial health of the client organization;
- Fund-raising expenditures are within the authority and control of the not-for-profit organization.

Further:

- It is in the best interest of clients that solicitation of gifts is undertaken by board members, staff, and other volunteers;
- Member firms do not engage in methods that mislead the public or harm the client, such as exaggerating past achievements, guaranteeing results, or promising unrealistic goals;
- Subsequent to analysis or study, a member firm should engage a client only when the probability for fund-raising success exists;

- Member firms should not profit directly or indirectly from materials provided by others, but billed to the member firms, without disclosure to the client;
- Any potential conflict of interest should be disclosed by the firm to clients and prospective clients.

And:

- Member firms will not acquire or maintain custody of funds and/or gifts directed to the client organization.

Courtesy of American Association Fund Raising Counsel, Inc., New York, New York.

STATEMENT OF PROFESSIONAL STANDARDS AND CONDUCT ASSOCIATION FOR HEALTHCARE PHILANTHROPY

All members shall comply with the Association's Statement of Professional Standards and Conduct:

Association for Healthcare Philanthropy members represent to the public, by personal example and conduct, both their employer and their profession. They have, therefore, a duty to faithfully adhere to the highest standards and conduct in:

I

Their promotion of the merits of their institutions and of excellence in health care generally, providing community leadership in cooperation with health, educational, cultural, and other organizations;

II

Their words and actions, embodying respect for truth, honesty, fairness, free inquiry, and the opinions of others, treating all with equality and dignity;

III

Their respect for all individuals without regard to race, color, sex, creed, ethnic or national identity, handicap, or age;

IV

Their commitment to strive to increase professional and personal skills for improved service to their donors and institutions, to encourage and actively participate in career development for themselves and others whose roles include support for resource development functions, and to share freely their knowledge and experience with others as appropriate;

V

Their continuing effort and energy to pursue new ideas and modifications to improve conditions for, and benefits to, donors and their institution;

VI

Their avoidance of activities that might damage the reputation of any donor, their institution, any other resource development professional or the profession as a whole, or themselves, and to give full credit for the ideas, words, or images originated by others;

VII

Their respect for the rights of privacy of others and the confidentiality of information gained in the pursuit of their professional duties;

VIII

Their acceptance of a compensation method freely agreed upon and based on their institution's usual and customary compensation guidelines which have been established and approved for general institutional use while always remembering that:

(a) any compensation agreement should fully reflect the standards of professional conduct; and,
(b) antitrust laws in the United States prohibit limitation on compensation methods.

IX

Their respect for the law and professional ethics as a standard of personal conduct, with full adherence to the policies and procedures of their institution;

X

Their pledge to adhere to this Statement of Professional Standards and Conduct, and to encourage others to join them in observance of its guidelines.

Courtesy of Association for Healthcare Philanthropy, Falls Church, Virginia.

AMERICAN PROSPECT RESEARCH ASSOCIATION

Statement of Ethics

As representatives of the profession, American Prospect Research Association (APRA) members shall be respectful of all people and organizations. They shall support and further individual's fundamental right to privacy. APRA members are committed to the ethical collection and use of information in the pursuit of legitimate institutional goals.

Code of Ethics

In their work, prospect researchers must balance the needs of their institutions/organizations to collect and record information with the prospects' right to privacy. This balance is not always easy to maintain. However, the following ethical principles apply:

I. **Fundamental Principles**

   A. **Relevance**

   Prospect researchers shall seek and record only information that is relevant to the fund raising effort of the institutions that employ them.

   B. **Honesty**

   Prospect researchers shall be truthful with regard to their identity, purpose and the identity of their institution during the course of their work.

   C. **Confidentiality**

   Confidential information pertaining to donors or prospective donors shall be scrupulously protected so that the relationship of trust between donor and donee and the integrity of the prospect research professional is upheld.

   D. **Accuracy**

   Prospect researchers shall record all data accurately. Such information must be verifiable or attributable to its source.

II. **Procedures**

   A. **Collection**
   1. The collection and use of information shall be done lawfully.
   2. Information sought and recorded may include all public records.
   3. Written requests for public information shall be made on institutional stationary clearly identifying the sender.
   4. Whenever possible, payments for public records shall be made through the institution.

5. When requesting information in person or by telephone, neither individual nor institutional identity shall be concealed.

B. Recording
1. Researchers shall state information in an objective and factual manner.
2. Documents pertaining to donors or prospective donors shall be irreversibly disposed of when no longer needed.

C. Use
1. Non-public information is the property of the institution for which it was collected and shall not be given to persons other than those who are involved with the cultivation or solicitation effort or those who need that information in the performance of their duties for that institution.
2. Only public or published information may be shared with colleagues at other institutions as a professional courtesy.
3. Prospect information is the property of the institution for which it was gathered and shall not be taken to another institution.
4. Prospect information shall be stored securely to prevent access by unauthorized persons.
5. Research documents containing donor or prospective donor information that are to be used outside research offices shall be clearly marked "Confidential."
6. Special protection shall be afforded all giving records pertaining to anonymous donors.

PRINCIPLES OF ETHICAL CONDUCT
FOR GRANTSEEKING PROFESSIONALS
JOSEPHSON INSTITUTE OF ETHICS (1991)

These are the ethical responsibilities of trustees, board members, employees and agents of grantseeking instituions:

I. Preservation of Public Trust

Help build and sustain public trust and the good reputations of their own organizations and the philanthropic community as a whole by consciously exemplifying the highest ethical standards and avoiding even the appearance of impropriety.

II. Public Purpose

Assure that funds raised by nonprofit public benefit corporations are used only to advance significant charitable or community purposes rather than the private interests of trustees, board members or employees of the nonprofit organization or its benefactors.

III. Honesty

Establish and preserve relationships of trust with grantmakers, the public, the government, and with others in the philanthropic community by: (1) being truthful, sincere, forthright, and, except where professional duties require confidentiality, being candid, straightforward and frank; and (2) not cheating, stealing, lying, deceiving, acting deviously, or intentionally misleading any person by omission, half-truth or other means.

IV. Personal Integrity

Demonstrate the highest standards of personal integrity by: (1) honoring and adhering to personal moral convictions with courage and character, regardless of personal, political, social and economic pressures; and (2) expressing and fighting for their concept of what is right and upholding their principles to the best of their ability.

V. Institutional Integrity

Demonstrate the highest standards of institutional integrity by: (1) consistently advancing organizational missions and values and overcoming temptations to

Source: Reprinted from *Ethics of Grant Making and Grant Seeking: Making Philanthropy Better* with permission of the Josephson Institute of Ethics © 1992.

alter or compromise institutional integrity in the pursuit of funding; (2) assuring that the process and substance of grantseeking activities are consistent with ethical principles; and (3) respecting the institutional integrity and missions of the grantmaking organizations with which they deal.

VI. Promise-Keeping

Demonstrate trustworthiness by: (1) keeping promises, fulfilling commitments and abiding by the letter and spirit of agreements; (2) interpreting contracts and other undertakings in a fair and reasonable manner and not so as to rationalize noncompliance or create justifications for escaping commitment; (3) exercising prudence and caution in making commitments, considering unknown or future factors which could make fulfillment of them impossible, difficult or undesirable; and (4) assuring that when commitments are made, the nature and scope of the obligations undertaken are clear to all parties.

VII. Loyalty, Objective Judgment, Avoidance of Conflicts of Interest

Demonstrate fidelity to their organizations and loyalty to their funders, beneficiaries, colleagues and subordinates by: (1) invariably exercising objective professional judgment based only on appropriate criteria—free of conflicts of interest and undue influences; (2) scrupulously avoiding transactions and relationships which may impair, or reasonably appear to impair, the ability to make decisions solely on the merits; (3) advancing and protecting the interests of those with legitimate moral claims arising from personal and institutional relationships; (4) safeguarding confidential and proprietary information learned in the course of their philanthropic activities; and (5) refusing to subordinate other ethical obligations such as honesty, integrity, fairness and the duty to make decisions on the merits, without favoritism, in the name of loyalty.

VIII. Fairness

Demonstrate fairness by: (1) establishing and complying with equitable and reasonable procedures for development of programs and pursuit of grants; (2) making all decisions with impartiality and professional objectivity based on consistent and appropriate standards; (3) demonstrating a commitment to justice, the equitable treatment of individuals and appreciation for diversity in all grantseeking and personnel actions; (4) exercising authority with openmindedness and a willingness to reveal all relevant information; (5) employing open, equitable, and impartial processes for gathering and evaluating information necessary to decisions; and (6) voluntarily correcting personal or institutional mistakes and improprieties.

IX. Caring and Concern for Others

Demonstrate a concern for the well-being of all stakeholders in their actions by: (1) striving to carry out grantseeking and managerial responsibilities with a firm commitment to maximize benefits and minimize harm; and (2) being caring, considerate and, to the extent compatible with official duties, kind, compassionate and generous in all actions and communications.

X. Respect for Others

Demonstrate respect by: (1) acknowledging and honoring the right of those affected by their decisions to autonomy, privacy, and to be treated with dignity; (2) treating others with courtesy and decency and avoiding conduct that is arrogant, capricious and arbitrary; and (3) assuring that grantmakers and other donors have all the information they need to make informed judgments.

XI. Responsible Citizenship and Civic Virtue

Exercise responsible citizenship by: (1) observing all applicable laws and internal policies, refusing to engage in artifice or schemes designed to circumvent their purpose and spirit; and (2) demonstrating civic virtue through social consciousness and a commitment to the well-being of their community.

XII. Pursuit of Excellence

Strive to perform their duties with excellence by: (1) persevering; being diligent, reliable, careful, prepared, and informed; and (2) continually seeking to develop knowledge, skills, and judgment necessary to the performance of their duties.

XIII. Personal Accountability

Demonstrate personal accountability by: (1) accepting personal responsibility for the foreseeable consequences of their actions and inactions; and (2) recognizing their special opportunity and obligation to lead by example.

XIV. Institutional Accountability and Stewardship

Exercise conscientious responsible stewardship over the resources and reputation of their organizations by: (1) accepting responsibility for the foreseeable consequences of institutional actions; and (2) acknowledging and honoring a duty to discourage, prevent or correct conduct by others that tends to undermine public trust in the nonprofit sector.

CHAPTER 11

Manager or Leader?

The most common question posed by nonprofit executives is: What are the qualities of a leader? The concept of leader both fascinates and bewilders us, as we sometimes imagine the leader as hero, embodied by such figures as Mahatma Gandhi, Nelson Mandela, Gloria Steinem, or Martin Luther King Jr. The truth is that few nonprofit organizations are led by eminent personalities, a fact that may be to their advantage. Yet, every nonprofit organization shares in common with those associated with renowned leaders the need for a vision to be formulated, articulated, communicated, and achieved.

This then is the *sine qua non* of a leader: to conceive and define the vision or mission of the institution. Although this cryptic job description is valid for every organization, the relation of leader to vision is absolutely essential for nonprofit organizations where their very existence is inextricably bound to fulfillment of a mission.

If vision is the core duty of leadership, what are the other characteristics of a leader? How do you recognize leadership potential? What's the difference between a manager and a leader and is the difference important in the nonprofit sector? What makes an effective leader? Can leadership be taught or is it a matter of an inborn trait that only can be developed?

Leadership defies easy analysis and is resistant to definition consensus. Theorists and analysts of organizational behavior dance close to understanding effective leadership by attempting to define it, describing its characteristics and tasks, and considering it from a historical perspective to learn how leadership has come to be interpreted. Perhaps the most compelling description of leadership is "the most baffling of the performing arts."[1 (p.xiv)] However refreshing that admission, it does little to help us understand the nature of leadership. Realizing that we are dealing with an elusive concept, the thoughtful manager will seek a more complete appreciation of the leader's role and responsibilities by looking at definitions that scholars and theorists have proposed.

LEADERSHIP DEFINED

When a word such as "leadership" moves from common usage to a more technical discipline, it often takes on new meanings. Researchers usually define leadership according to their particular conceptual background or field of interest, including traits, behavior, influence, interaction patterns, roles, and power. The following examples give a sense of the broad range of definitions.

Influence

Leadership is the ability to "perceive what is needed and what is right and know how to mobilize people and resources to accomplish mutual goals."[2 (p.50)]

"Leadership is all about making things happen that otherwise might not happen and preventing things from happening that ordinarily would happen."[3 (p.xiii)]

Leadership is "a process of social influence."[4 (p.1)]

Behavior

Leadership is the managerial activity through which managers maximize productivity, stimulate creative problem solving, and promote morale and satisfaction among those who are led.[5]

Power

Leadership is "domination or the exercise of power." It is the capacity "to make another person act in a particular way, whether or not that person wants to do so and whether or not he or she is aware of the domination."[6 (p.7)]

Leadership is the capacity to "command willing service from followers and, when leadership is not enough, to exercise effective domination by so arranging matters that followers willy-nilly do what the leader requires."[7 (p.10)]

Change

"The methods to bring about change may be technological, political, or ideological but the object (of leadership) is the same: to profoundly alter human, economic, and political relationships."[8 (p.132)]

Discussion

These various definitions contain common threads: individual and group relations, vision, influence, and acceptance. In sum, the leader must determine what must be accomplished and influence others to achieve that goal. This description of the leader is at once concrete and esoteric. Warren Bennis[9] likens this concept of leadership to the mythical god Janus, whose gift it was to look both ways—in and out, back and forth. The Janus Phenomenon occurs when the nonprofit leader must look one way for vision, another for the needs of constituent groups, and still another for implementation of the vision.

Throughout the first half of the twenieth century, leaders were most often thought of as those "great people," with bigger-than-life stories and accomplishments. All of us can think of a number of examples of charismatic leaders from government, churches, and business: Winston Churchill, John F. Kennedy, Ayatollah Khomeini, Pope John XXIII, Mother Theresa, Apple's John Sculley. Compared to the total number of people in leadership positions, however, these heroic leaders are few in number. By the late 1940s, studies at Harvard in human relations and group dynamics were confirming that very few leaders actually fit this charismatic-type description.[10]

The next trend to develop in the study of leaders and leadership focused on the behavioral dimension. According to this approach, if a person developed the skills and techniques to properly manage others, he or she would become an effective leader. This "transactional process" examined supervisor-subordinate relationships to determine the degree to which the needs of followers were satisfied as they met leaders' expectations.[11]

When behavioral theories proved too limited in predicting effective leader performance, investigators began to question whether a situation-specific approach would give greater insights into what makes an effective leader. Although this method was somewhat more helpful in guiding the development of managers, it really couldn't explain or predict a wide variety of leadership behaviors, especially for creative, visionary leaders.

This creation of vision and the ability to motivate followers to help realize the vision is termed transformational leadership, a key concept for our current interpretation of effective leadership. Marshall Sashkin[12] proposes that there are three aspects to visionary or transformational leadership. The first, construction of a vision, consists of creating an ideal image of the organization or function and its culture. This requires cognitive skills to think clearly, to "vision" over periods of years, to explain the vision to others, to extend the vision so it can be applied in a variety of situations, and to expand the vision to a broad range of circumstances. Then leaders must be able to turn their cultural ideals into organizational realities, which may involve policies and procedures. Finally, the leader must implement the vision through personal practices.

The vice-president for advancement at a large university just completed a meeting with his president when he heard, for the first time, a description of the new vision for the institution. "Within the next five years," he was told, "our university will become the best bachelors- and masters-granting university in the nation." No small challenge in a country beset with academic institutions claiming they're number one.

The vice-president worked with the president to develop a theme that could succinctly make this vision concrete. The "Excellence Initiative" was born. The vice-president met with the deans of each of the university's schools and the faculty senate to set the course for this initiative.

He also met with his key advancement staff to articulate the vision and develop a campaign that restructured the university's fund-raising appeals to the giving public. As "Partners in Excellence," contributors could now help make the vision a reality. The advancement office developed a document detailing this new approach and its requirements. This complete program description was subsequently used in preparation for meetings with community representatives and business leaders from whom support was to be sought.

Working with relevant staff members, the vice-president identified ways to track the program's effects and effectiveness. He monitored the initiative and worked with his staff and the president on further initiative modifications and enhancements.

The path to understanding what constitutes a leader is neither straightforward nor definitive. However, it is possible to identify some of the most essential characteristics of those who assume the role of leader.

- Leaders possess a vision of the potential for their group or organization.
- As the vision-makers, leaders are obligated to communicate this vision so it can be lived out by group members.
- With creativity and innovative thinking, leaders are challenged to develop alternatives of action as the vision becomes a reality.
- Leaders must work diligently to sustain the vision.

MANAGERS AND LEADERS

We need competent managers and long for great leaders.

Are there distinctions between managers and leaders that are important enough to make a difference in how people are attracted to and developed for either of these functions? Management and leadership are distinct but complementary modes of action. The essence of manager versus leader is not limited by the official title that the bureaucratic system bestows. Although there are distinct characteristics for each of these roles, managers can understand themselves and act as leaders; leaders can also manage. The leader can develop a budget, attend meetings, and delegate. The manager can lead a staff to excellent performance with a compelling vision of what can be accomplished through their efforts.

The complementary systems of manager and leader accomplish similar tasks but in different ways. Their similarities lie in deciding what needs to be done, establishing relations between people to meet some goals, and then monitoring the processes for effectiveness. In Table 11–1, a comparison is made of some of the most common characteristics attributed to managers and leaders. As in any list of this kind, distinctions are made between categories that may prove to be not quite as discrete in practice as in conceptualization. Most managers demonstrate some leadership skills, and most leaders occasionally find themselves managing.

Whether the management or leadership functions are fulfilled by a single person or more than one, several conclusions can be drawn from studies in this area:

- The processes and impact of managers and leaders are different.
- Both managers and leaders are needed in any organization. The daily routine must be handled, and someone must serve to question whether the routine should be done at all.

Table 11–1 A comparison of manager and leader characteristics

Manager	Leader
• Administrates	• Innovates
• Maintains	• Develops
• Relies on systems	• Relies on people
• Counts on control	• Counts on trust
• Does things right	• Does the right thing
• Emphasizes rationality	• Motivates, inspires
• Solves problems	• Generates problems
• Responds to needs	• Actively shapes ideas
• Operates efficiently	• Manages work that others do
• Coordinates and balances opposing views	• Opens issues to new options, risks, even dangers
• Prefers to work with people, with low-level emotional involvement in those relationships	• Works with ideas and is intuitive and empathetic in relationships
• Conserves, regulates an existing order	• Seeks opportunities for change
• Handles complexity with planning and budgeting	• Sets direction
• Organizes and staffs	• Aligns people

Source: Data from W. Bennis, "Leadership from Inside and Out," *Fortune,* Vol. 117, pp. 173–174, © 1988, Time-Warner Publications; and A. Zaleznile, "Managers and Leaders: Are They Different?" *Harvard Business Review,* Vol. 70, © 1992.

- Not everyone can excel at both leading and managing. Some who excel at management perform poorly when they are promoted to a leadership position. Others may have leadership potential that is never maximized because they never were accomplished managers.

Institutions can be well managed and poorly led. Strong leadership with weak management is not better and sometimes worse than the reverse. Leadership is not better than management and certainly not a replacement for it. The real challenge is to attract strong leadership and strong management and use them to complement each other.

THE FALLACY OF CHARISMA, THE PARADOX OF FOLLOWERSHIP

Leadership may not be defined by that special inspirational magic that is charisma, but some leaders are fortunate enough to posses this attribute. Charismatic leaders attract and inspire followers to make organizational changes that implement the leader's vision. They inspire through personal attributes such as empathy, trust, mutual respect, and courage.

Leaders with charisma are more likely to lead through persuasion rather than position. "Charismatic leaders typically have a vision for the organization they lead, strong convictions about the correctness of the vision, and great self-confidence about their ability to realize the vision, and are perceived by their followers as agents of change."[13 (p.529)] In the study of sources of power, charisma typically is not considered an independent means to effect influence, but a special example of appeal that complements other leadership characteristics.

Although it is easy to be attracted to the concept of the charismatic leader, not all those who embody this persona are people of integrity, as evidenced by such notables as Hitler, Stalin, and Mao. Clearly, it is not charisma alone that is essential for the leader. Mission and vision are the essentials; charisma serves as an adjunct. Charisma may inspire, but without those in the organization with the disposition to follow, the vision can never be implemented. Leadership really cannot be understood without examining followership, and the leader-follower relationship.

At the most essential level, a follower is someone who accepts guidance and does what he or she is told to do. But so do robots. Leaders require followers, but little creative progress can be made without followers who are enthusiastic, intelligent, and willing participants in the work of the organization. In reality, nonprofit leaders are shaped by input from all their constituents—staff, boards, foundations, and contributors. Pointing out one of the many paradoxes of the leadership phenomenon, Cronin states, "If we wish to have leaders to follow, we will have to show them the way."[14]

The followership role is one that a person may move in and out of, sometimes within a single day. Some effective followers may be dedicated full-time to the role of team member; others make their leader/follower preferences dependent on the situation. Followers with varying motivations can be more or less effective in an organization. In Robert Kelley's schema (see Figure 11–1), the most effective followers are active and exercise independent, critical thinking. The passive and uncritical employee lacks initiative and a sense of responsibility. The task is never completed at a more than minimal level. "Yes" people are only slightly more active but are purposely selected by some bosses weak in judgment and self-confidence. Alienated followers are critical and independent but more than likely to be cynical about carrying out their role. We all recognize survivors who seem to bend with the winds but never step out to take a risk or develop an innovative strategy.

Effective followers bring a mature, adult attitude to their responsibilities. They can succeed even in the absence of strong leadership. They are confident of their abilities and contributions, paradoxically possessing a sense of equality with leaders but demonstrating their capabilities in different circumstances. This is the group that is coming into prominence as companies become flatter, leaner organizations.

Kelley has identified four essential qualities of effective followers:

1. They manage themselves well.
2. They are committed to the organization and to a purpose, principle, or person outside themselves.

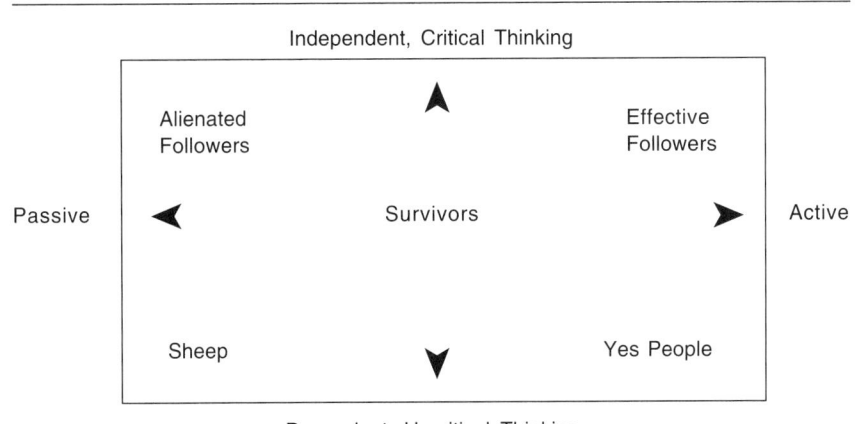

```
                    Independent, Critical Thinking
                                 ▲
        Alienated                                    Effective
        Followers                                    Followers

Passive     ◄               Survivors                   ►      Active

         Sheep                                       Yes People
                                 ▼
                    Dependent, Uncritical Thinking
```

Figure 11–1 A model of effective and less effective followers. *Source:* Reprinted by permission of *Harvard Business Review*. From "Some Followers are More Effective" by Robert E. Kelley, November/December 1988. Copyright © 1988 by the President and Fellows of Harvard College; all rights reserved.

3. They build their competence and focus their efforts for maximum impact.
4. They are courageous, honest, and credible.

In the course of research in preparation for writing a book, one author asked top-level managers whom he interviewed to complete a checklist of the characteristics they look for and admire most in a leader. In a separate study, he asked a similar group of executives about what qualities they value in a follower. Both sets of managers identified identical characteristics: honesty, competency, dependability, and cooperation.[15]

Considering all the words that have been written in praise of leaders, it is ironic that followers possess so much of the power. Sixty years ago, one insightful observer noted: "The decision as to whether an order has authority or not lies with the person to whom it is addressed, and does not reside in 'persons of authority' or those who issue orders."[16 (p.x)] Even charismatic leadership is insufficient until and unless the leader has developed effective followers who are empowered to implement the vision.

LEADERSHIP TRAITS AND SKILLS: THE RIGHT STUFF

"Leaders do not have to be great men or women by being intellectual geniuses or omniscient prophets to succeed, but they do need to have the 'right stuff' and this stuff is not equally present in all people . . . It takes a special kind of person to master the challenges of opportunity."[17 (p.525)]

In the first half of the twentieth century, when the concept of leader was still focused on the heroic or "great person" notion, studies concentrated on identifying traits that all leaders had in common. These traits included physical characteristics and personality traits: height, weight, appearance, alertness, originality, integrity, self-confidence, intelligence, cleverness. After many inconclusive findings, researchers finally concluded that universal leader traits did not exist. Rather, investigators began to examine how leaders performed within certain situations and the influence of followers and goals.

Instead of universal traits, the search was on for traits that could be at least associated with leaders. A comprehensive list of leadership characteristics was developed in the late 1940s that combined attributes of personal confidence, energy for the task, and a high level of stress tolerance[18]:

- strong drive for responsibility and task completion
- vigor and persistence in pursuit of goals
- venturesomeness and originality in problem solving
- drive to exercise initiative in social situations

- self-confidence and sense of personal identity
- willingness to accept consequences of decision and action
- readiness to absorb interpersonal stress
- willingness to tolerate frustration and delay
- ability to influence other persons' behavior
- capacity to structure social interaction systems to the purpose at hand

Current thinking takes a somewhat broader approach to leadership traits. Although key traits are identifiable, they don't guarantee that a person will perform as an effective leader. Rather than the ambiguous and subjective characteristics of charisma and creativity, the key traits more likely center on drive, motivation, integrity, cognitive ability, and knowledge of the business. Table 11–2 represents a composite list of leadership traits identified through studies in the profit and nonprofit arenas.

In a specific application of leadership traits, Tempkin[19] examines what characterizes the nonprofit leader: vision, a sense of reality, ethics, courage, commitment, cooperation—a list not unlike other in the field. However, her unique contribution is a 14-point checklist that managers can use to assess their readiness for nonprofit leadership roles (see Exhibit 11–1).

Table 11–2 Traits associated with leadership effectiveness

Intelligence	Personality	Abilities
• Judgment	• Adaptability	• Motivator
• Decisiveness	• Alertness	• Cooperativeness
• Knowledge	• Creativity	• Popularity and prestige
• Fluent speech	• Personal integrity	• Interpersonal skills
• Strategic thinking	• Self-confidence	• Social participation
	• Self-honesty	• Tact, diplomacy
	• Emotional balance and control	• Fairness
	• Independence (nonconformity)	• Ability to listen
	• Positive	• Willingness to communicate
	• Objectivity	• Productive
	• Courageous	• Educator
	• Commitment	• Goal setter
	• Dependable	• Visionary thinker
		• Competence
		• Influential

Source: Data from B. Bass, *Handbook of Leadership*, © 1982, Free Press and P. Drucker, *Managing the Non-Profit Organization: Principles and Practices*, © 1990, Harper Collins Publishers.

Exhibit 11–1 Are you a leader of tomorrow?

---

1. Can you list 10 ways the nonprofit sector will be different in 10 years from the way it is today?
2. Can you list 10 ways you have adapted your vision for your organization to the ways the nonprofit sector is changing?
3. Have you given up the idea that you can "do it all"? Do you delegate tasks whenever possible, giving people freedom to do those jobs in their own way?
4. Do you have specific criteria in place to evaluate how well your organization is meeting its goals?
5. Do you take a personal interest in everyone who works for your organization?
6. Do you take the time to identify and train people to become future leaders?
7. Do you schedule frequent get-togethers (lunches, office parties, etc.) that allow people in your organization to socialize and get to know one another?
8. Do you involve people in making decisions and setting goals for your organization whenever possible?
9. Do you give public, tangible recognition to workers when they do a good job?
10. Do you have a good idea of the reasons people are working for your organization and how you can help them satisfy those needs?
11. Do you make communication a top priority?
12. Do you have a suggestion box, monthly survey, or other formal mechanism to receive feedback from workers? Do you make it a point always to respond to such feedback within a day or so?
13. Do you create teams of workers to come up with solutions to problems?
14. Are you fair, compassionate, honest, ethical, and upbeat, and do you reward other workers for these qualities?

Source: Reprinted with permission from T. Tempkin, "Nonprofit Leadership: New Skills Are Needed," *Nonprofit World*, Vol. 12, No. 5, © 1994.

SITUATIONAL THEORIES OF LEADERSHIP

When behavioral scientists observed that inborn traits and behaviors alone could not account for universally effective leadership, they began to examine how both of these factors could be applied in differing situations. Could certain traits and certain behaviors be effective in some situations but not others?

Fiedler's Contingency Theory

As is often the case with bodies of thought that develop over a period of time, a radically new theory isn't always so radical after all. This is the case with Fiedler[20] who conducted research in the late 1960s, still attempting to incorporate trait theory and apply it to situations. He proposed that certain leader traits would be particularly effective in specific situations. This is a "contingency" theory because it is hypothesized that effective leadership is contingent upon whether there is a match between the particular traits of the leader and the particular situation where leadership is demonstrated.

The contingency theory of leadership was built around a unique profile, the least preferred coworker (LPC) measure of leader personality. It proposes that a leader's description of the person with whom he or she has had the greatest difficulty working reflects a basic leadership style. The LPC consists of 16 attribute sets, such as supportive-hostile, with an 8-point scoring scale (Exhibit 11–2). To calculate the score, ratings of the attribute set are added together. The results of this test determine whether a leader is primarily motivated by task or relationships. A low score was initially determined to be indicative of a person who is primarily motivated by relations; a high score was characteristic of a leader who is motivated by task success and task-related problems. Fiedler's later research modified the interpretation of the score to mean almost the opposite. High LPC leaders are now thought to value relations most highly. When good leader-follower relations are already accomplished, the relationship leader's behavior can become more task oriented. Conversely, low LPC leaders are now seen as valuing task accomplishment most highly. But when task accomplishment is assured, their behavior will become more relationship oriented.[21]

Fiedler's second premise is that the leader personality orientation or behavioral style that contributes most to group performance varies according to what he refers to as "situation favorability." Situations are thought to allow differing degrees of leader influence depending on three factors: the quality of the leader's relationship with subordinates; the leader's formal power to influence by such measures as rewards and punishment; and the degree of task structure.

Fiedler's theory has received considerable criticism since its initial development. Although it was never possible to prove the author's original belief that the LPC measure tapped an underlying, invariant personality dimension, the theory has survived for decades because of the plausible logic that leaders do affect subordinates' behavior and that different styles of leadership are more or less effective in different settings.

Hershey and Blanchard's Situational Leadership Model

A contingency theory that has inherent logical appeal for practitioners is that of Paul Hershey and Kenneth Blanchard.[22,23] Referred to as a "situational" leadership theory, it relies again on two dimensions of leader style and one dimension of the environment:

- the *leader's relationship behavior* by which the leader maintains personal relations with followers through open communication and supportive behavior.

Exhibit 11–2 Fielder's LPC Scale

Think of the person with whom you can work least well. This may be someone you work with now or someone you knew in the past. It does not have to be the person you like least well but should be the person with whom you had the most difficulty in getting a job done. Describe this person as he or she appears to you.

	8	7	6	5	4	3	2	1	
Pleasant									Unpleasant
Friendly	8	7	6	5	4	3	2	1	Unfriendly
Rejecting	1	2	3	4	5	6	7	8	Accepting
Helpful	8	7	6	5	4	3	2	1	Frustrating
Unenthusiastic	1	2	3	4	5	6	7	8	Enthusiastic
Tense	1	2	3	4	5	6	7	8	Relaxed
Distant	1	2	3	4	5	6	7	8	Close
Cold	1	2	3	4	5	6	7	8	Warm
Cooperative	8	7	6	5	4	3	2	1	Uncooperative
Supportive	8	7	6	5	4	3	2	1	Hostile
Boring	1	2	3	4	5	6	7	8	Interesting
Quarrelsome	1	2	3	4	5	6	7	8	Harmonious
Self-assured	8	7	6	5	4	3	2	1	Hesistant
Efficient	8	7	6	5	4	3	2	1	Inefficient
Gloomy	1	2	3	4	5	6	7	8	Cheerful
Open	8	7	6	5	4	3	2	1	Guarded

Source: Reprinted with permission from F.E. Fiedler and M.E. Chemers, *Leadership and Effective Management,* © 1974.

- the *leader's task behavior*, including organization and definition of the roles of followers, guidance, and direction.
- the *follower's readiness* to perform a task for function or to pursue an objective.

The key situational variable in this model is the follower, specifically the follower's maturity or readiness to perform. Hersey and Blanchard identify four combinations of task and relationship behavior (telling, selling, participating, delegating) and propose that each of these is particularly effective when matched with a specific level of subordinate maturity.

- *Telling:* High task/low relationship. The leader role is primary in defining roles, directing activities of followers.
- *Selling*: High task/high relationship. The leader makes the decision and explains it to followers, demonstrating directive and supportive behavior.
- *Participating:* Low task/high relationship. The leader and followers share decision making. The leader's role is to encourage and assist followers to contribute.
- *Delegating:* Low task/low relationship. The leader abdicates to the followers who make the decisions.

Followers' willingness to perform their tasks ranges from low to high in the following schema:

- unable and unwilling to take responsibility or insecure about the task
- unable but willing, which may reflect a need for skill development or leader guidance to improve their capacity for action
- able but unwilling or feel insecure about performing the task
- able and willing or able and confident

Although this model may appear at first to be more complex than it actually is, it has been shown to be valuable in illustrating the importance of the followers' role. To be effective, leaders must assess the readiness of their followers to be led; this level of readiness can be affected by the leader's actions.

Vroom-Yetton Decision-Making Model

If previous theories or models were thought to be complex, consider that the model developed by Victor Vroom and Phillip Yetton requires computer programming to fully understand it.[24] Fortunately, we can benefit from its essential principles without understanding every possible implication. This model proposes that specific criteria can be identified to determine whether and how the leader should involve followers in certain kinds of decisions situation.

Five main types of leader styles are distinguished in the Vroom-Yetton model and can be divided into three categories.

Autocratic Decision Making

The leader solves the problem or makes the decision using information available at the time, or the leader obtains the necessary information from followers and then decides on the solution. The leader may or may not inform the followers about the nature of the problem when their information is obtained.

Consultation

The leader shares the problem with the relevant followers individually, getting their ideas and suggestions but without bringing them together as a group. The leader then makes the decision that may or may not reflect the followers' influence.

The leader brings the followers together as a group and informs them about the problem. However, the decision that the leader makes still may or may not reflect the subordinates' influence.

Joint Decision Making

The leader shares the problem with a group of followers. Together, they generate and evaluate alternatives and attempt to come to a consensus on a solution. The leader-as-chairperson does not try to coerce the group to accept his or her solution; the leader is willing to accept and implement the group's decision.

Exhibit 11–3 illustrates the model's 11 contingency questions, which when combined with the appropriate behaviors from the above list, provide the leader with the appropriate situation-dependent prescribed leader behavior.

The value of the Vroom-Yetton model lies in its principle that leaders can vary their behavioral styles to match the requirements of different situations. In differentiating between the quality of a decision and its acceptability by followers, this model is also unique in acknowledging the possibility of conflict in the leader-followers' decision-making process.

House-Mitchell Path-Goal Theory of Leadership

A contingency theory with some similarities to the Hersey-Blanchard model, the path-goal theory asserts that subordinates will do what leaders want if leaders do two things: (1) Ensure that followers understand how to accomplish the leader's goals; and (2) ensure that followers achieve their personal goals in the process.[25] The leader's task is to assess the task environment and select those behaviors that will ensure that followers are maximally motivated toward organizational goals (vision).

Exhibit 11–3 Questions about problem attributes

1. Does the problem possess a quality requirement?
2. Do I have sufficient information to make a high quality decision?
3. Is the problem structured?
4. Is acceptance of the decision by subordinates important for effective implementation?
5. If I were to make the decision by myself, is it reasonably certain that it would be accepted by my subordinates?
6. Do subordinates share the organizational goals to be attained in solving this problem?
7. Is conflict among subordinates over preferred solutions likely?
8. How much prior information and ability do subordinates have?
9. Is there a time constraint upon problem solution?
10. How important is subordinate development?
11. How valuable is time in this situation?

Source: Reprinted with permission from P.B. Smith and M.F. Peterson, *Leadership, Organizations and Culture: An Event Management Model,* © 1988, Sage Ltd.

In a later version of this theory, four leader styles were identified:

1. *Instrumental* or directive: Leaders tell followers what to do, then schedule and coordinate the work. This is most appropriate when subordinates have low levels of training and their work is routine and ambiguous, at least in part. Because of their skills, advancement staff may not need the "how" information but, if supported, will be responsive to the challenge of work.
2. *Supportive:* The leader is friendly and considerate of the needs of followers. This style works best when followers have been doing highly routine work for a period of time.
3. *Participative:* The leader consults with followers, asking for opinions and considering the input. This is appropriate for situations in which the work and the experience of the subordinates is at a medium level of ambiguity.
4. *Achievement-oriented*: The leader establishes challenging goals for followers, expects excellent performance, and exhibits confidence that followers will meet expectations. This style is best matched to situations in which the work is highly innovative and unambiguous, and subordinates are highly skilled and experienced.

In selecting style, the leader must consider followers' level of perceived control, their knowledge, skill, and experience. In addition, leaders take into account the environment in which the tasks are to be performed. The environment in this context refers to the nature of the work group, the authority system within the organization, and the routine or ambiguous nature of each particular subordinate's tasks.

INFLUENCE, POWER, AND AUTHORITY

The foundations on which the leadership concept rests is the ability to influence followers, complemented by the followers' influence on leaders. This reciprocal relationship is important to understand in the development of effective leaders.

Influence seems like a relatively simple concept: the process by which one person has an effect on another. The complexity that arises when we examine "influence" comes from the processes by which the influence is exacted and the nature of the effect of this influence. Leaders can coerce followers or compel them with logic and vision; followers can perceive they are being forced into a direction or respectfully allowed to select their course of action. Furthermore, what is intended by the leader may not be the same thing as what is perceived by the follower.

Leaders are sensitive to two related concepts: power and authority. Power is the strength or force to control or coerce someone to do something, whereas power that is viewed as legitimate by subordinates is considered authority.[26] In the dynamic leader-follower relationship, there is a tension at the extremes between followers' desire for meaningful involvement in the organization's processes and their desire for the charismatic leader to determine directions. This active/passive conflict is highlighted in situations in which either the leader or follower oversteps a perceived boundary in the influencing process.

Which decisions should the leader make alone because of his or her authority? When should the staff participate in decisions and directions without this process making them all into mini-managers? When is the power of unilateral decision making the most efficient and effective course of action? The nonprofit manager has a rich collection of traits, skills, and styles to draw on in determining how to influence others in the pursuit of desired outcomes.

To the extent that the ability to influence is central to effective leadership, it is useful to understand how power is acquired. French and Raven[27] are recognized authors of one of the most well-known and useful classifications of the various bases of power. They propose that interpersonal power can be legitimate, reward, coercive, expert, and referent.

Legitimate Power

Legitimate power derives from a person's position in an organization. This more formal power accompanies the designation of manager; its authority is based on an established structure within a group. The leader, who is also manager, is advantaged by legitimization.

Reward Power

Reward power exists when a leader is able to influence because he or she can reward desired behavior. When managers recognize outstanding accomplishments, give a pay raise, or declare a holiday, they are exercising reward power. Reward and legitimate power work together; a manager with legitimate power has the ability to bestow rewards. Leaders often marry rewards and behavior.

Coercive Power

Coercive power is the opposite of reward power, that is, it is the authority to punish undesirable behavior. Rewards and punishment, as experience indicates, can both be powerful motivational tools.

Expert Power

Expert power capitalizes on the manager's knowledge, a key feature of leadership. Expert managers influence others because of their recognized knowledge of business, of a specialty field, or of their more generalized knowledge and ability to problem solve. Unlike legitimate, reward, and coercive power, experts are recognized on an individual basis rather than due to status that the organization has given them. Expert power in one field, however, does not ensure effective leadership capabilities. Highly skilled experts such as physicians are not necessarily the best candidates to be leaders, even with their ability to influence from their expert base. Advancement managers who are recognized for their achievement in matching organizational challenges to the dollar commitments of donors are often accorded expert power by staff and colleagues; acknowledgment of leadership may follow.

Referent Power

Referent power is exercised when a leader is able to influence because he or she is admired or emulated. Charismatic leaders are among those who demonstrate referent power.

Abuses of one type of power can diminish the effect of other power sources. An arrogant manager who consistently refuses to acknowledge the team's accomplishments will soon lose respect derived from referent power. Effective leaders acknowledge and incorporate, in their actions, various ways to influence others, adapting the sources of power to the needs of differing individuals and situations.

NATURE OR NURTURE: CAN LEADERSHIP BE TAUGHT?

From the time that the study of leadership shifted away from trait theory, there was great excitement in the behavioral science and management development fields. If leadership abilities did not develop from basic traits inherent in the individual from birth, perhaps leadership could be taught. After five decades of debate, organizational scientists are not entirely sure that is the case.

Psychological biographies of great leaders sometimes indicate that early experiences may have forced them to become somewhat isolated from others, less dependent on authority figures than on an inner sense of self. This self-reliance may account for the leader's later ability to "lean out from the mountain," take risks, and bear the consequences with little sensitivity to criticism or reward. But this early history is meaningless if the person does not possess talent, and talent is, by itself, no guarantee of achievement.

Even if the raw material of a potential leader can be recognized, the organization has to commit to a course to develop that individual's career path. Many recognized leaders had a series of opportunities early in life to try to lead, to risk, and to learn from successes and failures. Early promotions or lateral career moves are typical of eventual leaders. Formally or informally, students of leadership are usually either mentored within an organization, shown by example how to problem solve, and encouraged to mediate conflict and propose innovative strategies.

LEADERSHIP MODELS, THEORIES, AND THE ADVANCEMENT MANAGER

The nonprofit organization exists to fulfill a mission. Divining and articulating the vision behind the mission is the primary responsibility of the leader. Effective leadership is not such an elusive concept that it can be left to chance, nor should it be delegated to the good intentions demonstrated by dedicated management and followers. If we are to have effective leaders, we must use the findings of theory and research to sort out those controllable factors in the identification of potential leaders; their development within the organization; their most effective exercise of power; and their role in the development and relationship to followers. Leadership is not the province of an elite few who are born to this vocation.

If effective leadership requires a match between the person and the situation, then the study of leadership theory helps the manager to create the most advantageous correspondence between a person and their areas of responsibilities. In evaluating performance, leadership theory directs us to assess not only the person, but the tasks, relationships, and the situational factors that impinge on performance.

If leadership can't be taught but can be learned, nonprofit managers need insights from theory to identify the most effective ways to develop potential leaders. It may not be possible to identify potential leaders precisely, but nonprofit organizations can give those with recognized raw material the opportunities to develop themselves by exposure to the strengths and limitations of organizational leaders.

Leadership, management, and followership are vital as the internal organization initiates, influences, coordinates, and implements. Some of us will be leaders; some managers; others followers. And at different times, we may act in each of these capacities. The development of each of these critical roles is essential in determining to what extent the institution's vision will be achieved.

REFERENCES

1. T. Cronin, "Thinking and Learning about Leadership," in *Contemporary Issues in Leadership*, eds. W.E. Rosenbach and R. Taylor (San Francisco: Westview Press, 1989).
2. T. Cronin, "Thinking and Learning about Leadership," 50.
3. T. Cronin, "Thinking and Learning about Leadership," xiii.
4. W.E. Rosenbach and R.L. Taylor, *Contemporary Issues*, 1.
5. R.R. Blake and J.S. Mouton, *The Versatile Manager: A Grid Profile* (Homewood, IL: Richard D. Irwin, 1981).
6. F.G. Bailey, *Humbuggery and Manipulation: The Art of Leadership* (Ithaca, NY: Cornell Unviersity Press, 1988).
7. F.G. Bailey, *Humbuggery*, 10.
8. A. Zaleznik, "Managers and Leaders: Are They Different?" *Harvard Business Review* 70 (March-April 1992): 126–135.
9. W. Bennis, "Where Have All the Leaders Gone?" in *Contemporary Issues in Leadership,* eds. W.E. Rosenbach, and R. Taylor (San Francisco: Westview Press, 1989).
10. M. Sashkin, "Visionary Leadership: A Perspective from Education," in *Contemporary Issues in Leadership*, eds. W.E. Rosenbach, and R. Taylor (San Francisco: Westview Press, 1989).
11. J.M. Burns, *Leadership* (New York: Harper and Row, 1978).

12. M. Sashkin, "Visionary Leadership."
13. J.A. Conger et al., *Charismatic Leadership: The Elusive Factor in Organizations* (San Francisco: Jossey-Bass, 1988).
14. T. Cronin, "Thinking and Learning about Leadership."
15. J. Kouzes, "When Leadership Collides with Loyalty," in *Contemporary Issues*, eds. W.E. Rosenbach and R.L. Taylor.
16. R.E. Kelley, "In Praise of Followers," in *Contemporary Issues*, eds. W.E. Rosenbach and R.L. Taylor.
17. J.S. Rakich, *Managing Health Services Organizations*, 3d ed. (Baltimore: Health Professionals, 1992).
18. R.H. Stogdill, *Handbook of Leadership: A Survey of the Literature* (New York: Free Press, 1974).
19. T. Tempkin, "Nonprofit Leadership: New Skills Are Needed" *Nonprofit World* 12, no. 5 (1994): 35–39.
20. P.B. Smith and M.F. Peterson, *Leadership, Organizations and Culture: An Event Management Model* (Beverly Hills, CA: Sage Publications, 1988).
21. P.B. Smith and M.F. Peterson, *Leadership, Organizations and Culture*.
22. J.S. Rakich, *Managing Health Services Organizations*.
23. P.B. Smith and M.F. Peterson, *Leadership, Organizations and Culture*.
24. J.S. Rakich, *Managing Health Services Organizations*.
25. P.B. Smith and M.F. Peterson, *Leadership, Organizations and Culture*.
26. T. Cronin, "Thinking and Learning about Leadership."
27. J.R. French and B.H. Raven, "The Basis of Social Power," in *Studies of Social Power*, ed. D. Cartwright (Ann Arbor, MI: Institute for Social Research, 1959).

Chapter 12

Evaluating the Advancement Manager

Henry, the advancement manager for the community hospital, was no different from the rest of us; he dreaded going into that Thursday morning meeting with the CEO to get his annual performance evaluation. Overall, Henry knew his performance had been excellent in terms of the total amount of money raised. But he also remembered those difficult situations earlier in the year when staff turmoil nearly derailed a campaign. Then there were those press releases that weren't so well written and the budget that didn't get turned in exactly on time. The CEO made brief work of Henry's misery. "Henry," the CEO announced, "I've given you the highest score of anyone I've ever evaluated. You'll be getting a raise that will reflect how satisfied I am with your work." They shook hands and Henry left, pleased with the praise but confused about the message.

The legal system has ensured that employers don't fire employees without just cause that has been documented and explained, but the system is mute on another unjust practice, that of appraising employees without sufficient discussion, explanation, and coaching to provide real benefit. Henry left with a bigger paycheck but with little understanding of direction, expectations, his strengths, areas in need of growth, or plans for the following year.

When the leader communicates the organization's vision, he or she has taken only the first step. The vision will not translate into action unless the entire staff gets the message in a manner that influences the way they do their work every day. An effective performance management system can play a key role in improving the quality of an advancement manager's day-to-day work and in helping an organization achieve its vision.

> Performance management is . . . "a process for establishing a shared understanding about what is to be achieved, and how it is to be achieved, and an approach to managing people that increases the probability of achieving success."[1] (p.3)

- *A process*—Unlike the tedious, annual appraisal event of old, today's performance management system impacts managers' behavior, influences daily decisions, and is intended to assist in personal and professional development.
- *...for establishing a shared understanding about what is to be achieved, and how it is to be achieved*—If advancement managers are to direct their energies to excellent job performance, they need a target that is more than a vague ideal. It is important for them to know what constitutes success, both for the organization and for their role.
- *... and an approach to managing people*—It is not the abstract "personnel" but people who are the focus of performance management for the advancement function. This process targets the manager as an individual, as a team member, as the representative of his or her organization in the community, and as a part of the leadership team that shapes the vision.
- *... that increases the probability of achieving success*—Performance management focuses on the achievement of success for the advancement manager and on fulfillment of the nonprofit's vision and mission. Performance is significantly improved when managers are clear about their purpose, receive feedback on their performance, and are recognized for achievement of tangible goals.

FROM TRAITS TO SYSTEMS: THE EVOLUTION OF PERFORMANCE EVALUATION

This view of performance management as an integral process in support of the nonprofit organization's vision is a relatively new approach. For about as long as humans have been working in groups, people have been making at least informal appraisals of each other's performance. Starting in the 1920s and continuing through the 1950s, companies used psychological tests and aptitude surveys to determine which managers possessed the traits indicative of development potential.[2] With few tools to assess performance, the emphasis was on the psychological profile that would make the manager most adept at human relations skills.

By the 1970s, the assessment of "traits" was popular as the appraisal system. Unlike the trait theory of leadership, performance researchers did not believe that management traits were inborn; they were, instead, characteristics that could be taught through skill development. Douglas McGregor[3] authored a landmark article that highlighted managers' widespread resistance to the appraisal process, primarily because they had to make judgments about personality traits. He recommended a method that eventually became widespread in the 1980s, not only as an appraisal methodology but as an approach to management itself: management by objectives (MBO). MBO encouraged increased participation by the person being appraised and focused on individual performance against set goals.

The MBO revolution of the 1980s has essentially come to a standstill. As organizations call for improvements in the less quantifiable dimensions of quality, customer service, and teamwork, they have difficulty using an appraisal system that is limited to the measurement of targets that are largely numerical. Today's advancement managers are best served by the application of systems for performance evaluation that integrate personal achievement and organizational effectiveness. These systems incorporate the measurement of empirical results and demonstrated behavioral competencies. In this context, a competency is a "personal characteristic that is proven to drive superior performance."[4 (p.29)] A competency is the attribute that underlies an observable behavior. For example, the advancement manager may want to influence the performance of others (a competency based on motive). He or she may demonstrate this competency through a positive and engaging communication style with employees. In a competency-based schema, the output from the performance management process is not just the manager's rating. It is a documentation of accomplishments and performance in relation to agreed-upon goals and behavioral dimensions.

WHAT CONSTITUTES SUCCESS FOR THE ADVANCEMENT MANAGER?

In the most forward-thinking settings, performance management begins with the articulation of the organization's vision and the development of a strategy to make the vision a reality. Critical management competencies are then identified that are believed to be consistent with the employment of the strategy and, ultimately, the achievement of the vision.

In the process of developing an inventory of competencies for the advancement manager, the first steps require an assessment of what the successful incumbents do on a daily basis. What constitutes success for these particular managers? Although each list will vary by circumstances, a generic set of success factors can be developed by examining the following areas:

- *Attention to the bottom line.* In concert with the rest of the business world, nonprofit organizations share a focus on "ultimate results." However, for the nonprofit organization the most essential factors are not profit margins and stockholder returns. Advancement managers in these institutions are assessed on bottom-line factors such as the total amount of money raised, the breadth of press and electronic coverage the organization received, and the extent of community or government buy-in to the organization's stated direction.

- *Positioning of the advancement function within the organization.* Has the advancement manager been able to bring a high degree of credibility to his or her role within the organization? Has the advancement manager brought dignity to the position as perceived by those within the organization? To what extent do the key stakeholders such as other vice-presidents, deans, or the medical staff value this function?

- *Positioning of the institution within the community.* How successful has the advancement manger been in positioning the institution for its community? Do community members and key leaders view the organization as valuable, responsive, forward-thinking, influential, and a contributor to community life?

    Increasingly, the advancement manager is the face of the institution for the community; whether it is in making presentations at Chamber of Commerce or Rotary Club meetings, or attendance at a black-tie event in honor of AIDS activists, the advancement manager represents the entire institution. The credibility and integrity, business acumen, and insights he or she brings to these interactions creates an image of the organization for the community.

    Some nonprofit organizations function as if they aim to be the "best kept secrets in town." Others try to function without the benefit of input from those they are supposed to be serving. The advancement manager has a responsibility to fulfill both functions: to promote the institution and seek out opinions and feedback from the community.

- *Attracting and retaining quality advancement staff.* How is this manager's operation viewed within the advancement community? Has the manager been able to attract high quality, experienced, and well-respected staff, or does the staff largely consist of those who were fired from other organizations? Is the manager able to keep well-qualified and high-performing staff members?

- *Quality of written work.* Has the advancement manager been able to bring honor to the institution through the quality of his or her written work? How well has the advancement manager monitored the development, design, and quality of all the printed materials that describe the organization? To what extent do these materials reflect well on the institution?

- *Development of the advancement function.* The advancement manager may have been hired just to "raise money," but how successful has the manager been in elevating the institution's understanding of this position? Has the manager been able to provide valuable counsel to the CEO? Has he or she made contributions to the shape of the institution's larger vision and strategies? Has the manager brought respect and honor to the position, enabling the function and its staff to be perceived as having value to the organization as a whole?

ADVANCEMENT MANAGERS' FUNDAMENTAL COMPETENCIES

When the success factors for the advancement manager have been identified, a set of core competencies can be developed. As in the development of success factors, a list of competencies can be formulated by examining how superior-performing advancement managers function most of the time. If these competencies are scaled and codified, they can become quantifiable measures in the manager's assessment process. The more likely scenario is that they will serve as the discussion points in effective performance and development sessions. Core competencies for the advancement manager function might include the following inventory that has been adapted from one developed by the Hay Group for leaders[5]:

- *Knowledge of the local and larger community's* issues, needs, and events that could impact the organization or to which the organization could contribute in a mutually beneficial way.
- *Conceptual thinking* that allows the manager to identify underlying issues or connections between situations that are not obviously related. This ability helps the advancement manager to "put a face" on a campaign in such a manner that it has widespread appeal and is perceived as a valuable cause by potential contributors.
- *Skill in organizational influence* that enables the manager to understand the formal and informal ways in which the organization can change, and how he or she can effect that change.
- *Skill in the assessment of people*, which is required for the manager to select competent staff members and to match their competencies with specific job assignments.
- *Leadership*, demonstrated by the advancement manager, creates group cohesion, commitment, and motivation to work beyond the call of duty. It is the capacity to demonstrate "360-degree leadership," providing insights and direction to the larger organization, influencing the community, and communicating the institution's vision in such a way that others understand where the organization is headed, what their role is, and how they can contribute.
- *Impact and influence* that requires the manager to know how to persuade, convince, or influence others to support the organization's agenda.
- *A need to achieve,* which is demonstrated by high motivation for the individual, the advancement function, and the organization to succeed.
- *Self-confidence,* which is essentially the courage of conviction, despite rapidly changing landscapes, uncertain directions, and ambiguities so characteristic of growing institutions.

- *A sense of social responsibility* that enables the advancement manager to keep focused on the reality of the organization's mission and to use his or her power and influence to enable that mission to be achieved.
- *Curiosity and information seeking.* Successful advancement managers exhibit a curiosity that drives them to know more about people, things, and issues. Combined with their analytic and conceptual thinking, they are able to gain and communicate insights about future developments that could create opportunities or avoid problems for the institution they represent.
- *Developing and empowering.* The best advancement managers are those who can develop others. They manage with a coaching style that emphasizes shared responsibility and empowered staff. They make expectations clear and then give their capable staff the room to develop their own solutions and take action.
- *Listening and responding.* The advancement manager must be responsive to a number of stakeholders: the CEO, board of directors, the institution's other managers, community organizations, the advancement staff. The successful manager hears and understands the concerns and perspectives of each of these constituencies.
- *Initiating action.* The successful advancement manager is not satisfied with great ideas or even quick responses. He or she is able to take action to either prevent problems from ever occurring or create opportunities for the organization's future.

Generic competencies are adapted for specific settings and modified as the organization develops significantly new strategic directions.

Don Mettler founded his community organization 24 years ago to educate consumers about how to make more informed decisions about whether or not they apply home treatment or seek physician care for the most common illness and injuries. His organization developed educational materials such as a medical self-care book, a training program, and an electronic knowledge-based version of the book. The primary consumer market for these materials had been employers, especially large employee groups.

At a recent strategic planning retreat, Don and the key staff determined that their new vision was to provide customer-based solutions to address the overutilization concerns of health care institutions. The advancement manager was challenged to develop a campaign that would create a positive image of the organization as experts in medical education for consumers, particularly in the eyes of their new constituency: health care organizations that assume the risk and the cost for the care of a defined group of members.

The advancement manager's performance review resulted in the identification of several new key competencies for the year:

- current knowledge of the major risk-bearing health care companies in the organization's target market areas
- knowledge of the needs of this new constituency in relation to consumer education
- knowledge of sources for research funds to support demonstration pilots in medical self-care education for health care organizations
- identification of the new skills required by the advancement staff to appeal to this new constituency and preparation of development plans for staff

THE ELUSIVE NONPROFIT BOTTOM LINE

Nonprofit institutions have a particular challenge in giving performance and results the priority they justly deserve. The business sector lives and breathes profitability as a goal and constantly scans the economic horizon for shifting trends that may impact the financial forecast. Profit and loss may not be the only measure of performance, but they are at least concrete and drive the focus on performance management to impact productivity.

In a sense, both for-profit and nonprofit organizations share a concern about the bottom-line economics, whether it is specifically about profit or total amounts raised. However, the enlightened advancement manager is unique in never losing sight of the "why" of contributions. Funding is not sought in a vacuum but raised so the organization has additional resources to do the things that need to be done. The American Heart Association does not raise money so it can have a better financial statement than the American Cancer Society. It seeks funding to achieve its goals of heart disease prevention, education, and research. The advancement manager is in a unique position to keep the organization and the community focused on this reality of funding.

Carolyn, an advancement manager for a large community college, was asked to develop a campaign to raise funds so the college could acquire state-of-the-art, digital equipment for the campus television station. Carolyn's first reaction was one of skepticism. What could be so appealing about high-tech equipment that it could become a rallying point for contributors? If she couldn't get a handle on the heart of the campaign and shape it in some useful way, Carolyn knew the effort would not be successful.

After thoroughly investigating the topic in the literature and probing the chancellor's office for insights, Carolyn came up with a framework for the campaign that broadened its intent. This would not be just an ask to fund purchases of equipment. The campaign represented the college's commitment to provide its larger community with educational opportunities not tied to time and place. The equipment supported a major move toward the development of distance learning capabilities that would allow community members in more rural areas to participate in educational experiences as if they were on campus. It would meet the needs of the fast-paced business sector students who could not leave their job locations to complete a degree program. Groups in the community, including the disabled, who never before thought it was possible to pursue an education could now access an institution that was available to them when and where they lived. This more expansive vision gave the advancement manager the bottom line that would drive staff motivation, productivity, contributor interest, and a successful financial outcome.

The determination of which bottom line to operate from is a formidable, yet fundamental issue for nonprofit organizations. The museum must decide whether it is going to gauge success on the quality of its collection or the number of visitors who come to see its exhibits. The community hospital has to select performance indicators from among areas that may compete with each other: customer service, quality of care, occupancy rates, community image, revenues versus expenses. As institutions clarify their vision and strategies, the performance indicators selected should be consistent with this endeavor. It is a basic axiom that we, as individuals or institutions, will work to achieve in those areas that will be used to evaluate our performance. If "speed of service in the emergency room" is a primary indicator for the community hospital, then customer service may suffer. If performance for the advancement manager is defined as "total amount contributed," then the manager may be tempted to focus more on numbers and less on undergirding the institution's mission.

An agency that provides medical supplies for disaster relief received an offer of funding from a politician's constituency group for a project to send a group of physicians to teach surgical techniques to a hospital's medical staff in Croatia. This effort could be organized by the agency and was within the scope of its long-term vision. But neither the timing of the offer nor the location of the physician team were a match with the agency's priorities. This undertaking would mean pulling staff from other projects and focusing almost all of the agency's limited resources on launching this initiative over a three-month period.

The CEO and advancement manager carefully considered the short-term and long-term benefits and risks for the agency of refusing the politician's offer or accepting the offer and redirecting resources. Their eventual decision was to accept the funding but assign an independent observer to accompany the mission and evaluate each aspect, from selection and orientation of team members to the effectiveness of teaching techniques. The observer's report would be used by the agency when it began sending medical teams to its target country, Vietnam.

Peter Drucker[6] reminds us of two common enticements that occur when an institution is trying to operationalize its mission. As one of the "keepers of the institution's vision and mission," the advancement manager is in a position to be particularly affected by each of them. One temptation is to go for the easy results rather than for results that drive toward realization of the institution's mission. Without concerted effort, a university may receive substantial funds for designated giving, but it may suffer in overall accomplishments if it does not seek unrestricted funding as well. The community hospital does not consider primary research a priority, but it has the opportunity to update the computer systems in its outpatient department if it becomes a pilot site for a major drug intervention trial.

The opposite attraction is to be so taken with the organization's cause that the manager is overcome by a sort of reckless abandon in specifying what can be done. The attitude of "we will do whatever it takes" (to eradicate cancer, to educate our children, to relieve starvation in Ethiopia) is noble but can lead to a lot of false promises that can't be fulfilled.

Drucker believes that the common cause for both of these temptations is that the nonprofit organization does not get paid for performance, unlike businesses, in which performance is the currency returned for the customer's cash. Our accountability systems must be designed, however, to hold our institutional feet to the fire for fulfilling the organization's fundamental mission.

INFORMAL EVALUATIONS

Ask any of the vice-presidents and they'll tell you—to a person—that Charles, the advancement manager, talks way too much and delivers too little. "He's forever saying he's going to follow up and never does" is a typical rap sheet entry on Charles.

Colleagues evaluate the advancement function and its manger on a daily basis. Views held by the institution change in subtle ways that may not be formal or stated outright. To be in a position to shape the institution's mission, it is critical for the advancement manager to stay congruent with the nuances of change that occur in the setting and with his or her performance in relation to these changes. The manager needs to know if that last speech was on target with what the CEO had in mind for the new campaign, or whether that most recent press release did justice to the institution's renewed emphasis on nondiscrimination for the disabled.

To deal efficiently with performance feedback, the enlightened advancement manager can establish a reliable, yet informal evaluation system. Peers, staff, the CEO, members of the board, or others can provide valuable and timely feedback. "Good job, Charles, in detailing our community commitment at that breakfast meeting" may let Charles know that he is sufficiently on target to begin directing the writing of brochure copy on this topic. "I'm concerned about your lack of initiative on this project" is not the type of feedback that should wait for an annual performance evaluation meeting. As a trusted professional, the advancement manager can make mid-course corrections with timely, constructive criticism.

The pace of change within an institution is too swift to depend solely on the annual review for performance feedback. Managers often benefit from planned and periodic review sessions with the person to whom they report. These sessions, more structured than casual comments given "on the fly," will occur more frequently than the annual review. No ratings or comprehensive assessments are made; salary action is not a topic. The emphasis is on participative review, problem solving, and goal setting.

FORMAL EVALUATIONS

One of the first questions that arises in the process of developing a management appraisal system is whether to use input from a single person or several. The research evidence is clear: "The average of several evaluations made by equally competent raters is far superior to a single rating."[7 (p.200)]

The advancement manager serves many masters: the CEO, peers in the institution, staff, and donors. If managers receive honest, specific feedback from their bosses, colleagues, subordinates, and the community, they get a unique and valuable perspective on how their behavior affects others. In addition, when there is consensus input from a variety of sources, the manager is less likely to oppose recommendations on performance areas in need of change. The 360-degree feedback system is currently viewed by training professionals, consultants, and practitioners as the optimal tool for enhancing leadership and management capabilities.[8]

The first step in the 360-degree, or full-circle appraisal process, is the identification of competencies required by the advancement manager position. As discussed earlier, these competencies should be aligned with the institution's mission and reflect the behaviors and skills that predict success for this specific position.

In most instances, questionnaires are developed to gather information about the manager's behavior from those in a position to witness it on a regular and continuing basis. In addition, the advancement manager completes a self-assessment form. The results are summarized, and the CEO (presuming the advancement manager is in a direct reporting relationship to the person occupying this position) and manager meet to discuss the feedback.

Gary Yukl and Richard Lepsinger,[9] experts in management effectiveness, describe qualities of the full-circle appraisal that increase the likelihood that real behavior change will result from this process. These recommendations have been adapted for use by the advancement manager.

The Questionnaire

Well-researched

Items on the questionnaire should be known to be related to managers' effectiveness. Although organizational research can provide generalized indicators for management effectiveness, the specific competencies for effectiveness within the advancement function are not found in the literature. However, items can be developed from the competencies identified earlier in this chapter.

Behavioral

It is more difficult for respondents to give feedback when the behaviors are described in vague and general terms. "Represents the institution well" is more difficult to rate and does not give as much information back to the manager as "Articulates the institution's goals clearly when presenting at community functions." Specific items make it easier for the manager to make needed changes.

Positive

Behaviors should be described in positive rather than negative terms. "Doesn't listen to input from staff" is more difficult to respond to than "Encourages staff to give input and is responsive to their views." The difference may seem subtle, but a negatively worded statement is not as beneficial for a number of reasons: (1) evaluators are, in general, hesitant to report that the manager is ineffective (even if this is true some of the time); (2) managers are more likely to respond defensively to negative statements about them; and (3) the positively worded statements tell the manager precisely which behaviors are desired.

Personal

Whenever feasible, behaviors should be described in terms that relate to the person answering the questionnaire. For example, it is preferable to ask for a response to "This manager keeps me informed of changes in funding strategies" rather than "This manager keeps the vice-presidents informed of changes in funding strategies." Respondents should not be invited to guess about how the manager behaves with others. Of course, this recommendation is not appropriate for behaviors that involve more than one person ("Holds a celebration after the goals of a major campaign have been accomplished") or for behaviors the manager performs alone ("Reviews performance summaries for the advancement staff").

Multidirectional

Advancement managers use different forms of influence when dealing with their staff, the CEO, or community representatives. It would hardly be appropriate, for example, to include items that deal with delegation on a questionnaire used by the head of a community foundation. Multiple versions of the questionnaire may be necessary; each version should include only the behaviors relevant in that particular kind of relationship.

Administering the Questionnaire

Select Respondents Carefully

In most cases, advancement managers will be asked to furnish a list of people with whom the managers interact frequently and who are most critical to their effectiveness in their position. Even this simple step gives the manager a sense of control over the process, increasing the likelihood that he or she will be more responsive to the results.

Ensure an Adequate Number of Respondents

In larger institutions, the policy on performance appraisal may dictate the number of respondents required for this process. Given a choice, the number should be large enough to ensure adequate sampling and protect the confidentiality of the sources. Because some people invariably fail to return the questionnaire, the initial sample should be large enough to account for attrition in responses.

Explain How the Data Will be Used and Ensure Confidentiality

This issue may be more salient in organizations that are new to this type of appraisal process. However, direct reports or associates who are also social acquaintances may be reluctant to give entirely honest feedback without a reminder that individual responses will remain anonymous. Depending on the relationship, the CEO or person the advancement manager directly reports to may also be hesitant because, as the single person in the "boss" category, their feedback is obviously not anonymous. If the assessment is exclusively for developmental purposes, this is less of an issue.

Help Respondents Avoid Common Problems in Rating

Instead of recalling how frequently the manager demonstrated a specific behavior over the past several months, raters may be responding to a general feeling they have about the manager. When managers are well liked, they may get high ratings overall, despite the fact that in certain areas they are clearly deficient. Likewise, a manager who is not well liked may be rated negatively on behaviors he or she performs well. In a similar error, raters may believe that a manager is an effective communicator and rate him or her high on any scale thought to relate to communications; in truth, the manager may be excellent in one-to-one communications, but not nearly as effective in front of a group.

Short of rater training—a resource-intensive proposition—the next best approach is to alert raters to these potential biases and encourage them to rate behaviors accurately. Raters can be reminded of the importance of their feedback, especially for areas of improvement.

The Feedback Report

Clearly Identify Feedback From Different Perspectives

Behavior descriptions from different sets of sources—boss, staff, community representatives, donors—should be presented separately. When feedback from different sources is aggregated, the intrinsic value of full-circle assessment is lost. It is only natural that the advancement manager's responses vary in different settings. If the way in which he or she behaves with a certain set of stakeholders is detrimental, however, simply presenting an "averaged" description will lose the feedback that is most important for improvement.

Compare Feedback From Others with the Manager's Own Perceptions

The advancement manager's self-assessment may be a useful point of comparison. A high degree of agreement between the manager's ratings and those of others probably indicates accuracy in the evaluation. When a discrepancy such as a higher rating by the manager than by the raters is noted, it represents a difference in perception that merits exploration. A number of explanations may be plausible: the manager or the rater may be biased; the manager's behavior may not be visible to the rater; or the other raters may have interpreted the items differently.

Compare the Manager's Ratings to Norms

This is a feasible suggestion only when data are available from a large selection of managers with ratings on at least a portion of the scales used for the advancement manager.

Display Feedback for Items as Well as Scales

Most behavior scales or categories consist of several items. The behavior scale of "develops advancement staff" may consist of items such as "Identifies with you the priority areas for professional development"; "Encourages you to attend conferences and workshops on important subjects for your development"; and "Provides coaching to help you improve your job skills." Item feedback helps the manager to understand the scale scores by providing specific examples for each category. Feedback on individual items also reduces misinterpretations caused by missing data, which may be coded as "never does" or not counted at all.

Provide Feedback on Recommendations

One of the most helpful features of the feedback questionnaire is the information that describes not only what the manager does but what the respondent would like the manager to do. In particular, these recommendations indicate how many respondents say a certain behavior should be used either more frequently, the same amount, or less. For example, even though an advancement manager has a moderately high score on a behavior such as "timely follow-through on commitments," the CEO may prefer that the manager become even more timely on a consistent basis. Because it takes extra time to complete the recommendations section, these questions should focus on scales rather than individual items.

The advancement manager may receive only written feedback on the 360-degree assessment or, preferably, written feedback in addition to a discussion with the CEO. In whatever setting, the advancement manager should be reminded of the purpose and benefit of this type of assessment process. This is an important time to revisit the association between the institution's mission, effective leadership, and management. Strengths as well as weakness should be noted, and an improvement plan that addresses very specific behaviors can be developed. Together, these steps in the evaluation of the advancement manager will support the most informed approach to management development aligned with the institution's mission.

How have managers responded to this process? "It was the first time in my career that I'd ever had a sense of how I was perceived in the community," reported one museum advancement manager. "I couldn't believe how helpful it was to get that perspective. It made me look squarely at my strengths and the areas I need to work on to be a better manager. And it wasn't as painful as I had thought," commented another manager. Not everyone agrees with the painful part. "No matter what they say," cautioned one candid advancement manager, "any appraisal process is inherently difficult. The process may be as objective as possible and the results intended mostly for my development, but part of me becomes this kid again, afraid of the repercussions of a negative assessment."

Despite the very human side of performance assessment, the general consensus is that a thoughtful, well-planned, and educational process like 360-degree assessment can provide unique insights into institutional, staff, and customer expectations; identify areas of strength for the advancement manager to continue; and indicate directions for development.

TYING EVALUATION RESULTS TO REWARDS

Everyone has won and they all must have prizes.
—Lewis Carroll
Alice in Wonderland (1865)

It is safe to say that no one performs without rewards. Some managers, like many entrepreneurs, are motivated by intrinsic rewards, those that come from the activity itself rather than from what the person gains from engaging in the activity. Other managers are motivated by pay, status, career growth opportunities, or recognition. The key to the reward system for advancement management is to harness the energy of performance motivation and use it to drive the institution's strategies.

At first glance, it may appear unusual to recommend reward options for advancement managers—the primary target for this book's readership—because it is the CEO who would be giving the reward. However, as we observed earlier, leaders are often taught by their followers. When a manager has considered a full range of motivators, and understands which types of rewards are the most powerful drivers, the manager can let the CEO know his or her preferences. This saves a lot of guessing and perhaps misjudgments on the part of the CEO whose primary intention is to reward excellent performance.

Andrew, the community agency's advancement manager, had come through a most difficult year with remarkable success. Negative public reaction to a prominent voluntary agency's scandal that made the newspapers' headlines day after day threatened to spill over to Andrew's institution as well. In weekly meetings, the advancement staff reported that a significant backlash was building among contributors owing to the scandal. Foundations and employer groups, in particular, were slowing their contributions. Andrew realized the seriousness of this trend and mounted a successful counter-campaign to differentiate his agency and reassert its integrity and dedication to the community.

The CEO who monitored this six-month effort was enormously pleased with the results. Unable to reward Andrew with a significant pay raise, the CEO sought to express his satisfaction with the advancement manager's performance by other means. The CEO offered Andrew tickets to one of the most popular events in the city—opening night at the performing arts center—a "black tie affair." What the CEO did not know is that dressing up for formal gatherings was one of the most uncomfortable aspects of Andrew's job. He did it when he had to but often gave the black-tie assignment to another staff member. What was intended as a reward from the CEO was a poor match with what motivated Andrew's performance.

The difficulty in paying for performance in a nonprofit organization has been addressed in an earlier chapter. From among the possible nonmonetary rewards, advancement managers may be motivated by unique opportunities for growth and development. One CEO commended outstanding effort by recommending that the manager attend two conferences within the subsequent year. All expenses would be paid and no report would be required. "Go and learn" was the message from the CEO.

Another successful advancement manger was given an opportunity to participate on a hand-selected team, that for the next six months, would direct the larger institution's strategic planning efforts. Despite the effect of "more work for hard work," the paradox is that this reward was enormously satisfying for the manager. It represented recognition by executive management, confidence in her ability to contribute to the broader organization, an opportunity to work side by side with executive management, and career growth.

For some managers, there is little that is more satisfying than the opportunity to "shine," to tell their story in front of an audience of intelligent, willing listeners. One CEO rewarded his advancement manager with the opportunity to keynote a major conference. What terrorizes one manager may be the ideal reward for another. Another advancement manager was rewarded with an expanded job description that reflected a notable increase in authority. Pay, status, career opportunities, recognition, and further education are just a few of the rewards for the advancement manager to consider.

Whatever the reward, the key to its use is the linkage between performance expectations and rewards. When tangible or intangible rewards are provided, they should come with an explanation of why the reward is offered. This integration of purpose and reward directly supports repeated excellent performance. However, it is more likely that rewards will provide the incentive to work toward even higher levels of performance when the rewards are valued by the manager.

CAREER ADVANCEMENT

Data from the performance management process can be used to develop a career advancement plan for the advancement manager and to complete a succession plan for this position. The advancement manager may make a career change and become a foundation director. A relatively small number of advancement managers succeed to the role of CEO of their institutions. The majority who do make career changes usually move to a similar position in a more complex and challenging environment. For example, the advancement manager from a comprehensive university may assume the same position in a research university.

It is not uncommon practice for an organization to prepare a management personnel inventory, indicating future replacement needs and listing the candidates who may qualify for anticipated vacancies, immediately or after further development. Needs are often anticipated for the next five years; candidates are identified who may be considered for advancement based on performance, retirement plans, health, and projected organizational changes.[10] A formal, written assessment of a manager's potential for career advancement may include an inventory of the information illustrated in Exhibit 12–1.

Advancement managers in today's most effective nonprofit organizations understand and help shape their institution's vision. The identification of advancement management competencies ties vision to performance. Formal and informal evaluation is sought from all constituencies that have a stake in the manager's function. Rewards are tied to performance, with considerable thought given to pay and non-pay incentives that, on an individual basis, link performance with the rewards. Finally, development plans allow the manager to keep his or her sights on the next professional move that will make best use of the competencies gained in the current position.

Exhibit 12–1 Assessment of career advancement potential

- **Promotability/next assignment**
  Timing: Immediately promotable, ready within one to two years, ready within two to five years
  Position to which promotable within current or other area
- **Assessment of long-range potential**
  Level: CEO, president
- **Dimensions profile and rating**
  Decision making: Organizational influence, analysis, judgment, vision
  Managerial: Planning and organizing, delegation and control, quality and development of advancement staff, representation of advancement to organization
  Interpersonal: Leadership/influence, team building, negotiation, communications, community relations
  Personal: Initiative/innovativeness, entrepreneurial action
  Job knowledge skills: Professional advancement function
- **Career development**
  Present assignment
  Career preferences
  Career development plan

REFERENCES

1. T. Weiss and F. Hartle, *Reengineering Performance Management* (Boca Raton, FL: St. Lucie Press, 1977).
2. C. Fletcher and R. Williams, *Performance Appraisal and Career Development* (London: Hutchinson, 1985).
3. D. McGregor, "An Uneasy Look at Performance Appraisal," *Harvard Business Review* 35, no 3 (1957): 89–94.
4. T. Weiss and F. Hartle, *Reengineering Performance Management*, 29.
5. T. Weiss and F. Hartle, *Reengineering Performance Management*.
6. P. Drucker, *Managing the Non-Profit Organization: Practices and Principles* (New York: HarperCollins Publishers, 1990).
7. J.B. Miner and M.G. Miner, *Personnel and Industrial Relations* (New York: Macmillan Publishing Company, 1985).
8. G. Yukl and R. Lepsinger, "360° Feedback." *Training* vol. 32 (December 1995): 45–50.
9. G. Yukl and R. Lepsinger, "360° Feedback."
10. J.B. Miner and M.G. Miner, *Personnel and Industrial Relations*.

Index

A

Achievement, and motivation, 179–181
Advancement, definition of, 42
Advancement activities
  alumni relations, 67–70
  church relations, 65
  government, role in, 40–41
  government relations, 63–65
  history of, 39–40
  private philanthropy, 41–60
  public affairs, 60–63
  publications, 65–66
  structure of. *See* Organizational structure
Advancement of employees
  in-house strategies for, 178
  managerial advancement, 280–281
  and motivation, 177–178
Advancement managers
  attributes of effective manager, 267–268
  budgeting, 34–36
  competencies required of, 269–271
  evaluation function, 29–34
  evaluation of, 265–281
  hiring of, 4–5
  and organizational culture, 37–38
  personnel administration, 9–29
  planning function, 6–9
  representation function, 38
  responsibilities of, 5
Advancement office, divisions of, 44
Advancement staff
  growth over time, 41–42, 89
  internal staff, management structure, 90
  size of, 5–6
  span of control, 89
  staff relationships, 88–91
  and strategic planning, 163–165
Alumni relations, 67–70
  donor flowchart, 69
  independent and institutional program, 68, 69
  institutional service for graduates, 68
  models for, 67–68
  types of alumni activities, 67
American Association of Fund Raising Counsel, ethical code, 215
American Prospect Research Association, Codes of Ethics, 239–240
Annual fund
  direct mail, 54–55
  telefund, 55–56
Association for Healthcare Philanthropy, Statement of Professional Standards and Conduct, 237–238
Association of Professional Researchers for Advancement (APRA), 45

B

Benchmarks, 105–106
Blanchard, Kenneth, 255
Bonuses, 173
Budgeting, 34–36
  categories of expenses, 35

justifying augmentation requests, 36
mixed-model organization, 83–84
staff factors in, 35–36

C

Career path, 177
Caring, of ethical character, 230
CASE Code of Ethics, 215, 216
Census printouts, prospect research, 46
Centralized organization, 76–78
  example of model, 77
  features of, 76
  pros and cons of, 77–78
Challenging assignments, and motivation, 179–181
Change
  acceptance of, 193–195
  accommodation to, 191–192
  and departure of employees, 196
  evaluation of, 201–203
  external change, types of, 204–206
  implementation of, 200–201
  and looping, 203–204
  and negotiation, 192–193
  planning for, 199–200
  preparation for, 196–199
  readiness for, 206–208
  and resignations, 195–196
  resistance to, 191
Charisma, and leaders, 250
Church, relations with, 65
Civic virtue, of ethical character, 230–231
Classified advertisements, 11, 13
  problems of, 11, 13
Codes of Ethics, 214–220
  American Prospect Research Association, 239–240
  CASE Code of Ethics, 215, 216
  Josephson Institute of Ethics Principles of Ethical Conduct, 241–243
  Model Standards of Practice for the Charitable Gift Planner, 220, 223–224
  NSFRE Code of Ethics, 215, 217
  Standards of Membership and Professional Conduct, 233–236
  Statement of Professional Standards and Conduct of the Association for Healthcare Philanthropy, 237–238

Coercive power, 261
Committees, strategic planning committee, 148
Communication
  conflict resolution, 121–125
  interactional model, 111
  linear model, 111
  listening, 115–116
  negative/positive aspects, 118–121
  noise, 112–113
  nonverbal, 113–115
  public affairs related, 60–62
  responding, 116–118
  transactional model, 112
  See also Organizational communication
Compensation
  and hiring, 23
  and motivation, 27–28
  suggested salaries, 24
Competition, and strategic planning, 154–155
Computers
  acquisition of, 136–137
  converting to new system, 139–140
  database, 138–139
  database directors, 52–53
  database for prospect research, 46
  functions needed, 137–138
  increase in use of, 132–134
  Internet, 140–141
  new needs, dealing with, 143
  on-line uses, 140–141
  pre-evaluation, 134–135
  problems related to, 141–142
  software, 136–137
  in telefund, 56
Conflict, 121, 124–125
Conflict resolution, 121–125
  steps in, 122–124
Conflicts of interest, types of, 219–220
Conrad Teitel, 51
Contingency theory, leadership, 254–255
Crisis plan
  elements of, 63
  public affairs, 63
"Cumulative List," 43

D

Database directors, 52–53
  role of, 53

Databases
  prospect research, 46
  requirements of, 138–139
Decentralized organization, 78–81
  example of model, 79
  features of, 78, 80
  pros and cons of, 80
Decision-making
  job applicant, 21–22
  leadership styles for, 258
Decision-making model, of leadership, 257–258
Demographic data, and strategic planning, 154
Development officers
  keys to success of, 50
  monthly report form, 49
  for planned giving, 51, 52
  role of, 47–50
Direct mail
  cost factors, 54–55
  planned giving program, 54–55
  segmentation methods, 55
  supplement to telefund, 55
Donor Bill of Rights, 220, 221–222
Downward flow, organizational communication, 126–127
Drucker, Peter, 185, 272–273

E

Education, of planned giving officers, 51
E-mail, 137
Employee selection, 14–23
  current issues, 15
  job interview, 16, 18–22
  negotiation areas, 22–23
  screening process, 15–16
  search protocol, 17–18
Ethics
  Codes of Ethics, 214–220
  conflicts of interest, types of, 219–220
  definitions of, 211, 212
  Donor Bill of Rights, 220, 221–222
  ethical character, elements of, 228–231
  ethical conflict, dealing with, 213–214
  fiduciary responsibilities, 222, 225
  job-related ethical practices, 226–227
  legal aspects, 225

religious/philosophical views, 211–214
  rules-oriented approach, 227
  social ethic, 227–228
  See also Codes of Ethics
Evaluation by manager, 29–34
  of change, 201–203
  dimensions of, 30
  evaluation forms, 29–30, 31–33
  location factors, 34
  and manager's style, 33
  problems related to, 34
  as subjective process, 30, 33
Evaluation of manager
  and advancement potential, 280–281
  and bottom line, 271–273
  evolution of, 266–267
  feedback method, 277–279
  formal evaluation, 274–279
  informal evaluation, 273–274
  questionnaire method, 275–277
  and reward, 279–280
  success indicators, 267–268
Expert power, 261

F

Fairness, of ethical character, 230
Feedback method, evaluation of manager, 277–279
Fiedler, Fred, 254–255
Financial incentives
  approaches to, 174, 175
  bonus arrangements, 173
  and communication with staff, 176
  debate about, 175
  and motivation, 172–177
  pay-for-performance, 173, 174
Financial projections, strategic planning, 157–160
Firing employees, ethical practices, 226–227
501(c) organizations, 43
Followership
  and leaders, 251–252
  qualities of followers, 251–252
Formal evaluation, of advancement manager, 274–279
Foundation Directory, 46
Fund raising, 44–50

fund raisers, role of, 47–50
major gifts, 59–60
planned giving, 50–59
prospect research, 44–47

G

Goal-setting, 102–103
 and benchmarks, 105–106
 dollar goals, formula for, 87
 factors in, 87–88
 mixed-model organization, 86–88
 relationship to objectives, 103, 104
Government, 40–41
 impacts on change, 205
 lobbying, 64
 printed material from, 64
 public versus private support issue, 40–41
 relations with, 63–65
Grant writing, 52

H

Hershey, Paul, 255
Herzberg, Frederick, 186
History of organization, strategic plan, 151–152
Home page, on Web, 140–141

I

Informal evaluation, of advancement manager, 273–274
In-house training, 25–26
Interactional model, communication, 111
Internet, 140–141
 home page, 140–141

J

Job announcements, 13
Job description, 10–11
 components of, 11
 example of, 12
Job interview, 16, 18–22
 beginning interview, 18
 decision-making, 21–22
 as discovery process, 20
 interview panels, 21
 legal issues, 19, 20–21, 226
 negotiation areas, 22
 note-taking, 21
 questions, types of, 19–20
 and résumé, 18
Job security, 170–172
Josephson Institute of Ethics Principles of Ethical Conduct, 241–243
Justice, of ethical character, 230

K

Knight Ridder, 46

L

Lateral flow, organizational communication, 128–129
Leaders/leadership
 and charisma, 250
 compared to managers, 248–250
 contingency theory, 254–255
 decision-making model, 257–258
 dimensions of, 246–248
 and followership, 251–252
 least preferred coworker measure, 255, 256
 path-goal theory, 258–259
 power of, 260–262
 situational model, 255, 257
 teaching of, 262
 traits of effective leaders, 252–254
Least preferred coworker measure, 255, 256
Legal issues
 ethical behavior, 225–227
 job interview, 19, 226
Legitimate power, 260–261
Linear model, communication, 111
Listening, in communication, 115–116
Lobbying, 64
Looping, and change, 203–204

M

Major gifts
 major gift officers, 59

subunits for giving, 59
Management
  benchmarks, 105–106
  definition of, 2
  example of functioning, 2–3
  goals, 102–103
  mission statement, 94–96
  objectives, 103–105
  policy statement, 98–101
  priority, 106–107
  procedures, 101–102
  vision of institution, 96–98
Management by objectives (MBO), 267
Manager
  compared to leaders, 248–250
  definition of, 3
  See also Advancement managers
McGregor, Douglas, 184, 266
Mentoring programs, 178
Mission statement, 94–96
  basic commitments, 95
  importance for advancement manager, 95–96
  stability over time, 94–95
  in strategic plan, 152–153
Mixed-model organization, 81–88
  advancement of personnel, 84–85
  areas of cooperation, 83–84
  budget, 83–84
  example of model, 82
  goal-setting, 86–88
  unit-based priorities, determination, 85
Model Standards of Practice for the Charitable Gift Planner, 220, 233–234
Motivation, definition of, 170
Motivation of employees, 26–29
  and achievement, 179–181
  and advancement, 177–178
  and challenging assignments, 179–181
  concrete motivators, 27–28
  dimensions of, 26–27
  and employee needs, 26
  financial incentives, 172–177
  job security, 170–172
  meeting method, 27
  oral approval, 28
  promotion, 28–29
  and recognition, 181–184
Motivation theories, 184–187

Theory X, Theory Y, Theory Z, 184–186
two-factor theory, 186

N

Networking, and recruitment, 14
Noise, in communication, 112–113
Nonverbal communication, 113–115
NSFRE Code of Ethics, 215, 217

O

Objectives, 103–105
  and benchmarks, 105–106
  characteristics of, 103
  identification of, 103
  income strategies, 104–105
  relationship to goals, 103, 104
  strategic plan, 160–161
Organizational communication
  downward flow, 126–127
  lateral flow, 128–129
  printed communication, 125
  upward flow, 127–128
Organizational culture, 37–38
  effects of, 37
Organizational structure
  centralized organization, 76–78
  decentralized organization, 78–81
  foundation-focused structure, 74
  lines of authority, 71–74
  mixed-model organization, 81–88
  nominally distant foundation, 74
  reporting relationships, 72, 73, 75
  and staff relationships, 88–91
Organization chart, advancement staff, 7, 8
Ouchi, William, 185

P

Path-goal theory, leadership, 258–259
Pay-for-performance, 173
Personnel administration, 9–29
  importance of, 10
  job description, 10–11
  motivation of employees, 26–29
  recruitment, 11, 13–14

training, 23–26
Philosophy, and ethics, 212–214
Planned giving, 50–59
  database directors, 52
  development officer, 52
  direct mail solicitations, 54–55
  planned giving officers, competency of, 51
  special events, 56–59
  telefund, 55–56
Planning, 6–9
  benefits of, 9
  for change, 199–200
  strategic planning, 8, 146–166
  tactile planning, 8–9
  See also Strategic planning
Pledge forms, 56, 57
Policy statement, 98–101
  advancement manager, role of, 100–101
  characteristics of, 98
  importance of, 99
  and nonprofit organizations, 100
  types of policies, 100
Power, 260–262
  coercive power, 261
  expert power, 261
  legitimate power, 260–261
  referent power, 261–262
  reward power, 261
Praise, as motivation, 28
Printed communication
  organizational communication, 125
  public affairs, 60–61, 62
Priorities, 106–107
  meaning of, 106
  and scale of importance, 106–107
Private philanthropy, 41–60
  advancement staff, growth of, 41–42
  fund raisers, role of, 47–50
  fund raising, 44–50
  major gifts, 59–60
  planned giving, 50–59
  prospect research, 44–47
  taxation, 42–44
Procedures, 101–102
  goals of, 101, 102
  prescriptive nature of, 101
  rigidity of, 102
Professional meetings, recruitment through, 14
Programs, strategic plan, 161–163

Promotion, as motivation, 28–29
Prospect management, 47
Prospect research, 44–47
  databases, 46
  general information from, 46
  professional organizations, 45
  prospect management, 47
Public affairs, 60–63
  crisis plan, 63
  and internal politics, 60
  printed communication, 60–62
  public affairs officers, role of, 61–62
Publications, 65–66
  advanced electronic methods, 66
  affecting factors, 66
  personnel for, 65–66

Q

Questionnaire method, evaluation of manager, 275–277
Questions, in job interview, 19–20

R

Recognition of employees
  forms of, 182–183
  and motivation, 181–184
  time off as, 183
Recruitment, 11, 13–14
  classified advertisements, 11, 13
  employee selection, 14–23
  job announcements, 13
  ongoing interviewing, 14
  and professional meetings, 14
  through professional press, 13
  word of mouth, 14
Referent power, 261–262
Religion, and ethics, 211–212
Representation, and advancement managers, 38
Resignations, and change, 195–196
Respect, of ethical character, 228–229
Responding, in communication, 116–118
Responsibility, of ethical character, 229–230
Revenue Act of 1917, 42
Reward power, 261
Robert Sharp Co., 51

S

Salary, equity in arrangements, 172, 174
Satisficers/dissatisficers, and motivation, 186
Screening process, employee selection, 15–16
Section 170 of tax code, 43
Situational leadership model, 255, 257
Situation analysis, strategic planning, 150–151
Software. *See* Computers
Special events, 56–59
  characteristics of, 58
  pros/cons of, 58
  staff for, 59
  taxation, 58–59
Staff. *See* Advancement staff
Standards of Membership and Professional Conduct, 233–236
Statement of Professional Standards and Conduct, Association for Healthcare Philanthropy, 237–238
Strategic planning
  and advancement staff, 163–165
  and competition, 154–155
  critical issues, 155–157
  definition of, 146–147
  and demographic data, 154
  elements of, 8
  elements of plan, 149
  financial projections, 157–160
  history of organization, 151–152
  implementation of plan, 166–167
  and macro-environment, 153
  management roles in, 147–149
  mission statement, 152–153
  objectives, 160–161
  planning committee, 148
  programs, 161–163
  situation analysis, 150–151
  time line, 165

T

Tactile planning, elements of, 8–9
Taft Group, 46
Taxation, 42–44
  "Cumulative List," 43
  501(c) organizations, 43
  maximum and lesser deductibility, 43
  Section, 170
  special events, 58–59
  tax-exempt organizations, 43–44
Telefund
  direct mail as supplement, 55
  management of, 56
  planned giving program, 55–56
  pledge forms, 56, 57
  recording responses to calls, 55–56
  script, 56
  types of callers, 55
Theory X, Theory Y, Theory Z, of motivation, 184–186
Time line, strategic planning, 165
Training, 23–26
  for advancement, 178
  benefits for employees, 25
  ethical practices, 226
  importance of, 24
  in-house training, 25–26
  types of programs, 24–25
Transactional model, communication, 112
Trustworthiness, of ethical character, 228
Turnover, problem of, 29
Two-factor theory, of motivation, 186

U

Upward flow, organizational communication, 127–128

V

Vision of institution, 96–98
  impact of, 97–98
  meaning of, 96
  vision activities, 96
  vision task force, 97
Vroom, Victor, 257

W

Who's Who, 46

Y

Yetton, Phillip, 257